From Christian Science to Jewish Science

From Christian Science to Jewish Science

Spiritual Healing and American Jews

ELLEN M. UMANSKY

OXFORD
UNIVERSITY PRESS

2005

OXFORD
UNIVERSITY PRESS

Oxford New York
Auckland Bangkok Buenos Aires Cape Town Chennai
Dar es Salaam Delhi Hong Kong Istanbul Karachi Kolkata
Kuala Lumpur Madrid Melbourne Mexico City Mumbai
Nairobi São Paulo Shanghai Taipei Tokyo Toronto

Copyright © 2005 by Ellen M. Umansky

Published by Oxford University Press, Inc.
198 Madison Avenue, New York, New York 10016

www.oup.com

Oxford is a registered trademark of Oxford University Press

Library of Congress Cataloging-in-Publication Data
Umansky, Ellen M.
From Christian Science to Jewish Science: spiritual healing and American Jews / Ellen
M. Umansky.
p. cm.
Includes bibliographical references and index.
ISBN 0-19-504400-2
1. Jewish Science—History. I. Title.
BM729.J4U53 2004
296.7'1—dc22 2004004041

9 8 7 6 5 4 3 2 1

Printed in the United States of America
on acid-free paper

To my sons,
Abraham, Ezra, and Seth Kannof
For their love, encouragement, ongoing interest in my work,
and much appreciated patience
and to
Doris Friedman and Abraham Goldstein
of blessed memory
Whose words and lived examples helped me to understand
far more than any sermon or book could have
the teachings of Jewish Science

Preface

This book is the first major study of a little-known movement called Jewish Science. Based on ideas formulated by a number of Reform rabbis during the early twentieth century, it sought to counter the growing influence of Christian Science among American Jews by offering Christian Science's dual promise of happiness and health within a specifically Jewish context. To date, very little has been written on the Jewish attraction to Christian Science, and no published articles or books have explicitly focused on Jewish Science either as a philosophy of Judaism or as a religious movement. Extensive interviews and/or correspondence with Jews who became Christian Scientists, members and former members of Jewish Science groups, family members of Jewish Science leaders, scholars working in related fields, and contemporary rabbis and social workers interested in Jewish healing thus became essential components of my research. So was a lengthy questionnaire sent to members of the Society of Jewish Science in Manhattan. Well over half of the sixty questionnaires that I distributed were filled out and returned to me.

Much of this work is based on unpublished or not easily accessible material. I am therefore indebted to many people without whom this study simply could not have been written. Because I began researching this book so long ago, I am afraid that some names may unintentionally be omitted. If so, my deepest apologies to those whom I've failed to thank but should have. First and foremost, I want to thank Rebecca Alpert, whose early encouragement and generosity convinced me that a book on Jewish Science not only needed to be written but in fact *could* be written. Learning from Fannie Zelcer at the American Jewish Archives that Rebecca had written a 1977 doctoral dissertation entitled "From Jewish Science to Rabbinical Counseling: The Evaluation of the Relationship between Religion and Health by the American Reform Rabbinate," I found Rebecca's phone number in Philadelphia, called her, and talked to her at length about her unpublished dissertation, which I subsequently purchased through University Microfilms in Ann Arbor, Michigan. While only a few pages of Rebecca's dissertation focused on Jewish Science, I was fascinated by her discussion of the larger historical and religious context out of which Jewish Science emerged. I was also anxious to read the material by or related to Rabbi Alfred Moses, Rabbi Clifton Harby Levy, and Rabbi Morris and Tehilla Lichtenstein, the central figures in the history of Jewish Science. Rebecca apparently had saved the material that she had gathered and, with her own scholarly work moving in a different direction, offered to give this material to me. A short time later, my husband, Alan, and I drove down to Philadelphia for Rebecca's dissertation files. Thus, I was fortunate to begin researching this book not only with access to private correspondence and primary source material that I might not otherwise have attained but also with a tremendous sense of collegiality and trust from a fellow scholar who has long since become a friend.

Invaluable to this project has been the ongoing support I have received from members and officers of the Society of Jewish Science. Indeed, without the help of David Goldstein, in particular, my chapters on the society would have been far sketchier and consequently, I believe, less insightful. From the beginning, David gave me full access to the society's files, graciously answering my many questions, and for well over a decade has continued to send me material that I have requested or that he thought might be of interest to me. For two months, during the summer of 1985 (when I was pregnant with my first son, Abraham), he met me at the train station in Hicksville, Long Island, several times a week, drove me to the society's offices in Plainview, where I immersed myself in the society's archives, and drove me back to the train eight hours later. I will long remember his enthusiasm and kindness, as well as the many lunches we shared.

So too will I remember driving to Queens and then riding into Manhattan with Doris Friedman to attend Jewish Science services. Even without listening to her tapes of Tehilla Lichtenstein's sermons, I can conjure up a vision of Doris leading the healing service and reading a sermon by Morris or Tehilla Lichtenstein, always standing straight, enunciating clearly, and speaking from the heart. Our long conversations helped me gain enormous insight into Jewish Science, as did the few, but lengthy, conversations I had with Abraham Goldstein. Both of them truly embodied the teachings of Jewish Science. So did Helen Miller Harwood and her sister-in-law, Sarah Rosenfeld, whom I saw regularly at services and interviewed at length, and so do Jack Botwin and Mildred Goldstein, whose positive outlook on life continues to inspire me to-

day. My greatest thanks to Immanuel and Michael Lichtenstein for their treasure trove of family reminiscences; their cousin, Margaret Sackton Rosan, for
sharing personal records, including her mother's two-volume family history,
with me; and Kate Friedman, Harry Hauptman, Evelyn Diamond Saldick, and
Bertha Schwartz, past and present members of the Society of Jewish Science,
for their openness and assistance.

Among the more difficult chapters to research was that on Rabbi Alfred
Geiger Moses. Without the enthusiastic assistance of Phyllis Feibelman, lifelong member of Sha'arai Shomayim in Mobile, Alabama, and a distant relative
of Moses, and Robert Zietz, the temple's archivist, the time that I spent in
Mobile would have proved to be far less fruitful. I especially appreciate Phyllis
arranging my taped interview with her father, Samuel Brown, and her recent
assistance in helping me to gather additional information for this chapter. My
thanks to Mindy Agin, who has long since graduated from Emory University
but who, while she was still an undergraduate, assisted in my research, even
going to Mobile with me. Thanks too to the other Emory undergraduates Martin Wisse, Michele Ostrow, and Tammy Indianer, who helped me at various
early stages of this study, and to Mark Bauman, the first-rate editor of *Southern
Jewish History*, who encouraged me to write an essay for the journal focusing
on Alfred Geiger Moses, drawing on material included in the first two chapters
of my book. His careful and critical reading of my work led me to make a
number of substantive and stylistic changes that greatly strengthened the essay.
I then incorporated many of those changes, along with other minor ones suggested by the journal's outside readers, into my book.

Just as the Board of Trustees minutes from Sha'arai Shomayim proved
invaluable to my work on Alfred Geiger Moses, so the Board of Trustees
minutes from the Bronx's Tremont Temple was of enormous help in ascer-
taining information about Clifton Harby Levy's early rabbinic career. My deepest thanks to Alan Hochberg and Rabbi Steven Klein of Scarsdale Synagogue–
Tremont Temple for so generously making the records of Tremont Temple
available to me. Additional thanks to Ruth Herman, whose mother was a devoted member of Levy's Centre of Jewish Science, for sharing with me relevant
newspaper clippings, photographs, center publications, and decades worth of
memories.

During the many years it took to complete this book, the American Jewish
Archives in Cincinnati continued to be an important resource. My thanks to
Jacob Rader Marcus and Fanny Zelcer, who aided in the beginning stages of
this work; archivist Kevin Profitt and Camille Servizzi; and Gary Zola, current
director of the Marcus Center, for their recent, much appreciated, assistance.
I also want to thank Sue Levi Elwell and Steve Elwell for their home hospitality
during an early visit to Cincinnati, as well as Jonathan Sarna, a member of the
Hebrew Union College–Jewish Institute of Religion (HUC-JIR) Cincinnati faculty until 1990, who, during my visits to the archives, continued to encourage

me, took me out for dinner on more than one occasion, and arranged for me to present my early work on Jewish Science to a forum of HUC-JIR faculty and graduate students. Finally, I am indebted to Tom Edsall of the 19th Shop in Baltimore and Susie Kessler of the National Jewish Healing Center in New York City for their help in completing the collection of photographs assembled for this book's publication.

There have been many colleagues and friends who have long been supportive of my work. I am indebted to David Blumenthal at Emory University, for long ago teaching me how to organize a book and write an introduction; my friends, Ali Crown and David Edwards, who have followed this book's progress since the years we were at Emory together; those at Hebrew Union College–Jewish Institute of Religion who took a genuine interest in this work, especially Kerry Olitzky, Larry Hoffman, Larry Kushner, David Sperling, and David Ellenson (who has been among my most enthusiastic and valued supporters since our graduate school days at Columbia University).

In light of the fact that currently I am the only full-time faculty member in Judaic Studies at Fairfield University, I feel particularly fortunate to have colleagues with whom I can discuss my work. As the organizational shape and content of this book unfolded, I very much appreciated the questions, critical comments, and constant support of John Thiel, Paul Lakeland, and Patricia Behre. I am also grateful to Timothy Law Snyder, dean of the College of Arts and Sciences, and Orin Grossman, Fairfield's academic vice president, not only for their encouragement but also for their strongly worded advice about staying away from campus during my sabbatical leave in the spring of 2003 in order to devote my full attention to this book. That with few exceptions I was able to follow their advice speaks volumes about my assistant, Elaine Bowman, who efficiently and effectively ran the Bennett Center for Judaic Studies in my absence, Patricia Behre, who genuinely seemed to enjoy the many responsibilities thrust upon her as acting director, and my colleague Philip Eliasoph, who, understanding that I temporarily needed to absent myself from campus debates, valiantly carried on without me.

During the many years in which I have been researching and writing this book, I have been surrounded by friends and family who respected my work schedule, even when it meant talking to or seeing one another less than we would have liked. They have continued to ask questions about the book's content and never stopped believing in me or in this book's imminent completion. I especially want to thank my longtime friends Stephan Loewentheil, Stephanie Stern, Gail Goodman, and Don Aslan; my many Edgemont and synagogue friends, with whom I wish I could have had lunch more often; Ben Ornopia, for his invaluable help at home; and John Cleary, who constantly reminds me of the important connection between mind and body. I also want to thank my wonderful family, who have long provided me with great emotional and intellectual support. I especially want to thank my nephew, Marc Levy, for his enthusiastic assistance, invaluable suggestions, and considerable computer expertise; my sisters, Amy Kahn and Myrna Levy, and my cousin, Meryl Katz, for their interest and patience; my aunt, Diana Laub, for her many important, critical questions; Alan Kannof and my children, Abraham, Ezra, and Seth Kannof, for giving me the space and the time to write, even when my daily writing hours supposedly were to have ended; and Dorothy Umansky, my mother and closest friend, who, for over fifteen years, has enthusiastically and patiently awaited this book's publication. Finally, my deepest gratitude to my editor, Cynthia Read, for her encouragement, suggestions, and ongoing interest during the many years it took to complete this work. As other writers will attest, those of us who have worked with Cynthia are fortunate indeed.

Divided into seven chapters, this book begins with a lengthy discussion of the attraction of tens of thousands of American Jews to Christian Science during the late nineteenth and early twentieth century and the ways in which Jewish leaders and organizations, especially members of the Central Conference of American [Reform] Rabbis, attempted to meet what they simultaneously perceived to be a threat and a challenge. Chapter 2 focuses on Rabbi Alfred Geiger Moses of Mobile, Alabama, who first named and formulated concepts that he identified as those of "Jewish Science." In a slim volume published in 1916, and a greatly reworked and expanded 1920 edition, Moses sought to create both a spiritual renaissance among American Jews and a direct counterattack against the growing allure of Christian Science. Resisting appeals by readers to help create and serve as leader of a group grounded in the teachings of Jewish Science, Moses left it to the Reform rabbi Morris Lichtenstein to transform Jewish Science from a set of ideas into a specific, Jewish religious movement. Chapter 3 details the creation of the Society of Jewish Science in New York City, which Lichtenstein helped create and led from 1922 until his death in 1938; chapter 4 focuses on what he understood to be the content and religious significance of Jewish Science.

Chapter 5 explores the teachings and work of another Reform rabbi, Clifton Harby Levy, who, in December 1924, helped establish and served as leader of a second Jewish Science group, the Centre of Jewish Science. Chapter 6 focuses on Tehilla Lichtenstein and the Society of Jewish Science. It includes a discussion of her religious and family background, her assumption and model of leadership, her understanding of Judaism and Jewish identity, and the development of the society during her thirty-five years as leader. Finally, chapter 7 begins with a description of works written during the late 1940s and 1950s by such religious leaders as Rabbi Joshua Loth Liebman and the Reverend Norman Vincent Peale that shared many of Jewish Science's concerns and practical suggestions. It then details the building and dedication of the society's synagogue in Old Bethpage, Long Island, in 1956, and includes a brief history of the society since Tehilla Lichtenstein's death. This study concludes with a discussion of recent religious innovations and developments within the American Jewish community that are similar in nature and intent to those proposed over eighty years ago by the founders and formulators of Jewish Science.

Contents

Chronology

1875   Publication of *Science and Health with Key to the Scriptures*, by Mary Baker Eddy

1879   Establishment of First Church of Christ, Scientist, in Boston

1911   B'nai Brith passes a resolution excluding from membership Jews affiliated with Christian Science

1912   Central Conference of American (Reform) Rabbis resolves that any Jew subscribing to Christian Science teachings will henceforth be regarded "as a non-Jew in faith"

1916   Publication of *Jewish Science*, Alfred Geiger Moses

1920   Publication of Moses' substantially revised second edition of *Jewish Science*

1920   Founding of the First Society of Jewish New Thought in New York by Lucia Nola Levy and Bertha Strauss, with Alfred Geiger Moses as honorary president

1922   Rabbi Morris Lichtenstein assumes leadership of the society founded by L. N. Levy and B. Strauss, which, at his instigation, is renamed the Society of Jewish Science

1924   Rabbi Clifton Harby Levy helps found and assumes leadership of the Centre of Jewish Science in New York

1925   Publication of *Jewish Science and Health*, by Morris Lichtenstein, the "textbook" of the Society of Jewish Science

1927   Annual meeting of the Central Conference of American Rabbis includes series of papers and prolonged discussion on Jewish Science and spiritual healing

1938   In late November, Tehilla Lichtenstein succeeds her husband as leader of the Society of Jewish Science

1953   S. Pereira Mendes helps found and serves as leader of the short-lived New Thought synagogue in Los Angeles

1956   The Society of Jewish Science formally dedicates its newly built synagogue in Old Bethpage, Long Island (which closes in 1977)

1962   The Centre of Jewish Science closes after the death of its leader, Clifton Harby Levy

1973   Abraham Goldstein, chairman of the Society of Jewish Science, succeeds Tehilla Lichtenstein as leader, a position held until his death in 1998

1991   The Jewish Healing Center (currently known as the Bay Area Jewish Healing Center) opens in San Francisco

1992   Founding of Elat Chayyim as a transdenominational Jewish retreat center for healing and renewal

1994   The Nathan Cummings Foundation helps establish the National Center for Jewish Healing

1996   The Society of Jewish Science opens its new headquarters on East 39th Street in New York

From Christian Science to Jewish Science

Introduction

Nearly twenty years ago, in Boston, at the annual conference of the Association for Jewish Studies, a fortuitous meeting sparked my interest in Jewish Science, a religious movement of which I had absolutely no prior knowledge. While I no longer remember the exact circumstances under which I first met the American Jewish historian Jonathan Sarna, our brief conversation stands out vividly in my imagination. Walking over and introducing himself to me, he began by praising my groundbreaking work on Lily Montagu, the founder of the Liberal Jewish movement in England. Although at the time we were both assistant professors, in the early stage of our academic careers, Jonathan had already published three books and numerous articles, several of which I had read and greatly admired. He apparently was familiar with my work as well, not just on Lily Montagu but on other nineteenth- and twentieth century women who, like her, became unordained Jewish religious leaders.

After discussing my nearly completed second book on Lily Montagu (an annotated sourcebook of her selected writings), Jonathan said, "When you've finished your work on Lily Montagu, I have another woman for you to write about." His intention was clear. He knew of another Jewish woman in whom he thought I'd be interested and about whom I was particularly qualified to write. "Who?" I asked. He replied, quite simply, "Tehilla Lichtenstein." After I admitted that I had never heard of her before, he shared with me the little that he knew about her. Tehilla Lichtenstein, he said, succeeded her husband, Reform rabbi Morris Lichtenstein, as leader of the Society of Jewish Science, a Jewish religious group that sought to stem the growing tide of Jews attracted to Christian Science. In so doing, she became the first American Jewish woman to serve as spiritual leader of an ongoing Jewish congregation.

Having previously done extensive research for a chapter on women and Jewish religious leadership that was included in *Women of Spirit: Female Leadership in the Jewish and Christian Traditions* (1979), coedited by Rosemary Ruether and Eleanor McLaughlin, I was surprised that neither the archival nor published materials on which I had drawn mentioned Tehilla Lichtenstein. I couldn't help but wonder whether she was as little known as Jonathan Sarna seemed to be suggesting, or whether there was material that for some reason I simply had failed to discover. At the same time, I was surprised that I had never heard about Jewish Science, given its historical ties to American Reform Judaism, the movement with which I have been affiliated since childhood and one of my major fields of academic interest and research.

What Jonathan Sarna didn't know was that several years earlier I had taught a course at Princeton University on "Female Religious Leadership in America." One of the leaders on whom we focused, discussing her *Science and Health with Key to the Scriptures* in great detail, was Mary Baker Eddy. Having since reread *Science and Health* several times, I continue to be struck by the centrality of Jesus to Eddy's theology of healing. Yet for some reason, when I first read *Science and Health*, I was left with a very different impression. What struck me then was Eddy's emphasis on God's immanence, along with a this-worldly theology and a positive view of human nature. I remember thinking at the time that despite Eddy's denial of the reality of matter and her consequent disbelief in the efficacy of medicine, there were a number of basic beliefs concerning God and human nature that Jews and Christian Scientists shared. Were Jews, I wondered, ever attracted to Christian Science? I would later discover that the answer was an emphatic yes—at least tens of thousands of late nineteenth- and early twentieth-century Jews had been drawn to the teachings of Christian Science.

Genuinely curious to learn about Tehilla Lichtenstein and the movement that she had led, and eager to correct what I saw as a serious omission in my aforementioned chapter on female religious leadership, I decided that my next research project would focus on Tehilla Lichtenstein. After reading the few published essays, newspaper articles, and rabbinic responses that I could find on the Jewish attraction to Christian Science, I called Fannie Zelcer, the chief archivist of the American Jewish Archives in Cincinnati. Having done a considerable amount of research there on more than one occasion, I knew that Fannie would know what materials on Jewish Science, if any, the archives contained. Much to my delight, she told me that the archives had recently acquired the sermons of Tehilla Lichtenstein. It is unclear whether they had been catalogued and available to researchers when I was there gathering materials for my chapter in the Ruether and McLaughlin book. In any case, I quickly arranged a trip to the American Jewish Archives in Cincinnati, where I read as many of Tehilla Lichtenstein's two hundred sermons as I could, photocopied many others, and discovered that the archives had other holdings that would further illuminate my study of Jewish Science. I began to envision far more than a scholarly article. Indeed, I proposed to write the first in-depth study of Tehilla Lichtenstein and the Society of Jewish Science.

Within a year, I realized that a work focusing on Tehilla Lichtenstein was premature. The book that first needed to be written was one focusing on the Jewish attraction to Christian Science, subsequent responses by Jewish communal leaders, and the attempt by several individuals, including Tehilla Lichtenstein, to combat the inroads that Christian Science had made through the counter movement of Jewish Science. This book aims to be such a study.

In 1916, in direct response to the growing influence of Christian Science within the American Jewish community, Reform rabbi Alfred Geiger published a work titled *Jewish Science: Divine Healing in Judaism*. He maintained that its aim was to create a renaissance within the American Jewish community by awakening religiously apathetic Jews to Judaism's spiritual possibilities, thus combating the inroads already made by Christian Science. While the book's first edition equated Christian Science with belief in God as healer, the greatly expanded 1920 edition placed greater focus on Mary Baker Eddy's denial of the reality of the body's organs and functions. Asserting that the body was real, just as sickness was real to the sufferer, he maintained that the teachings of Christian Science needed to be rejected, for they were contrary to reason. In the book's second edition, Moses called Jewish Science an "applied psychology of Judaism," equating divine healing with the power of autosuggestion.

Later formulators also acknowledged the significance of modern psychology. Yet to them the theological insights of Jewish Science were at least as important as the psychological. To Rabbi Morris Lichtenstein and his wife, Tehilla, leaders of the Society of Jewish Science in New York City, Jewish Science was grounded in belief in God as a nonsupernatural power, or "divine mind," within every human being. Each of us, they insisted, has the capability to tap this inner power through such methods as visualization and affirmative prayer in order to overcome worry and fear and achieve happiness, health, calm, and other states of personal well-being. Drawing on Jewish literary and liturgical sources in their sermons and published writings, they made the Jewish context of Jewish Science clear. This context was further illuminated through religious school classes and weekly Sabbath and holiday services held in Manhattan, and from 1956 to 1977, at the society's synagogue in Old Bethpage, Long Island, as well.

The Reform rabbi Clifton Harby Levy, who helped establish and led the Manhattan-based Centre of Jewish Science from 1924 until his death in 1962, emphasized the efficacy of both affirmative and petitionary prayer. While he also focused on God as healer, he drew on more traditional images of divinity, describing prayer as a feeling of closeness to God rather than a feeling of one's own internal power. An active member of the Central Conference of American [Reform] Rabbis (CCAR) until his death, he helped popularize the ideas of Jewish Science within the Reform movement. He created educational programs on Jewish Science for use by Reform congregations, delivered a major address on spiritual healing at the annual CCAR conference in 1927, and kept alive within the CCAR issues concerning medical and religious cooperation. In 1937, thanks to the efforts of Clifton Harby Levy and others, Hebrew Union College in Cincinnati offered as part of the rabbinic school curriculum its first elective course in pastoral psychology. A course in pastoral counseling has long since become a requirement in the rabbinic program of its Cincinnati, New York City, and Los Angeles campuses, and similar courses are now offered at other rabbinic institutions.

While as a movement Jewish Science remained numerically small, the teachings of Alfred Geiger Moses, Morris and Tehilla Lichtenstein, and Clifton Harby Levy had a direct impact on thousands of American Jews. Thanks to the Society of Jewish Science in Manhattan, which has retained a small yet devoted membership, the works of Morris and Tehilla Lichtenstein are particularly accessible. The society has kept Morris Lichtenstein's books in print, published an edited volume of Tehilla Lichtenstein's sermons, and publishes the *Jewish Science Interpreter* eight times a year, which regularly includes the Lichtensteins' sermons.

Predating the current Jewish interest in spiritual healing by over seventy years, Jewish Science has remained a largely unwritten chapter in both the history of Reform Judaism in the United States and American Jewish history as a whole. It is my hope that this book will spark future scholarly interest in the ideas, individuals, and historical and religious developments it describes, and help illuminate what the formulators of Jewish Science rightly understood to be the deep-seated connection between Judaism and spiritual healing.

I

Christian Science and American Jews

In March 1911, a headline in the weekly Jewish newspaper the *American Hebrew* declared: "International Order of B'nai B'rith Excludes Christian Scientists." Reporting on B'nai B'rith's annual convention in San Francisco, the *American Hebrew* described in detail the attention paid to the growing numbers of American Jews who had begun to affiliate with Christian Science. These Jews diligently studied Mary Baker Eddy's *Science and Health with Key to the Scriptures*, first published in 1875, regularly attended Christian Science services, availed themselves of Christian Science practitioners, and eventually joined the Christian Science Church. By an overwhelming majority, members of B'nai B'rith voted to exclude such Jews from their fraternal order on the grounds that it was impossible for one to be both a Jew and a Christian Scientist.

Attempting to explain why such a resolution was necessary, the *American Hebrew* argued that "nowadays there is growing to be so great a laxity and want of firmness among Jews, even those who have strong Jewish feelings, that they seem to consider they can belong to any movement whatever its theological tendency, and yet claim the right to call themselves Jews."[1] Included among these were Jews affiliated with Christian Science, Unitarianism, and Ethical Culture. Yet Ethical Culture, it insisted, had been a "comparative failure," while Unitarianism posed a relatively minor threat. Only Christian Science had made serious inroads within the American Jewish community, and thus, it cautioned, the American rabbinate needed "to do more constructive work," beginning with a recognition of the reasons why so many Jews had been "led astray" by Christian Science teachings.

Throughout the second and third decades of the twentieth century, many educated Jews and Christians attempted to answer this question. Sermons on "Why Jews Turn to Christian Science" could frequently be heard from liberal Jewish and Christian pulpits, scholarly papers addressing this topic were delivered at annual meetings of various Jewish religious organizations, and pamphlets such as Samuel Deinard's *Jews and Christian Science*, published in 1919, attempted to explore the relationship between the two in greater detail. While some non-Jews, like Henry Frank, the author of *Why Is Christian Science Luring the Jew away from Judaism?* also published in 1919, celebrated the Jewish defection to Christian Science as a sign that Jews were beginning to free themselves from "the circumstances of ceremonial limitation, the narrowness of race consciousness and bigotry and every anachronistic vestige of antiquity" and merge in "the one religion that sometimes must conquer and crown all humankind,"[2] that is, Christianity, most writing on this theme attempted to be more objective. Both Jews and Christians concurred that there were three major reasons why Jews were attracted to Christian Science: the first physical, the second social, and the third spiritual in nature.

Like most non-Jews who joined Christian Science, Jews often found themselves initially attracted to it because of its promise of health, peace, and comfort. In an age of rapid urbanization, and the anxiety and tension that observers maintained went with it, many American city dwellers, both men and women, found themselves suffering from such ideational or functional illnesses as neurasthenia (nervous exhaustion) and hysteria. Hysteria was especially widespread among urban middle- and upper-middle-class women between the ages of fifteen and forty, with symptoms that included nervousness, depression, fatigue, headaches, pain, seizures, and even paralysis.[3] Whether hysteria was a disease that had some identifiable cause or was simply a functional illness frequently used by late nineteenth- and early twentieth-century women as a way of consciously or unconsciously expressing dissatisfaction with their lives, hysteria became one of the classic diseases of the era and one for which many nineteenth- and early twentieth-century women sought relief through practitioners of such mind cure faiths as Christian Science.

Given the fact that most American Jews were both middle-class and city dwellers, it should come as no surprise that Jews were said to be especially prone, or, as one contemporary observer put it, were "notorious sufferers" of nervous or functional disorders.[4] Published pamphlets, books, and sermons claimed that there were vast numbers of Jews going to medical clinics and/or mind cure practitioners. At the same time, local Jewish newspapers throughout the United States regularly carried advertisements for products promising to cure such illnesses, indicating that manufacturers at least perceived there to be an excellent market for these products among American Jews. Between 1880 and 1907, one could find in almost any newspaper in America, Jewish or not, ads for such products as Dr. Putnam's Syrup Pectoral, "for coughs, cold, croup, and asthma," and his Rheumatic Mixture, "the only known remedy" for rheumatism; Samaritan Nervine, which promised to cleanse the blood and quicken sluggish circulation, cure paralysis, and clear one's complexion; and Ayer's Sarsparilla, an "absolute cure" for scrofula (a disease manifesting itself as eczema, boils, ulcers, tumors, and physical collapse), kidney and liver diseases, tuberculosis consumption, and "various other dangerous or fatal maladies." Ayers also featured ads for its Cherry Pectoral, with testimonials by physicians claiming that it was invaluable in treating diseases of the throat and lung, for its Hair Vigor, for its Ague Cream against malaria, and for its pills for headaches, back pain, digestive troubles, and typhoid fever.

Between 1880 and 1907, two of the most widely read Jewish newspapers in the United States, the *American Israelite* (published in Cincinnati) and the *American Hebrew* (published in New York City), devoted much of their advertising space to such products. In any single issue, one could find advertisements for such "remarkable cures" as Hall's Hair Renewer; Scott's Emulsion, for consumption, bronchitis, coughs, colds, and wasting diseases; Cuticura Soap, for "humors of the blood and skin"; Pond's Extract ("invaluable" for catarrh, hoarseness, rheumatism, toothaches and ulcers); Kidney-Wort ("the sure cure for kidney diseases, liver complains, constipation, piles and blood diseases"); Hood's Sarsaparilla, for liver and kidney trouble; and Hunt's Kidney and Liver Remedy, recommended not only for problems with the kidney and liver but also for headaches, general debility, heart disease, and diabetes. Also featured were regular ads in the *American Hebrew* for Samaritan Nervine and in the *American Israelite* for Dr. Miles's Nervine (plus his liver pills and heart cure) as well as for many of the products manufactured by Dr. Putnam and by Ayers. Equally popular were advertisements for elastic trusses for hernias, electric corsets and belts (guaranteed to cure pains, aches, or general lack of energy), and medicinal pads, such as the Improved Excelsior Kidney Pad, for all diseases of the kidney, bladder, and urinary organs; Dr. Holman's Liver Pad, for malaria, yellow fever, seasickness, diarrhea, and various children's diseases; and the Electric XX Pad, which evasively guaranteed a "variety of medical applications for various illnesses" and claimed to have made seventy-five thousand cures during 1883 alone! Food products were similarly extolled in terms of their curative value, from Epp's Cocoa (which guaranteed "a constitution [that] may be gradually built up until strong enough to resist every tendency to disease") to breakfast cereals that claimed credit for saving the health of hundreds of men, women, and children, and teas that promised to cure both constipation and headaches, to all kinds of mineral water that claimed to cure Bright's disease (diseases of the kidney), to Bovinine, a raw food that promised to create new blood and permanently cure "nervous prostration and debility." Among the more intriguing products advertised were Cactus Blood Cure, a blood purifier said to have been discovered by Brazilian Indians, and Dr. H. James's Cannabis Indica, available in pill or ointment form and prepared in Calcutta from the best native hemp, as a remedy for consumption, bronchitis, asthma, colds, nasal problems, and nervous debility.

Many manufacturers made a special appeal to women. Ads for Kidney-Wort, Hunt's Kidney and Liver Remedy, Hop Bitters, Ayers Hair Vigor and Sarsaparilla, Bovinine, Scott's Emulsion, and Johann Hoff's Malt Extract continually emphasized the special benefits that women might receive from using their products. Some ads, like those for Beecham's Pills, promised to "restore females to complete health" (though what they might have been suffering from was unclear), while others, like Johann Hoff's, which claimed to restore strength to nursing mothers, were more narrowly focused. Both the German Electro Galvanic Belt (advertised in the *American Hebrew*) and Dr. Gregg's Electric Belt (advertised in the *American Israelite*) claimed to cure physical "female complaints" due to the sensitive nature of the female nervous systems, while Warner's Tippecanoe ensured women's deliverance from the "deadly power" of physical decline and nervous exhaustion that had come to enslave them. Though by the second decade of the twentieth century these ads were fewer in number, they continued to be prominently featured in local newspapers throughout the 1920s. Self-proclaimed specialists in various forms of nervous and chronic diseases similarly placed ads offering to cure such illnesses in person, by the sale of remedies they had manufactured, and/or by sharing, usually for a price, the secrets of their curative powers.

Letters, diaries, and published testimonials by Jews who "went over" to Christian Science further attest to the physical appeal of what Jewish leaders derisively labeled the "Christian Science cult." Many sought relief from "nerve troubles," others from more physical ailments, including broken bones, terminal illnesses, and what doctors had diagnosed as poor health in general. In her memoirs, Clara Lowenburg Moses, a New Orleans Jewish woman who lived from 1865 to 1951, recalled that in 1914, when her brother-in-law was stricken with leukemia, she and her sister had him treated by a Christian Science practitioner under whose care he got better. "When we left [for an extended visit to] ... Asheville, North Carolina," she wrote, "we got another healer to treat him there. The doctors said there was no cure, that these healings occurred but that he would only live a few years at most." Yet she and her sister retained confidence in their Christian Science teacher in New Orleans, who claimed that it was through her healing and work with him that Clara's brother-in-law had improved. Consequently, while they continued to seek medical attention for him, Clara Moses, her sister, Helen, and her sister's daughter, Marguerite, began to read Mary Baker Eddy's *Science and Health with Key to the Scriptures* and portions from the "Old and New Testament" aloud for hours each day, hoping that Helen's husband would regain his health completely. Clara similarly tried to get her sister-in-law, Medea, who suffered from fainting spells, to "take up Science study," but Medea lost all faith in the New Orleans practitioner who sought to heal her when, in the middle of silent concentration, he apparently fell asleep and began to snore, an event that Clara Moses described as an "unfortunate accident" that prevented her sister-in-law from realizing the benefits that one could receive from Christian Science.[5]

Testimonials from Jews who became Christian Scientists during the late nineteenth and early twentieth centuries occasionally appeared in the *Christian Science Journal*. One such testimonial, appearing in the February 1902 edition of the *Journal* in article form and entitled "Christian Science and the Jewish People," was written by Jacob S. Shield of Warsaw, Indiana. Admitting to his early skepticism about the healing powers of Christian Science teachings, he went on to describe how he and his wife, after years of unsuccessful medical treatment, decided to leave their skepticism behind and seek the aid of a Christian Science practitioner. The results, he maintained, were "not only gratifying but amazing." His wife was cured of spinal disorder, hay fever, dyspepsia, and other physical ailments, and he was not only relieved of a compound inguinal hernia for which he'd worn a truss for eleven years but also, "after wearing glasses for sixteen years . . . was able to lay them aside" and do all of his work without them. Eventually, through Christian Science, every member of his family was cured of the illnesses that plagued them, leading them to conclude that "Christian Scientists knew more about curing the sick than [did] the medical profession."[6]

A similar, though less sensational, testimonial appeared in the *Christian Science Sentinel* in April 1912. Henry Deutsch, a former Jew who had joined Christian Science, appealed to his former coreligionists to join the church, as he had. While Judaism, he maintained, had been unable to offer him the slightest relief from the excruciating stomachaches from which he had suffered for years, Christian Science, by revealing the false nature of these pains, cured him completely. For many Jews, it seems, the major allure of Christian Science lay in its seeming ability to heal all illness. One Southern woman who long ago left Judaism for Christian Science wrote to me as follows:

> Forty years ago I was in the depths of despair with a problem that
> the doctors could not help, altho[ugh] they tried. A friend gave me a
> Christian Science pamphlet to read, which was so full of truth and
> love and encouragement, that my healing was instantaneous—all
> the frightening symptoms disappeared and I was truly reborn. . . .
> Christian Science *saved my life* and that's why it is my way of life, as
> well as my religion.[7]

While these sentiments may well echo the experiences of many, perhaps most Jews who became affiliated with Christian Science, there were also Jews, as some observers noted, who joined Christian Science primarily for social reasons. To these religiously indifferent Jews, Judaism appeared to be outdated.

Its rituals and observances not only seemed obsolete but also helped militate against the full integration of Jews into American life. As letters and testimonials written by Jews during the first few decades of the twentieth century reveal, many who joined Christian Science, especially those from Eastern European backgrounds, came from traditional Jewish homes. Believing that it was impossible to be both Orthodox and modern, many abandoned Orthodoxy for either Conservative or Reform Judaism, and others abandoned religious faith all together, while some, sensing that religious affiliation, though voluntary, was part of the American way of life, chose church affiliation over synagogue affiliation, hoping that it would elevate their social standing. Among the latter group, hundreds, if not thousands, joined Christian Science.

Among German Jews, most of whom had been born in America and whose parents, if not grandparents, had been born in the United States as well, joining Christian Science or, for that matter, converting to Christianity in general wasn't a means of becoming fully American, as it was for many eastern European immigrants and their children, but of socially elevating themselves while outwardly affirming their own, deeply felt American self-identity. For many who had been raised as Reform Jews or had long affiliated with the Reform movement conversion simply meant a change of outward identity. Having abandoned most if not all of the ceremonies and ritual observances of traditional Judaism, (sporadically) attending synagogue services that were almost exclusively in English, and largely ignorant of Jewish teachings, including Jewish theology, many American Reform Jews simply equated Reform with Jewish accommodation and adaptation to modernity. Though few went so far as to convert to Christianity, many of those that did believed, as the nineteenth-century German poet Heinrich Heine once wrote, that conversion was the "ticket price of admission" into modern society. Thousands of Jews, especially those from highly assimilated Reform backgrounds, paid this price gladly.

No longer viewing Judaism as an all-encompassing way of life, many may have found the transition from Reform Judaism to Christian Science to be particularly easy, for, as the American Jewish philosopher and educator Horace Kallen noted in 1916, this transition demanded "only a change in the formula of belief, in the way of talking, not in the way of living."[8] The end result was a newfound opportunity to mix in previously inaccessible socioeconomic circles. An editorial in the *American Hebrew* (dated April 4, 1913) noted:

> Christian Science is, or up to very recent times was a fashionable fad adopted by many persons in so-called "society." The leaders of the movement are shrewd persons, who make the social element a strong appeal to their congregants. This side of the movement has evidently had its attraction for Jews and Jewesses who are religiously indifferent but have a craving for outside society. In other words, much of the new tendency is pure snobbery.[9]

Both sympathetic and hostile contemporary observers spoke of the genteel environment associated with Christian Science. Many, especially those who joined Christian Science, spoke of the warmth of the church and its members, in sharp contrast to the coldness of the synagogue and of their fellow Jews. They also spoke of Christian Science's rapid growth and its increasing prosperity. As one observer noted, to be a Christian Scientist meant that one was part of a congregation whose members included the "richest, the most refined, and the [most] cultured people from every community" in America.[10] Whether or not this observation was true, many Jews may well have shared this perception.

In addition, as others maintained, many American Jews found the newness of Christian Science particularly appealing. Having been founded by Mary Baker Eddy in 1879, Christian Science was free of any past associations with anti-Semitism and anti-Jewish persecution. While, as a number of Jewish writers pointed out, Eddy's *Science and Health* continually contrasted Christian truth with rabbinic error, the church itself had never taken part in any anti-Jewish legislation. Nor had it circulated anti-Jewish propaganda[11] or massacred Jews in the name of religion.

Finally, as Samuel Deinard noted in 1919, many found Christian Science to be a particularly easy and convenient way to escape from Judaism, one that was relatively inoffensive to relatives, friends, and former Jewish associates because of the often heard, but deceptive, argument that one could simultaneously be a Jew and a Christian Scientist.[12] Christian Scientists, it seems, helped foster this misconception. Jews who began attending Christian Science meetings were repeatedly told that one did not have to abandon Judaism to receive the blessings of Christian Science and that joining Christian Science would in fact make one a better Jew. Jacob Shield wrote to his former coreligionists in the *Christian Science Journal:*

> [Christian] Science does not require either the Jew or the Gentile to repudiate or renounce anything that is good or practical in other religions. Instead of taking away any of these it adds to their very essence, and instead of converting the Jew to something that has always been his enemy, it blends him with his fellow-man in a union of purified hearts, and brings a refining and regeneration which all must undergo, Christians as well as Jews.[13]

Throughout the first few decades of the twentieth century, other articles and pamphlets, all written by former Jews, similarly maintained that adherence to Christian Science did not necessarily mean abandoning Judaism. These arguments were repeated not only by Jews who personally had few qualms about abandoning Judaism but wanted to retain familial ties but also by Jews who joined Christian Science for spiritual reasons yet still wanted to identify themselves, socially if not religiously, as Jewish.

Modie and Lena Spiegel, the maternal grandparents of the writer Paul Cowan, were among such people. In his autobiography, *An Orphan in History*, Cowan describes the kinds of justifications they offered to themselves and to others in explaining their adherence to the teachings of Christian Science. Joining the church in 1910, the Spiegels, who lived near Chicago and had formerly been members of Emil Hirsch's radical Reform congregation, Sinai Temple, insisted that they hadn't converted to Christianity. Instead they were simply students of Christian Science, a church without crosses or clergy and with a concept of Jesus as healer but not as divine. "Many people, including my grandparents," Cowan observes, "argued that the act of accepting the inner discipline of Christian Science—which meant using prayer and meditation to arrive at the faith that a divine power, not doctors, could heal the sick—made them stronger people and better Jews."[14] Though Modie Spiegel died with a picture of Jesus Christ in his breast pocket, during his lifetime he insisted that Jesus was not the son of God but quite simply the world's greatest Jew.

The argument that one simultaneously could be a Jew and a Christian Scientist was repeatedly used both by missionizing Christian Scientists and by Jews seeking to justify to themselves and others that "going over" to Christian Science was different from going over to Catholicism, Episcopalianism, or even Unitarianism. In fact, however, as Rabbi Max Heller, the spiritual leader of Temple Sinai in New Orleans and president of the Reform movement's CCAR from 1909 to 1911, pointed out, one could not justifiably claim to be a Jew and a Christian Scientist, since membership in the church required that one formally abjure membership from any denomination or religious group to which one previously had belonged. Jews had to produce a certificate of dismissal from their former rabbis before they could join Christian Science.[15] Yet the fact that many Jews continued to perpetuate this argument betrays the fundamental ignorance of most American Jews concerning Christian Science. Most learned of Christian Science and of the Jewish attraction to it not from sermons or published essays or from reading *Science and Health with Key to the Scriptures* (which is overwhelmingly Christian both in content and tone) but from listening to others selectively talk about Mary Baker Eddy and her teachings. Jews who joined Christian Science, seeking to make peace with themselves and their families, had a great deal at stake in perpetuating this falsehood, while others, whose attraction to Christian Science probably was limited to visiting a practitioner, attending a few meetings, and reading parts of *Science and Health*, were honestly unaware of what membership in the church entailed.

The fact is, most Jews who were attracted to Christian Science deeply wanted to believe that one could be a Christian Scientist and a Jew, for unlike those who joined for purely social reasons, most did not join to free themselves of Judaism but to find in Christian Science the kind of spirituality that Judaism seemed to be lacking. While undoubtedly the initial attraction of hundreds, if not thousands, of Jews to Christian Science was physical, what Christian Science offered was spiritual sustenance, only part of which was relief from physical pain. Many Jews who first went to Christian Science in order to be healed by one of its practitioners stayed in it long after the symptoms of the illness from which they had been suffering had disappeared. Their reason for initially going to Christian Science may have been physical, but their reasons for actually joining the church were spiritual in nature.[16]

Undoubtedly, there were some Jews who joined the church for social reasons, yet such Jews were relatively few in number. While Jewish-authored sermons, newspaper editorials, essays, and even books continually made reference to such Jews, Jews who actually joined Christian Science did not describe their "conversions" primarily as social. This isn't to say that Jews who turned to Christian Science failed to recognize the socioeconomic benefits that accrued to them as a result of their action. However, I have yet to find a letter, essay, or general testimonial that cites the social aspects of membership as the major reason, much less the sole reason, for joining Christian Science.

What's more, like Paul Cowan's grandparents, most Jews who joined Christian Science discovered that their new coreligionists did not socially accept them. Thus many—again like Cowan's grandparents, who helped found the all-Jewish Lake Shore Country Club—may have religiously identified with Christian Science yet, by necessity or choice, primarily socialized with other Jews. This seems to be particularly true in the North, where social differences between Christians and Jews, especially those of eastern European origin, and even between eastern European Jews and Jews of German extraction, remained great at least through the first three decades of the twentieth century. Most, like the wealthy Jewish New York matrons to whom writer Elizabeth Stern refers in her semiautobiographical novel *I Am a Woman—And a Jew,* went alone every Sunday to the Christian Science Church, though "they, in no way, had social contact with the non-Jewish members . . . of the church. They had no wish for that contact."[17] In the South, where there were far fewer Jews and where social integration between Jews and non-Jews had to a great extent already been achieved, Christian Science may well have provided Christians and Jews with a new ground of meeting, but again, this ground was more spiritual than social.

In short, then, while the promise of relief from physical suffering may well have initially attracted thousands of American Jews to Christian Science and while the hope of social elevation may well have led other, religiously indifferent Jews to formally identify with the teachings of Mary Baker Eddy, most Jews who studied her teachings and eventually affiliated themselves with the Christian Science Church did so because of the vitality and intensity of religious faith they found there. Searching for spiritual guidance, they began to attend Christian Science services. Finding happiness, peace, and God as creator, many decided, albeit reluctantly, to sever their religious ties with Judaism and formally affiliate with Christian Science.

Contemporary observers acknowledged that of all the reasons why a Jew might join Christian Science, it was the spiritual that was most compelling. Rabbi Max Heller forcefully maintained that modern Jews needed

> to lay hand to heart and to confess that Christian Science has caught us napping; it discovered the starving children in our household and fed their imaginations on air-blown sugared soufflés of its topsy-turvy philosophy. . . . [But the truth is] our faith does lack in vitality and intensity; our pulpits and our religious schools lay too much stress on knowledge and conduct, too little on the spirituality that must underlie a mellowing atmosphere of strong faith, daily prayer and poetic observance; it is the merest shadow of an ever fading reminiscence.[18]

Thus, he concluded, we have only ourselves to blame, for it has been our apathy and indolence toward spiritual values as well as our "feverish intoxication over material pursuits" that has led to this large-scale defection.

Stephen Wise, the (Reform) rabbi of New York City's Free Synagogue, similarly pondered the question of why Jews turn to Christian Science in a sermon delivered in 1920. Like Heller, Wise admitted that the Judaism of his day had become "religionless" (sic) and that the "inadequate spiritual character of the synagogue" had helped alienate thousands of American Jews. Again, like Heller, Wise maintained that American Jews had turned to Christian Science because of "a very real spiritual hunger and unrest" that Orthodoxy was incapable of satisfying and Reform had done nothing to meet. To counter this threat, he insisted, the synagogue needed to become respiritualized, leading to a "renascence of faith in the place of the organized rationalism and unorganized materialism of [American] Jews."[19] Mordecai Kaplan, a Conservative rabbi and author and later the founder of Reconstructionism, a movement that attempted to reconstruct the bases of American Jewish life using the sociological model of the organic community, similarly asserted that Jews "should not have to go to Christian Science to obtain the spiritual food which acts as an anodyne and restorative." Taking note of the great number of Jews who seemed to be joining Christian Science churches, Kaplan insisted that "peace of mind and the spirit of faith in the healing influence of the Divine Presence," which thousands of his coreligionists seemed to have discovered in Christian Science, could be found within Judaism itself.[20]

Kaplan's assumption that the appeal of Christian Science was primarily spiritual, an assumption shared by Heller, Wise, and other American rabbis who began to write about the "astonishing" numbers of Jews who had found comfort in the teachings of Mary Baker Eddy, was frequently given expression in the American Jewish press. In September 1913, for example, the *American Hebrew* published a satirical piece entitled "Some New Types of Jewish Womanhood," which presented a "Mrs. He[y]" as prototypical of the newly emerging

Jewish Christian Scientist. Mrs. He[y]—the focus of the piece—was depicted in marked contrast to Mrs. Aleph, who joined Christian Science in order to move in good society; Mrs. Beth, who was completely materialistic, celebrated Christmas and Easter, and belonged to a Reform temple but rarely attended; the cultured and educated Mrs. Gimel, who was member of a Reform temple but worshiped elsewhere; and the wealthy Mrs. Daled, who insisted that her husband join a Reform temple although he missed the Orthodox *shul* in which he'd been raised. Mrs. He[y] was an ardent Christian Scientist who talked about the illusion of matter, the Allness of Spirit, and human error "with a glibness that confound[ed] all opponents." While insisting that "the rabbi is wrong, oh absolutely wrong, when he declares that Christian Science and Judaism are incompatible" and that she had in fact become a better Jewess since joining Christian Science, she sent her children to Christian Science school, even though, the author added, poking fun at Christian Science's claim that illnesses were not real but rather the result of faulty thinking, they missed three successive Sundays last winter because of severe attacks of imaginary measles.[21]

As this piece illustrates, Jewish reactions to the defection of thousands, if not tens of thousands, of American Jews to Christian Science during the first few decades of the twentieth century were usually cynical and often hostile. Yet these reactions also revealed an underlying sentiment, continually voiced in the American Jewish press, that the success of Christian Science indicated that there was a "craving for faith" among American Jews to which the organized Jewish community had been indifferent. Letters and testimonials by Jews who were or had been attracted to Christian Science bore out the suspicion that what most Jews sought from Christian Science was not social status or even relief from physical pain but rather the spiritual guidance that Reform, Conservative, and Orthodox synagogues had failed to offer.[22]

Jews who turned to Christian Science often spoke of their search for a spiritual home. More specifically, they yearned for teachings that would infuse them with a sense of God's reality and with what they and, later, Morris Lichtenstein, the leader of the Society of Jewish Science in New York City, identified as peace of mind.[23] Recognizing their own spiritual needs, many found themselves willing to overlook what one Jewish woman, who later left Christian Science to become a member of Morris Lichtenstein's society, described as a personal "restlessness and reluctance to accept the Christian atmosphere" of Christian Science.[24] Though some Jews, unable to overlook this atmosphere, subsequently left the church, many found themselves with "nothing spiritual to turn to" within the organized Jewish community or, as another former Christian Scientist put it, without the "spiritual sustenance" that Christian Science provided.[25]

In short, a comparison of letters and essays written by Christian Scientists or former Christian Scientists of Jewish extraction with those written by church members who were Christian by birth reveals that Jews primarily joined Christian Science for the same reason that Christians did, namely, as Jean McDonald has written, because they found in Christian Science a spiritually satisfying concept of God.[26] In her essay "Mary Baker Eddy and the Nineteenth-Century 'Public' Woman," McDonald argues that in the past most scholars, including feminist scholars, have theorized that Mary Baker Eddy and other nineteenth- and early twentieth-century women were attracted to Christian Science not because of its intrinsic theological merit but because it satisfied their personal needs for status and power within a male-dominated society. Thus, scholars have argued that Eddy saw Christian Science as a way to gain power and that her followers were attracted to a movement that made available leadership roles elsewhere denied them. Women were particularly attracted to Christian Science, the argument continues, because it offered them an escape from their traditional, social, political, and religious roles.

Yet, as McDonald convincingly maintains, these kinds of arguments are of questionable historical validity, clearly influenced by and serving to reinforce the traditional (male) view of public women as those in rebellion against women's accepted (private) sphere. Critics of Mary Baker Eddy, for example, have claimed that her articulation of Christian Science was not motivated by a search for truth but by her envy of maleness, as well as her own personal ambition for power and glory. In fact, however, as McDonald writes, there is no evidence that these charges are warranted. On the contrary, she argues, Eddy's articulation of Christian Science did not develop out of a desire for power but out of her own unwillingness to accept Christianity's traditional resignation to suffering in this life with hope of attaining salvation in the next.

This belief led to the consequent, sincerely held conviction that disease and other human illnesses were not inherent in Creation but rather the result of alienation from God. While one may question McDonald's argument in favor of the more traditional, sociopolitical view of Eddy, it is more difficult to refute her conclusion, based on letters in the *Christian Science Journal*, that the followers of Eddy, those who are of greatest interest to us here, came to Christian Science in order to satisfy a very real intellectual and spiritual hunger. As these letters reveal, hundreds of thousands of American men and women, Jews and Christians, found particularly appealing Eddy's concept of a mother-father God of love, goodness, and compassion, as well as her answer to the question *If God is good, why is there suffering?* (Answer: there isn't; suffering is an illusion.)

In reading *Science and Health*, the textbook of Christian Science, one is immediately struck by the centrality of Christ in Eddy's teachings. As the son of God whose incarnation as Jesus of Nazareth indicated the oneness of God and humanity, Christ serves as the divine principle that, through the atonement, has made reconciliation with God possible. Affirming belief in both the crucifixion of Jesus and his resurrection as proofs of God's love, truth, and

FIGURE I.I. Mary Baker Eddy. Courtesy of the Mary Baker Eddy Collection.

goodness, Eddy maintained that "we are not Christian Scientists until we leave all for Christ."[27] To do so, according to Eddy's teachings, was to leave behind the corporeal and the mortal, to rid oneself of material beliefs, including beliefs in the reality of matter, illness, sickness, evil, and even death, and to embrace God as spirit and truth as spiritual power. To follow Christ, then, was to acknowledge that God is mind and that "all that Mind, God, is, or hath made, is good, and He made all. Hence evil is not made and is not real."[28]

For Eddy, one was able to follow Christ in two ways: first, as a disciple of the human Jesus, who revealed through example that healing powers and the overcoming of sickness and death are not only divine but human powers, possessed by us all; and second, as a follower of the divine Christ, the son of God and divine consciousness or power within us, who is the source of love, truth, and eternal life. Eddy's insistence that God is "All-in-All," or spirit, led her to conclude that drugs and other forms of material medicine were unnecessary, for the medicine employed by God was mind, "God's remedy for error of every kind." It is mind alone, she maintained, that can diagnose and destroy disease, for only mind focuses on the true, mental cause, of all illness. Speaking

of mind as a curative principle, she therefore maintained that spiritual practitioners, those who recognized the true cause of illness, were more efficacious
as healers than the physician who, by "examining bodily symptoms, telling the
patient that he is sick, and treating the case according to his physical diagnosis,
would naturally induce the very disease he is trying to cure."[29] Indeed, she
contended, "we cannot serve two masters nor perceive divine Science with the
material senses. Drugs and hygiene cannot successfully usurp the place and
power of the divine source of all health and perfection."[30] If only this truth
were perceived and accepted, all of humanity, she insisted, through the merits
of Christ, might well be redeemed.

Most Jews who joined Christian Science ignored Eddy's Christocentrism,
focusing on Jesus as healer and exemplar of the human potential to overcome
sin, sickness, and death. Among those who acknowledged the centrality of
Christ in Eddy's teachings, some reluctantly accepted this centrality, believing
that what they gained from Christian Science was worth the discomfort over
constantly invoking Christ's name. Others chose to selectively emphasize
Christ as truth rather than as son of God or savior. Undoubtedly, the optimism
of Eddy's teachings, what William James described as the religion of healthy-
mindedness, appealed to many thousands of Jews, as it did to many thousands
of Christians. Stripped of its Christian character, Christian Science rested on
a number of religious beliefs that Jews and Christians shared: belief in God as
creator, father, source of justice, mercy, wisdom, love, truth, and goodness, and
one in whose image we, as humans, have been created. Though Eddy herself
emphasized God as mind, principle, or spirit more than she did God as being,
the connection that she made between the nature of God and the nature of
humanity possessed a strange, though to some Jews and Christians not incom-
prehensible, sort of logic. If God is spirit, she wrote, and we are created in the
divine image, then we must be spiritual beings (as opposed to spirit itself,
which would falsely imply that we were God). In other words, because we are
created as reflections of the divine, we can only reflect that which is in the
divine nature. Sin, sickness, and death are as foreign to our true nature as they
are to God's. Reaffirming, then, the traditional Jewish and Christian belief in
the essential kinship between God and humanity, Eddy took this belief a step
further, declaring, in opposition to both traditional Jewish and Christian teachings, that spirit is the only real substance and that sin, sickness, and death are
unrealities, untrue "because they are not of God."

For some Jews, who may have found little comfort in Judaism's vague
discussions of a future world to come, Eddy's pronouncement of death as
unreal must have been particularly appealing. "If you or I should appear to
die," she wrote,

> we should not be dead. The seeming disease, caused by a majority
> of human beliefs that man must die, or produced by mental assas-

sins, does not in the least disprove Christian Science; rather does it evidence the truth of its basic proposition that mortal thoughts in belief rule the materiality miscalled life in the body or in matter. But the forever fact remains paramount that Life, Truth, and Love, save from sin, disease and death.[31]

Equally appealing was the optimism with which Eddy approached suffering, sickness, and evil. Declaring that all were unrealities produced by the mortal mind, Eddy instilled in her followers personal confidence and hope that they could be overcome if one recognized their true illusory nature. That some illnesses from which followers of Mary Baker Eddy suffered were indeed mentally produced and thus cured through mental and spiritual aids undoubtedly helped increase the church's appeal.

Some critics have pointed to the impersonal nature of Eddy's God.[32] Yet there is no evidence to suggest that Christian Scientists themselves viewed God in this way. While the concept of God as power, truth, or spirit may sound impersonal, the images Eddy used to convey this concept, in particular her image of God as both father and mother, were extremely personal in nature. Many who joined remarked on the great sense of nearness they felt to a "tender Father-Mother" and to "a God whom they could 'at last' understand because the proof of His reality and power in healing showed that He [was] not just a supernatural person to whom one [could] pray" but an ever perfect and harmonious principle of all being.[33] What Christian Science seemed to provide was greater knowledge of the divine and of God's spiritual laws, a knowledge that led many of those who followed Eddy's teachings to truly feel, for the first time, that they indeed were among God's children.

Though Christian Science has always kept its records closed to public examination, national census reports reveal that between 1906 and 1926, the years of Christian Science's greatest growth, church membership increased from eighty-five thousand to over two hundred thousand men and women.[34] Within the American Jewish community, interest in Christian Science closely followed this period of growth. As Christian Science gained adherents among the general, non-Jewish population, so it gained adherents among Jews. How many Jews it attracted, however, still remains uncertain. In a paper presented in May 1912 to members of the CCAR, Rabbi Maurice Lefkovits maintained that the number of Jews who had formally affiliated with Christian Science was "infinitesimally small."[35] He estimated that the figure was less than one twenty-fifth of 1 percent of the total American Jewish population, a population that by 1912 numbered approximately three million. If Lefkovits's estimate was accurate, by 1912 slightly more than twelve hundred Jews had formally identified themselves as Christian Scientists.[36] Not all Reform rabbis, however, concurred with Lefkovits's admittedly low estimation (and indeed, Lefkovits himself never explained how he arrived at such a figure) and by 1917 the CCAR began to view the defection of Jews to Christian Science with great alarm. Rabbi William Rosenau, spiritual leader of Congregation Oheb Shalom in Baltimore and president of the CCAR from 1915 to 1917, publicly spoke out against the "many worthy men and women" who had left Judaism for entrance into the Christian Science Church, while Rabbi Stephen Wise maintained that although the number of Jews turning to Christian Science might not be as large as was commonly believed, the numbers were "considerable enough to be disturbing and arrestive [sic]."³⁷

Admitting to being astonished by the number of Jews who were attracted to Christian Science, Wise guessed that there were probably few Christian Science churches in America without Jews among their members. This conversion, he warned, was more serious than those in the past, primarily because of the sincerity with which the teachings of Mary Baker Eddy were being embraced. Throughout the 1920s and 1930s, some rabbis continued to insist that reported figures on the number of Jews who had joined Christian Science were greatly exaggerated. Yet a significant number spoke out from the pulpit against the "growing numbers of Jews" who had done so. In 1928, Rabbi Louis Gross estimated that in Greater New York one hundred thousand Jews had become Christian Scientists, while Rabbi Samuel Felix Mendelsohn, writing in 1936, asserted that seventy thousand Jews in New York City alone had become members. This figure is not inconsistent with an earlier figure—from a column in the London Jewish Chronicle in 1924 that "reputably estimated" that sixty thousand Jews in New York City had joined Christian Science.

The numbers cited by E. G. Homrighausen in his study "Evangelism and the Jewish People," published in 1950, are far greater. According to Homrighausen, "perhaps two hundred thousand" Jews became Christian Scientists during the early decades of the twentieth century. In explaining later how he arrived at this figure, which he took to be conservative, Homrighausen maintained that it had been given to him by Conrad Hofman, former secretary of the International Missionary Council (an organization that was later incorporated into the World Council of Churches), who was in charge of the Presbyterian Church's missionary work in connection with Jews during the 1950s.³⁸ There are no records, however, indicating how Hofman himself arrived at this figure. Neither do there seem to be other contemporaneous reports that substantiate Hofman's claim.

In short, there seem to be no reliable statistics concerning the number of Jews who took an active interest in, much less joined, Christian Science. As John Appel maintained in his 1969 study of Jewish attraction to Christian Science,

all available figures are suspect because they originate entirely from Christian clergy or rabbis with vested interests in the statistics. One group wished to minimize Jewish memberships in Christian Science; a second to impress readers with the alleged dangers arising from Jewish defections to Christian Science and to publicize their own efforts to slow or reverse this drift; a third to show prospective evangelists that Jews who were willing to embrace Christian Science ought to be ready for the true salvation found in more orthodox Christian denominations.[39]

In light of these various motives, I suspect that the number of Jews who actually joined Christian Science between 1906 and 1926 lies somewhere between four thousand and forty thousand. The former figure assumes that the number of Jews who became Christian Scientists never exceeded 1 percent of the American Jewish population, yet grew beyond one twenty-fifth of 1 percent, perhaps to as much as one tenth, out of a Jewish population that by 1926 had grown to approximately four million. The latter figure assumes that at least some claims of far higher figures were based on fact yet also assumes that if by 1926, as national census reports reveal, Christian Science claimed a membership of two hundred thousand, no more than one-fifth of its members (if that) would have been Jews.

In either case, however, the impact of Christian Science on the American Jewish community was significant, both in terms of the numbers of Jews that it attracted and the response it elicited within the American Jewish community. In part at least, this response reflected a genuine concern for numbers—that is, the fear, especially among the Reform rabbinate, that Christian Science would help deplete the American Jewish population. Yet it also reflected an awareness that those joining Christian Science included those whom the Jewish community could ill afford to lose, men and women who by and large were not previously unaffiliated but were active community organizational and financial supporters.

Over one half, and perhaps as many as two-thirds, of the Jews who joined Christian Science were women. Indeed, most non-Jews who affiliated with Christian Science were women as well. Yet, as Jean McDonald observes, it would be erroneous to characterize (or dismiss) Christian Science as a women's movement, first because thousands of men were also attracted to Christian Science and, second, because the roles that men occupied were not insignificant. On the contrary, many men succeeded in becoming church leaders. If one looks at letters, testimonials, and other personal records of Jews who joined Christian Science, one similarly finds that many of its most enthusiastic Jewish supporters were men. Undoubtedly, they joined for many of the same reasons that women did. Yet it may well be that among Jews in particular, Christian Science had a special appeal to women, not because, as John Appel implies, women more frequently suffered from mental and physical ailments than did men but because Jewish women found within Christian Science a rare opportunity to fully develop their own spiritual nature.

Most of the Jewish women who joined Christian Science knew little of the intellectual, theological, and liturgical tradition they had left behind. As women, many possessed a religious education that was minimal at best. Few could read Hebrew, and even fewer could understand it. Their participation in public worship was limited, and, whether from Orthodox or Reform backgrounds, they were unable to assume spiritual leadership roles. Few were encouraged to read the classics of Jewish literature, even in translation. Indeed, the study of religious texts was viewed as a male pursuit. While the religious education of men from Reform backgrounds was far less rigorous, and less traditional, than the education of Orthodox men, sending one's sons to religious school received a higher priority than sending one's daughters among all segments of the American Jewish population. There were exceptions, of course. But on the whole, what Christian Science provided Jewish women, for the first time, were religious texts that they not only could study but were expected to study. Written in English, these texts were easily accessible. With key concepts clearly stated and often repeated, they were comprehensible as well.

Christian Science took women's spiritual nature seriously. While a woman reading early rabbinic writings might feel, with justification, as though she were trespassing, overhearing conversations and teachings written by and for men, Eddy's *Science and Health with Key to the Scriptures* was meant to be read by men and women. Its author was a woman who claimed for herself divine revelation. The notion that God had chosen to speak through a woman must have had tremendous appeal to many Jewish women whose own previous understanding of religious truth was what had been handed down by God to Abraham, Isaac, Jacob, Moses, and the Hebrew (male) prophets and further preserved and transmitted by (male) rabbis extending over a period of several generations. Moreover, Eddy's message was that each one of us, male or female, is capable of gaining and transmitting religious truth, for such truth depends not, as it does in the rabbinic view, on years of disciplined study, but on the emotional—as well as, perhaps, the intellectual—recognition that the divine principle is ever present within the human consciousness, leading sin and disease to lose their reality "as naturally and as necessarily as darkness gives place to light and sin to reformation."[40]

Eddy constantly maintained, in a way that Judaism often did not, that both men and women are spiritual beings, capable of achieving spiritual consciousness through study and prayer. Her image of God as mother and father reiterated her conviction that both men and women are created in God's image. Moreover, her institution of a church in which leadership was assumed not by ordained ministers but by lay men and women, offered women the rare opportunity to occupy a number of public leadership roles. These roles included serving as a Christian Science lecturer, spiritual practitioner, and teacher. That no woman succeeded Eddy as the organizational leader of Christian Science must have been relatively unimportant to the many thousands of women who continued to find inspiration in Eddy's life and teachings. The fact is, even after her death, Eddy continued to remain the church's leader, with *Science and Health* still serving as its authoritative textbook and the rules of church governance established by Eddy still in operation.

While one often thinks of Christian Science as a Northern movement, Christian Science did, in fact, gain appeal among many late nineteenth- and early twentieth-century Southerners, Christians as well as Jews. On the whole, Christian Science took root in the South somewhat later than in the North. Yet Christian Science groups were created in the South only seven years after the establishment of the First Church of Christ, Scientist, in Boston, in 1879. According to Carolyn Cobb, in 1886 Julia Bartlett, a follower of Mary Baker Eddy, moved from Boston to Atlanta and began a class in the teachings of Christian Science. Among those to whom she offered spiritual aid was Sue Harper Mims, who soon after organized a regular Christian Science meeting in her home. Wealthy, sophisticated and cultured, Mims and her husband, Major Livingston Mims (who, in 1901, was elected the city's mayor) numbered among Atlanta's leading citizens. Having gained prominence not only as the wife of Major Mims but also as founder of the Shakespeare Club, the first cultural club organized in Atlanta, Sue Mims later became known throughout the South, and eventually throughout the United States, as a Christian Science teacher, practitioner, and lecturer and as the founder of Atlanta's first Church of Christ, Scientist. One of Christian Science's first four lecturers and one of the first two women appointed to the lecture board of the mother church in Boston, she and Mary Baker Eddy, who called Sue Mims "the Queen of the South," maintained a warm association and enjoyed an ongoing correspondence with one another for many years.[41]

As Sue Harper Mims recorded in her diary, Christian Science quickly became the most important aspect of her life, and she actively sought to share this faith with others. The Science group she first organized in her home, consisting of four other people, steadily grew in size and soon moved to larger quarters. In the fall of 1898, ground was broken for the establishment of a church, which soon attracted two hundred members and claimed the interest of many more. Consequently, in 1914, a year after Sue Mims's death, construction of a larger building, hailed by the *Atlanta Journal* as one of the "very finest churches of any denomination in the whole south," was completed.[42] During the latter years of her life, Mims continued to lecture on Christian Science throughout the United States. After one such lecture in Detroit, delivered before an audience of five thousand people, a reporter asked: "Mrs. Mims, tell me how a woman of your age can make her voice carry as you have done to the farthest seat of the upper gallery of this vast auditorium, when young men with big voices cannot do it?" She is said to have replied, quite straightforwardly, that the "voice of Truth" knew no limitations.

According to a lengthy article in its local newspaper, the *Times-Picayune*, New Orleans was the first city in Louisiana to establish a Church of Christ, Scientist. Gaining its charter in 1895, the church included as members those who had begun to meet in informal groups or clusters as early as 1887, the year in which a copy of Eddy's *Science and Health* apparently was first brought to New Orleans. Members of the group both studied Eddy's work and practiced its teaching. Despite efforts by opponents to make the practice of Christian Science illegal throughout the state, and despite the frequent legal persecution of Christian Science practitioners, a law was passed by the turn of the century specifically permitting the practice of Christian Science within the state of Louisiana. By 1930, numerous Christian Science churches and societies had come into existence throughout Louisiana, with small but active membership lists of men and women.[43] Newspaper articles, diaries, and references in the *Christian Science Journal* indicate that Christian Science churches were also established in various cities in North Carolina, South Carolina, Arkansas, Tennessee, and Alabama. Here, as elsewhere, one was able to learn about Christian Science by attending weekly services, reading *Science and Health*, talking to a local practitioner, and going to one of the many Christian Science lectures delivered throughout the North and South during the late nineteenth and early twentieth centuries.

We have only a small number of letters, sermons, and diaries indicating that Jews were among those that attended these lectures. Yet given the fact that thousands of Jews from the North and South eventually joined Christian Science, we can surmise that many did attend, just as we can surmise, again from letters, diaries, and sermons, that thousands of Jews read *Science and Health*, attended Science meetings, and sought the aid of practitioners who promised them relief through spiritual healing. Jews who joined Christian Science included immigrants and native-born Americans of both eastern European and German extraction. While numerically more Jews of eastern European descent actually joined the church than did German Jews, in terms of percentages of the population (by 1917, two million eastern European Jews versus a few hundred thousand of German-Jewish extraction), Christian Science apparently had equal appeal among both segments of the American Jewish community. Similarly, it succeeded in attracting both Orthodox Jews, or those who were Orthodox by birth (usually of eastern European extraction), and those Jews, usually of German extraction, who affiliated themselves, or had previously affiliated themselves, with Reform.

Like most non-Jews who joined, most of the Jews who turned to Christian Science were urban and middle- to upper-middle-class. Thus, the immigrants who joined were not new arrivals but those who had already begun, or had completed, the process of Americanization. Jews who were attracted to Christian Science, again, like non-Jews, included both laypeople and members of the clergy. One highly publicized occurrence was the defection of a Reform rabbi, Max Wertheimer, to Christian Science in 1900. Wertheimer, the rabbi of Temple B'nai Yeshurun in Dayton, Ohio, declined reappointment in 1899, apparently because of his growing attraction to non-Jewish forms of spirituality, including theosophy, spiritualism, and Christian Science. Subsequently, he resigned as a member of the Central Conference of American Rabbis (CCAR) and joined the Christian Science Church. According to Rabbi David Eichhorn, writing in 1938, Mary Baker Eddy herself financed Wertheimer's study.[44] As might be expected, the number of rabbis who were attracted to Christian Science was relatively small. Yet as late as 1912, despite rabbinic leaders like Max Heller insisting otherwise, there apparently were a number of Reform rabbis who maintained from the pulpit that one could be both a good Jew and a Christian Scientist.[45]

Jewish reaction to the increasing numbers of Jews who were attracted to Christian Science ranged from indifference to hostility. For the most part, Orthodox rabbis met the defection of Jews to Christian Science with silence, perhaps reasoning that this defection was no worse than the "defection" of Orthodox Jews to secularism or Reform. While most Conservative leaders maintained a similar stance, some, most notably Mordecai Kaplan, voiced concern over the implications of this defection. Writing in the *Menorah Journal*, Kaplan faulted Judaism itself for leading thousands of Jews to erroneously believe that only through Christian Science could one discover the healing influence of the divine presence. To counteract this influence, he suggested that a reconstructed Judaism, meaningful to present and future generations, consciously "include among other things a regimen for the care of the body with a view to the prolongation of life and the proper fulfillment of man's physical and mental functions." Kaplan went so far as to assert that "it would not even be out of place to include suggestions for making proper use of mental influence on physical health."[46]

Reactions from Reform rabbis were both more sustained and more vociferous. By the end of the nineteenth century, leading Reform rabbis like Isaac Mayer Wise began to denounce Christian Science as charlatanry, staunchly maintaining that he didn't believe in Christian Science any more than he believed in theosophy, spiritualism, Christology, or the infallibility of any person, church, or book. Spiritualistic mediums and Christian Scientists who profess to cure disease through practitioners and mental training, Wise wrote in 1898, "are one and all, without exception, willful and deliberate cheats who prey on the weakness of humanity purely for the sake of gain."[47] What's more, he maintained (in 1900), "it is almost incredible that Jews who regard themselves as of more than average intelligence should have recourse to Christian Science," a religion of "pure quackery" that is "rapidly assuming the proportions of an epidemic delusion."[48] References to Christian Science by other Reform rabbis were similarly hostile. While acknowledging that Christian Science seemed to be meeting a spiritual need that some Jews felt they could not find in Judaism, many shared Max Heller's feelings of pity and scorn for those Jews who had taken up Christian Science "with avidity, out of love for the bluish-gray haze of unintelligible twaddle which [their] female savior has managed to spin around the simplest utterances."[49] Though Heller's contempt may well have been genuine, it was in all probability motivated by the fact that Heller, like other early twentieth-century Reform rabbis, perceived Christian Science as a threat not only to the American Jewish community in general but also, and more directly, to the Reform movement itself.

There were several reasons for the latter fear. First, many believed that while Orthodoxy was primarily losing adherents to Reform, Reform was losing adherents either to agnosticism or Christian Science. Thus, Jewish attraction to Christian Science directly threatened Reform Judaism, robbing it of real or potential members. Second, since Reform prided itself on being the Judaism of the future, many Reform rabbis, if not the CCAR as a whole, came to believe that it was the responsibility of the Reform movement to meet the challenge posed by Christian Science. Indeed, many felt that only Reform could provide a solution, since it alone was capable of revitalizing American Jewry's spiritual life. And finally, many in the Reform movement recognized that Jewish defection to Christian Science gave credence to a charge leveled at Reform throughout the early decades of the twentieth century, namely that Reform Judaism was in trouble, beset by difficulties, shortcomings, and disintegrating influences it could not overcome. The defection to Christian Science could be seen, and was seen, as a visible sign of Reform's spiritual stagnation.

By 1912, the CCAR, in agreement with the conclusions of Maurice Lefkovits's paper "The Attitude of Judaism toward Christian Science," passed a resolution maintaining that "Jewish adherence to Christian Science implies abjuration of Judaism." Any Jew subscribing to Christian Science teachings, it continued, would henceforth be regarded "as a non-Jew in faith."[50] Five years later, Rabbi William Rosenau, in his presidential address, asked members of the CCAR whether they ought to do something "to prevent further entrance of Jews into the Christian Science church" and recommended that a paper be read at the CCAR convention the following year with suggestions as to how the influences of Christian Science might best be counteracted. He himself advocated "the employment of means adopted by the Christian Science Church in dealing with Jews, as long as these means are not opposed to good and authentic Jewish practice."[51]

The CCAR Committee on the President's Message apparently did not share Rosenau's sentiments as to the urgency of the issue, concluding that the 1912 resolution was an adequate response. Yet in the years that followed, a number of Reform rabbis searched for ways to take more concrete action. One idea, supported by the majority of CCAR members, was to revitalize Reform Judaism by reemphasizing its notion of the Jewish mission, a concept embedded in the ideology of nineteenth-century classical Reform. This mission, as understood by Reform Judaism, was to bear witness to the reality of God and to spread God's moral teachings to all of humanity. It was the belief of many that if this concept could be communicated to American Jews, and its importance underscored, Christian Science would seem less attractive, first, because Jews would discover within Judaism itself the opportunity to develop their spiritual nature, and second, because Jewish men and women would realize that personal happiness, health, and peace of mind were not in and of themselves sufficient. Between 1917 and 1925, when the CCAR once again took up the issue of Jews and mental healing, scores of sermons and papers were delivered by Reform rabbis focusing on the mission idea. Some, like Samuel Schulman, the rabbi of Temple Beth-El in New York City and a former president of the CCAR, emphasized the importance of bearing witness to God, while others, like Stephen Wise and Kaufmann Kohler, focused on the necessity of serving God by serving others.

In sermon after sermon, Samuel Schulman spoke about the spiritual values of Judaism and the need for a spiritual revival. "What we need to-day," he wrote, "is a vitalization of simple faith in God, of loyalty to the heritage of our fathers, of the religious consciousness of the Jew."[52] He spoke of converting Jews to Judaism and of actively encouraging all Jews to search their hearts and return to God. In a series of essays on the Jewish mission published between 1918 and 1924, Schulman maintained that Jews were primarily spiritual people who had been chosen to serve as God's instruments, bringing others to an awareness of God's reality and of his moral teachings. For Schulman, as for many other Reform Jews, this mission could only be carried out through the geographical dispersion of the Jewish people, making the return of the Jews to the land of Israel not merely undesirable but in opposition to that which God intended. He spoke of creating a Jewish culture "permeated, fructified, shaped, if you will, by the Jewish religious consciousness," divorced from any sense of separate nationalistic identity, and he asserted, with confidence, that if such a culture were to be created, Jews would no longer seek to lose themselves in alien churches but would enthusiastically commit themselves to working for the realization of Israel's prophetic ideals and hopes, convenanting themselves once again to the one spiritual God of humanity.[53]

Responding to a paper on the Jewish mission delivered at the 1919 CCAR conference by Rabbi Kaufmann Kohler, the president of Reform Judaism's rabbinical seminary, Hebrew Union College (HUC), Schulman said that in his opinion the demand of the hour was not to "justify Reform Judaism's emphasis on the mission idea . . . [but] to convert the Jew in life to this idea of a mission." We need to make clear, he continued, that this idea is by no means antiquated. Rather, it should inspire us to begin a period of spiritual reconstruction, supplementing the critical, analytical, rationalistic, and opportunistic work of Reform with "a deliberate determination to build up spiritual values in the consciousness of the Jew," recognizing that the religious life, as essentially personal faith, is sorely in need of revitalization. "It does not do us any good," he concluded,

> merely to rail at the thousands of Jews who turn their back on the wells of living waters, on the God of their fathers and go to seek satisfaction for their emotions and mystic longings to wells which we hold contain no water, and change the living God for what we consider an idol, because it is, in the main, an untruth. [Instead] we must ask ourselves whether, through appealing to the intellect and to ethics, which are primarily concerned with the relations of man to man, we have not kept shut up our own wells of living waters? We must ask ourselves whether we have not, through this neglect, starved our people emotionally and spiritually?[54]

Believing that the answer to these questions was yes, Schulman insisted that both the priestly and the prophetic elements of Judaism needed to be maintained, for righteousness without God, he asserted, is self-righteousness, as "ethically imperfect and eventually disintegrating" as is a God-consciousness that ignores the importance of moral action.

In a lengthy address delivered to members of the CCAR in 1919, Rabbi Julian Morgenstern, professor of Bible at HUC (and later its president), described ways in which this Jewish spiritual consciousness might best be reawakened. He maintained that Reform's spiritual stagnation could be attributed to the fact that American Reform Judaism had not freed itself from its German roots. If, he continued, an increasing number of Jews are seeking personal comfort and help in Christian Science it is because we have failed to recognize that the "conventional phrases of pious dogma and theology" that were part and parcel of German Reform Judaism do not speak to American Jews, who, like other Americans, seek to find in religion the answer to problems that affect them as individual men and women, such as the meaning of life, the divine purpose of suffering, the efficacy of prayer, and the truth regarding the future. Like other Americans, we demand that religion satisfy our individual spirit, our "mystical needs and cravings." A truly American Judaism must therefore minister to the individual as well as to the group, answering the "call of the heart as well as of the head," replacing "cold theology and bloodless rationalism" with the language of warm feeling and emotion, enabling its adherents, "like Moses of old, to commune with God face to face, as a man communes with his friend."

The reason, he asserted, we have not been successful in checking the drift of Jews to Christian Science is that we have pursued the wrong course. Rather than denouncing Christian Science Jews and reading them out of Judaism, as we have done, and exposing the incompatibility of Judaism and Christian Science, as we have done as well, we might better ask: what is wrong with Reform

Judaism, what is lacking in Reform that would lead so many of its adherents to Christian Science? In other words, does American Reform completely minister to the daily spiritual needs of its adherents and if not, how might these spiritual needs best be met? To live as American Jews, he concluded, we must correlate Judaism with Americanism, recognizing that while we may "pray in the past as Jews, we work and aspire in the present as Americans." To revitalize the prophetic spirit and to ensure that the divine mission of Israel be fulfilled, Morgenstern suggested the creation of a new American Judaism that would "evolve along the lines of simple, positive living." As he envisioned it, this new re-formed and restated Judaism would remain identifiably Jewish yet at the same time would become a creative and strengthening force in the daily lives of its adherents.[55]

A year later, Rabbi Leo Franklin of Michigan, in his presidential address to members of the CCAR, reported that at a recent meeting of the CCAR Executive Committee, a delegation of women from the (Reform movement's) National Federation of Temple Sisterhoods requested that the CCAR publish a book of Jewish meditations and prayers. Their hope was that by drawing on Jewish sources, such a book might help hold on to those leaving Judaism for Christian Science, "ignorantly believing" that Judaism was incapable of satisfying "the cravings of their souls."[56] While Franklin, members of the executive committee, and the CCAR special committee appointed to evaluate the president's message all strongly supported the publication of such a book, there is no evidence that such a project was ever completed. A committee to compile the book was appointed, with Henry Berkowitz serving as chair, but illness forced Berkowitz to resign, and there appears to be no mention of the committee or this project in records of subsequent CCAR meetings.

While Franklin made no explicit mention of the mission idea in his presidential address, Harry Ettelson, delivering the 1920 conference sermon, took the concept of mission as his focus. "The very effort to transform our mission into an actual and active program," he maintained, "will not only restore dignity and potency to the mission-idea itself, but by self-reaction will make Judaism meaningful for the Jew, giving the Jew more to do of, for and by Judaism."[57] These views were reaffirmed at the 1921 CCAR conference, with Leo Franklin speaking, in his presidential address, on ways the rabbi might better stimulate the spiritual life of his community, and Rabbi Louis Witt, in his conference lecture, discussing the importance of transforming the synagogue from a secular, rationalistic institution into one capable of promoting "inspirational access to the Unseen," teaching its members to interpret their own self-realization in terms of both "the realization of human good and the hunger for God."[58]

The importance of the Jewish mission, as interpreted by Reform, was reiterated at subsequent CCAR conferences. Rabbi Edward Calisch, in his 1923 presidential message, claimed that the sole object of this mission was "the stressing and conserving of the spiritual life," while Rabbi Abram Simon, in his presidential message a year later, spoke of humanity's "gnawing hunger and burning thirst . . . for the bread and the waters of the living God." Yet along with these sentiments went the conviction that the reawakening of Jewish religious consciousness meant more than a growing awareness of God's presence. As Rabbi Harry Ettelson put it, the true beauty of the soul could only come about through the realization of divine and human ethical power.

To better stress its commitment to moral action, the CCAR decided in 1918 to change the name of its Committee on Synagogue and Industrial Relations to the Commission on Social Justice. While the commission, at least in its earliest years, did little more than issue tracts, platforms, and other formal statements on the CCAR's support for the implementation of a minimum wage, an eight-hour work day, safe and sanitary conditions for working people, the right of labor to organize, adequate workmen's compensation, and so on, the commission gave expression, in words if not in deeds, to the Reform movement's belief that social justice was an integral part of its religious mission. This idea was clarified and discussed at length by Kaufmann Kohler in the aforementioned paper delivered in 1919 at the CCAR's annual meeting. "Religion," he asserted, "must be *life*, a life of *service*, not self-seeking solicitude for happiness, either here or hereafter."[59] Our mission, he continued, can only be achieved if we live and work in and with the world, actively promoting social justice. Sharing this vision of a reconstructed, socially active Judaism, Rabbi Louis Grossman, as president of the CCAR, maintained that religion was not a creed but a social organization that needed to go beyond its theological and congregational origins to carefully examine and act on the social and industrial problems confronting the world in which we live. Our mission, he said, is one of morality, and thus our task is to persuade the world to emulate our virtues and to make them the "springboards for civilization."[60]

Subsequent presidential addresses, similarly focusing on ways Judaism might respond to the postwar crisis, emphasized the contribution that Jews might make to humanity in terms of strengthening its moral fiber. These addresses also reminded Reform rabbis of their duty to the Jewish community, maintaining, as Edward Calisch put it in 1922, that our religious mission is to consecrate "our life, our loyalty and our love . . . to the ideal of ethical monotheism."[61] These sentiments could be heard not only at rabbinical conferences but also from the podium and the pulpit. Perhaps the most eloquent spokesperson for these ideas was Rabbi Stephen Wise, the founder and spiritual leader of the Free Synagogue in New York City.

Often attracting hundreds of men and women to his Sunday Carnegie Hall lectures, Wise repeatedly proclaimed the social message of the Hebrew prophets as central to Judaism, and for that matter, to Christianity. To Wise, one could not achieve a right relationship to God without first attaining a right relationship to one's fellow human beings. He thus defended the importance of social programs and openly spoke of ways such programs might best be implemented within a democratic political system. Among the causes that Wise defended were women's suffrage, better hours and more sanitary conditions in the work place, the abolition of child labor, greater religious tolerance as part of the American ideal, the liberalization of American divorce laws, and the founding of an American Jewish Congress to help combat anti-Semitism and to convey the common purpose and will of American Jewry. He enthusiastically supported Woodrow Wilson's decision in 1917 to enter World War I, although he admitted that before then he, like so many Americans, had felt that no war could be justified. Similarly, he openly supported Wilson's efforts after the war to achieve world justice. Finally, unlike many, if not most, in the Reform rabbinate, Wise actively worked to help rebuild Palestine as a Jewish state; he helped to found the Federation of American Zionists as early as 1897 and later, in 1918, was elected president of the Zionist Organization of America.

Although Stephen Wise rarely spoke of the mission idea, perhaps because of its identification in the minds of many with a position of anti-Zionism, he repeatedly called for the "reformation of the Jew." Such a reformation, he insisted, rested on the reclamation of Judaism's spiritual message as well as its moral ideals. What is needed, he said in an address on liberal Judaism delivered in 1920, "is not to restore the use of phylacteries, but to bind on the heart of the Jew the obligation in all essentials of feeling and thinking, and living and dreaming as a Jew."[62] For Wise, this sense of moral and social obligation represented the core of Judaism. He thus denounced Christian Science, and those Jews who had gone over to it, as seeking the prolongation of life rather than the "rightness of living." Unlike Judaism, Wise maintained, Christian Science tells its adherents that one can *be* well instead of insisting that they *do* well. It wrongly stresses love over justice and erroneously emphasizes the good that is to be granted one in life rather than the best that ought to be exacted from one. Wise's major objection to Christian Science was that it imposed on its adherents no new duties or burdens, that it offered no new responsibilities and made no new demands. The best way to combat its influence, he advised, was through a spiritual revival and a moral rebirth, making clear to those who might otherwise be attracted to Christian Science that Judaism, and indeed true religion in general, has no awards to make or bounties to bestow. "If ever there was a time in the world," he proclaimed at the end of the World War I,

> when religion needed to be voiced and interpreted in terms of duty
> and obligation, when it was needed to make religion a duty and duty
> a religion, that time is now. . . . This is the aim of religion—not to
> save people from pain or to spare them burdens but to make them
> bear every burden and endure suffering with courage and dignity
> and nobleness.[63]

While many Reform rabbis viewed the promulgation of the Jewish mission idea or, as Stephen Wise put it, the message of the Hebrew prophets, as a means of successfully combating the inroads that Christian Science had made within the American Jewish community, a handful of rabbis proposed a more far-reaching solution. It was their belief that the influence of Christian Science could best be checked both by promulgating the idea of a Jewish mission and by creating a new countervision of happiness and health set within a specifically Jewish context. The first to advocate this solution was a Southern rabbi named Alfred Geiger Moses. To underscore both the Jewish and scientific nature of his vision, and to gain the attention of those attracted to the teachings of Mary Baker Eddy, he identified his own teachings as Jewish Science.

2

Alfred Geiger Moses, New Thought, and the Applied Psychology of Judaism

In direct response to the growing influence of Christian Science within the American Jewish community, Alfred Geiger Moses (1878–1956), the rabbi of Reform congregation Sha'arai Shomayim U-Maskil El Dol (Congregation of the Gates of Heaven and Society of the Friends of the Needy), in Mobile, Alabama, formulated and disseminated teachings that he identified as those of "Jewish Science." First articulating his views in a slim volume published in 1916 titled *Jewish Science: Divine Healing in Judaism*, Alfred Moses maintained that the aim of his book was to create a spiritual renaissance within the American Jewish community by restoring to the modern Jew "the art of genuine prayer."[1] He believed that such a renaissance would serve the dual purposes of awakening religiously apathetic Jews to Judaism's spiritual possibilities and helping stem the growing tide of Jews who claimed adherence to the teachings of Christian Science.

Although Jews settled in Mobile as early as 1724, it wasn't until 1841 that the newly established Sha'arai Shomayim purchased its first burial ground. Three years later, it formally became incorporated as a congregation. By the late 1840s, membership had grown sufficiently to warrant hiring a rabbi, and services were held in the Turner Verein Hall on St. Emanuel Street, formally dedicated as a synagogue in December 1846.[2] Several years later, the growing and prosperous congregation dedicated its new synagogue on Jackson Street, where it remained for over fifty years.[3] During Alfred Geiger Moses' tenure as rabbi (1901–1940), the congregation erected a larger, architecturally impressive synagogue on Government Street, where members continued to worship through the early 1950s. Subsequently, a temple was built on the more suburban Spring Hill Avenue, where the congregation continues to worship today.

By 1855, there were approximately 250 Jews in Mobile.[4] According to temple records, just over one hundred belonged to Sha'arai Shomayim, while a significantly smaller number belonged to a second congregation formed as a result of inner dissension among Sha'arai Shomayim members.[5] By 1905, Sha'arai Shomayim, still Mobile's largest Jewish congregation, boasted a membership of six hundred. Yet, out of a general population of approximately fifty thousand, the Jewish community remained relatively small.[6]

Alfred Geiger Moses was born on September 23, 1878, to Rabbi Adolph and Emma Isaacs Moses. His father, Adolph Moses (1840–1902), was born in Poland and raised in a traditionally religious home. Adolph began his studies under the tutelage of his father, Rabbi Israel Baruch Moses, was educated in Polish *yeshivot* (schools of higher Jewish learning), and later attended the Jewish Theological Seminary in Breslau, headed by Rabbi Zechariah Frankel, a proponent of moderate religious reform. It was in Germany that he subsequently came under the influence of the more religiously liberal Rabbi Abraham Geiger, the major philosophical spokesperson of the Reform movement and the man after whom he later named his son. Adolph Moses arrived in the United States in 1870 and briefly served a congregation in Montgomery, Alabama, before becoming rabbi of Sha'ari Shomayim in Mobile (1871–1881) and Congregation Adath Israel of Louisville, Kentucky (1882–1902). He distinguished himself as a gifted scholar and talented writer. He was the author of *The Religion of Moses*, published in 1894, and *Yahvism and Other Discourses*, a collection of his essays, edited by his successor Hyman G. Enelow, published in 1903. He also edited, with his equally prominent brother, Rabbi Isaac Moses, numerous textbooks for Jewish children.

Identifying with the more radical wing of American Reform Judaism, Adolph Moses placed great emphasis on the universal nature of Judaism and, more generally, of all true religion. In order to underscore his conviction that Judaism was neither a national nor tribal religion, he adopted the term *Yahvism* in its place. It was Moses' hope that by emphasizing faith in the biblical God as universal creator, king, lawgiver, and savior, Yahvism would attract non-Jews while losing those Jews who were Jewish in name alone. Consequently, he believed, Yahvism would succeed where Reform Judaism had failed. Though Reform spoke of a universal messianic age of brotherhood and peace in which all would acknowledge the reality of the one true God, its retention of such tribal concepts as that of the chosen people and its tacit acceptance of nonreligious men and women as Reform Jews limited Reform's effectiveness in bringing this messianic age to fruition. In contrast, Judaism as Yahvism would represent a new "Church of Humanity," grounded in the universal vision of the biblical prophets and based on the mutual respect, union, and universal

FIGURE 2.1. Rabbi Adolph S. Moses. Published with permission of the Jacob Rader Marcus Center of the American Jewish Archives, Cincinnati, Ohio.

love of those who had formerly identified themselves either as Christians or as Jews.[7] In the fall of 1885, Adolph Moses was one of the fifteen Reform rabbis who met in Pittsburgh to deliberate and adopt the platform that became the ideological foundation of Reform Judaism for the next fifty years. In fact, it was he who enthusiastically moved for the adoption of this "able and wonderfully liberal document"[8] that would later have a deep influence on the religious thought of so many Reform rabbis, including his son.

Alfred Geiger Moses received his early education in Louisville. He then attended the University of Cincinnati, earning a bachelor of arts degree in 1900, and HUC, from which he received rabbinic ordination in 1901. That same year, he moved to Mobile, serving as rabbi of Sha'arai Shomayim until 1940, and rabbi emeritus from 1940 to 1946. In June 1915 he married Birdie Feld of Vicksburg, Mississippi, who later gave birth to their only child, Shirley. A noted teacher, orator, scholar, and writer, Alfred Geiger, in addition to his two books on Jewish Science, published several historical monographs, including a history of the Jews of Mobile. According to temple records, he also spoke at "hundreds of service club and other meetings, and gave many Jewish Chautauqua-sponsored lectures throughout the area."[9]

It is conceivable, but unlikely, that Moses' interest in the formulation of Jewish Science stemmed from the drift of Jews to Christian Science within his own community. While a Christian Science group apparently was formed in Mobile as early as 1897, becoming incorporated in July 1902, its membership was small in number.[10] Several Jews eventually joined Christian Science, despite Alfred Geiger Moses' claim that not a single Jew in his community had done so. However, there is no indication either in the *Mobile Register* or the congregational records of Sha'arai Shomayin that Christian Science ever posed a threat to the Mobile Jewish community.[11] Although the reasons remain unclear, Christian Science seems to have had relatively limited appeal among the Jewish and non-Jewish population of Mobile. Jews looking for social advancement through church affiliation, for example, were more likely to join the local Methodist, Episcopal, or Baptist churches than to become affiliated with Christian Science.

Moreover, most Mobile Jews probably recognized that such social conversions were unnecessary. By the early twentieth century, the Jews of Mobile enjoyed extremely cordial relations with their non-Jewish neighbors. For the most part, they were socially accepted, even by the local elite, and their religious differences were viewed with tolerance, if not mutual respect. As Leon Schwarz—the president of Sha'arai Shomayim from 1932 to 1934 and at one time county sheriff and mayor of Mobile—maintained, most Jews living in Mobile during the late nineteenth and early twentieth centuries felt, as did his father, that they had come to Mobile to live among their Gentile neighbors and to be one of them, sharing all of their troubles and differing in religious faith alone.[12]

A number of Jews in the community apparently did join Christian Science for physical and spiritual reasons. Yet the vast majority of Mobile Jewry in the late nineteenth and early twentieth century either identified themselves as Reform, affiliating with Sha'arai Shomayim, or saw themselves as religiously indifferent. Indeed, minutes of meetings of Sha'arai Shomayim's Board of Trustees during this period reveal great concern over the number of Jews who remained religiously unaffiliated, a number reaching as high as two-thirds of the Mobile Jewish population. Sermons delivered by Alfred Moses during the first two decades of the twentieth century repeatedly stressed the importance of "spiritual Judaism," freed of ceremonial laws yet existing "for the glorification of God in acts of humanity, kindness, charity and intellectual growth."[13] Explicitly invoking the concept of religious mission, Moses urged his congregants to bear witness to the living faith of their ancestors and to transform that faith into action, making their congregation the "pride of every Jew of Mobile," one that might encourage both affiliated and the unaffiliated Jews to consecrate themselves to God.

FIGURE 2.2. Alfred Geiger Moses, during the early years of his tenure as
rabbi of Congregation Sha'arai Shomayim in Mobile, Alabama. Courtesy of
the Spring Hill Avenue Temple, Congregation Sha'arai Shomayim.

As superintendent of Sha'arai Shomayim's Sabbath School, which by 1916
boasted an enrollment of one hundred, Alfred Moses attempted to instill in
the students a knowledge and love of Judaism and to assist their parents in
creating a Jewish atmosphere within their homes. To do so, he offered to provide parents with literature on ways of keeping the Sabbath and the holidays
and said that he and the teachers of the Sabbath School would gladly give
special instruction to those parents who had "no exact knowledge of the methods of Domestic Worship."[14] Reports to the synagogue's standing committee
on religion from both the Committee on Home Ceremonies and the Committee on Temple Attendance, dated November 1915, reveal that the leaders of
the congregation put great effort into combating what they perceived to be
spiritual apathy among the Mobile Jewish community in general by instituting

ways in which members of Sha'arai Shomayim might set a religious example for the community as a whole.

An examination of the minutes of Board of Trustees meetings, committee reports, and sermons and articles written by Alfred Geiger Moses from his election as rabbi in 1901 through the 1920s underscores the concern of Moses and the lay leadership of Sha'arai Shomayim about religious indifference among Mobile Jewry. In none of these records, however, are there any references to Christian Science. Indeed, in his book on Jewish Science, published in 1916, Moses maintained that while Jews throughout the country were deserting the synagogue to join the Christian Science "cult," this new faith did not pose a major threat to the Jewish community in which he lived. Claiming to have cultivated the teachings of Jewish Science within his own congregation, he boasted of having succeeded in discouraging otherwise interested Jews from joining the Christian Science Church.[15]

Unfortunately, no records remain describing the ways in which these teachings were cultivated. Leon Schwarz prided himself on being a close friend of Alfred Moses and in fact was a member of Moses' wedding party. In his reminiscences, Schwartz describes some of the activities Moses pursued as rabbi of Sha'arai Shomayim, including his work on behalf of B'nai Brith, but makes no mention of either Christian or Jewish Science.

Similarly, Samuel Brown, a past president of Sha'arai Shomayim who knew Alfred Moses well, remembers that among the members of Sha'arai Shomayim interested in Christian Science, there was the general impression that Moses' concept of Jewish Science was a substitute for Mary Baker Eddy's teachings. This impression was formed not from the content of Alfred Geiger Moses' sermons or lectures but from his writings. What's more, Brown's recollection is that members of the congregation did not view Moses' formulation of Jewish Science as particularly directed at them but at members of the American Jewish community as a whole, those for whom Christian Science did indeed hold great attraction.[16]

While in part, then, Alfred Moses' desire to create a spiritual renaissance within the American Jewish community may have been stimulated by the religious apathy he observed in Mobile, his formulation of Jewish Science as a direct counterattack against Christian Science needs to be seen within a broader context. As a Reform rabbi and a member of the CCAR, Moses was well aware of the Reform rabbinate's increasing concern over the growing number of Jews who were joining Christian Science. Explicitly referring to the CCAR's recently having considered this problem, Moses maintained in the 1916 edition of *Jewish Science* that his work was intended to be a spiritual weapon with which the Reform rabbinate as a whole might fight Christian Science. Like the Reform rabbis Morris Lichtenstein and Clifton Harby Levy, who, in the early 1920s, helped organize and assumed leadership of Jewish Science groups in New York City, Alfred Geiger Moses viewed Jewish Science

FIGURE 2.3. Government Street Temple, Congregation Sha'arai Shomayim, Mobile, early twentieth century. Courtesy of the Spring Hill Avenue Temple, Congregation Sha'arai Shomayim.

as both a critique of American Reform Judaism and a solution to what he perceived as Reform's limitations.

In the 1916 edition of his work, Moses made this critique of Reform clear. Referring to the "considerable heart-searching" of members of the Reform rabbinate and others in attempting to find ways of combating the influence of Christian Science within the Jewish community, Moses asserted that the only solution was "to educate the growing generation in the true Jewish doctrine, and to teach not only the abstract, but the *practical* value of faith." To him, Jewish Science met both of these demands and, as such, offered the spiritual means "by which Christian Science [might] be fought from the Jewish stand-point."[17] The "true Jewish doctrine," as Moses understood it, rested on the teachings of classical Reform as embodied in the Pittsburgh Platform of 1885. Equating Judaism with ethical monotheism, Moses, like the authors of the platform, viewed Judaism as a religion, based on faith in God and on the efficacy of prayer. Denying that modern Jews were members of a separate Jewish nation, he maintained that the quintessence of Judaism could be found in the Ten Commandments, whose teachings, combined with those of the prophets, underscored universal truths that could be apprehended by all people.

Like many other late nineteenth- and early twentieth-century Reformers, Alfred Moses spoke of the "God-idea" rather than of a supernatural, transcendent deity. Indeed, the God-idea was central to his understanding of Jewish Science as a science or wisdom that was Jewish in origin and that revealed the reality of divine healing as unfolded throughout the history and literature of the Jewish people. For Moses, the Jewish scriptures, embodying the "supreme expression of the God-idea," contained the first and original message or principle of divine healing. This principle, reiterated in liturgy and in other Jewish writings, rested on the power of faith to cure sickness and to assist the individual in achieving perfect health. It is the "pure idea of faith," Moses wrote, that contains within it the power to make men and women both strong and happy. It may not move mountains, he admitted, "but it is a powerful lever in lifting the sick and despondent to the higher level of Health and Happiness," creating "new interest and enthusiasm, and teach[ing] the value of spiritual joy as against temporal pleasure."[18]

Recognizing that faith in a benevolent God was in many ways a projection of the believer, Moses equated faith with the power of autosuggestion. Though to the mind of the believer it is God alone who is the source of all healing, in fact, healing occurs because the human mind "has the unique or peculiar function of being able to suggest to itself ideas which work themselves out in the sub-conscious self." It is this subconscious self or mind, he continued, that "is the real mind in which man lives, moves and has his being, and by which all bodily functions are controlled and disciplined." Without denying the benefits of medical science, Moses staunchly maintained that

> all strong suggestions help in the healing process. The good physi-
> cian realizes this truth, and it is a trite saying that "Confidence in
> the physician is half the battle of the patient." The sick man who
> has faith in his doctor already helps himself. At some stage of his
> treatment, the invalid must receive in addition to drugs or surgical
> relief powerful suggestions that intensify and strengthen his hope of
> recovery.[19]

For Moses, the power of faith lay in its emotional and driving force based on the absolute conviction of the individual that his or her beliefs were true. Divine healing, in other words, did not depend on the truth of the individual's beliefs (though they indeed might be true) but on the intensity with which they were held. For Moses, then, the ultimate value of the God-idea rested on its "moral motive-power," which, as a power of goodness, was a source of health, exerting great influence over mind and body.

Moses incorporated his understanding of the God-idea and its moral motive-power into his broader understanding of the Jewish mission. To bear witness to God, he maintained, was to rely on divine providence through faith in the reality of God and of God's healing power. Thus, as God's chosen people constantly proclaiming their divine mission, Jews "should be the last to discourage the use of those spiritual agencies that help the body as well as the mind and heart."[20] His implicit criticism here may well have been against those Reform rabbis who continually stressed the importance of the Jewish mission without emphasizing its practical implications. Indeed, in 1919 he made this criticism more explicit in his response to Kaufmann Kohler's CCAR address on the mission of Israel. While acknowledging that he shared Kohler's belief in the centrality of the mission idea, he criticized Kohler for omitting any pragmatic suggestions as to how this idea might best be implemented. Opening his remarks with a reference to his father, Rabbi Adolph Moses, he said:

> My father, who stood with Isaac M. Wise in the working out of his
> life's dream, detached the messianic idea from the historic side and
> followed it as a pragmatic question. He believed the philosophy of
> Judaism based on its past was capable [of being] and should be un-
> folded to the gentile world. He died disillusioned. But I believe the
> methods of the churches are worthy of copy and emulation. Let us
> not waste our efforts on discussion only. Let us try to do something
> definite, something that will stimulate thought—something that will
> bring results.[21]

Evidently, Alfred Moses envisioned Jewish Science as a pragmatic means of implementing the Jewish mission as he and many other late nineteenth- and early twentieth-century Reform rabbis understood it. Emphasizing that his intent was not to start a new religious movement but simply to demonstrate that the teachings of Jewish Science were identical to those of (Reform) Judaism, he conjectured that Reform had previously deemphasized or ignored divine healing because it had exalted reason and logic while minimizing emotion and sentiment. Without these, modern Jews had lost their "prayerful sense." Thus, they were ignorant of prayer's efficacy and power. His intent was to restore the art of prayer and its influence on every day life by emphasizing the importance of emotion in stimulating divine worship. In so doing, he hoped to make Judaism "a living reality and an ever-present help" by once again filling its synagogues with genuine believers.

It is no coincidence that in responding to Kaufmann Kohler's CCAR address on the Jewish mission, Alfred Moses invoked the memory and life's work of his father. Although his own future vision of Judaism was less universal than that of Adolph Moses, he too was committed to seeking a way in which the Jewish mission, as understood by Reform Judaism, might best be fulfilled. His hope was that by bringing about a spiritual renaissance within the American Jewish community, Jewish Science would result in greater dedication to the Jewish mission and, more broadly, to a greater belief in the efficacy of prayer. As Rabbi Emil Leipziger later noted, the fact that he was the son of Adolph Moses, "one of the *Gedolim* [great men] of the unfolding history of

Reform Judaism," greatly affected Alfred Moses throughout his career, serving as a "constant challenge to his own abilities and ideals."[22] Alfred Moses' concern for the spiritual vitality of Judaism and his efforts to preserve this vitality may well have been a concern that he not only shared with his father but learned from him. Thus, Jewish Science, as originally presented in 1916 and revised in 1920, may well have reflected Alfred Moses' desire to continue the spiritual work initiated by his father.

It is also possible that Alfred Moses' focus on God as healer and Judaism as a source of happiness and health stemmed from the physical and mental health problems from which he long suffered. As early as March 1903, less than a year and a half after assuming the pulpit of Sha'arai Shomayim, Moses (then twenty-five years old) asked of the Board of Trustees that he be temporarily relieved of his duties and granted an extended vacation for health reasons. Acting on the recommendation of Moses' physician that such a vacation be granted, the board approved the request. Though it is unclear how long this vacation lasted, it was not until March 1904 that the board resolved to recommend to the congregation that Moses be given a three-year contract. This suggests that Alfred Moses' vacation may have been as long as a year.[23] While the records of the Board of Trustees make no further mention of his health, there apparently were intervals when his mental life "became clouded by emotional confusion,"[24] and by 1940 he resigned as rabbi of Sha'arai Shomayim. According to Sam Brown, who later visited Moses in the state mental institution where he died in 1956, his mental illness progressed slowly, extending over a number of years, and eventually led to total mental incompetence. It may well have been, then, that Alfred Moses' interest in spiritual healing was primarily personal in nature, stemming from his earlier physical problems and perhaps, though this is not documented, from the fear that he was beginning to suffer, or was prone to suffer, from mental illness.[25]

Moses himself maintained that he first became interested in divine healing in 1914. A couple in Mobile whose one-year-old daughter had become very ill called him and asked him to perform a change of name ceremony for their daughter. Never having heard of this ceremony before, Moses was told by them that the ceremony was a Jewish ritual that invoked God's help as healer. The person performing the ritual was to pray to God as the restorer of health and then to change the name of the individual in need of divine assistance. While skeptical, Moses agreed to perform the ritual; much to his surprise, the child improved almost immediately, even though the child's physicians maintained that there was no hope of recovery. Although Moses subsequently learned of other instances in which the same ritual was performed, in some cases proving successful and in others not, the recoveries that did occur conclusively proved to him that Jewish Science, or the wisdom of divine healing, was effective and therefore should "recommend itself to all zealous Jews."[26]

Moses devoted a major part of his work to refuting the claims of Christian

Science, contrasting them to those of Jewish Science and revealing the anti-Jewish bias of Mary Baker Eddy's work. As friends and critics later pointed out, it was the latter aspect of his book that was most valuable both to those Jews who were attracted to Christian Science but uncomfortable about joining the church and to those searching for specific Jewish arguments against Eddy's teachings. Moses discussed at length Eddy's explicitly Christian understanding of faith, including her belief in Christ as the messiah, her exaltation of Christian Science's pure and spiritual understanding of the Godhead versus Judaism's more materialistic conception, and her celebration of Jesus' life as proving that God is love, in contrast to Jewish theology, which gives "no hint of the unchanging love of God." Citing specific pages from *Science and Health*, he carefully and convincingly sought to prove that Eddy's anti-Jewish bias was so great that no "self-respecting Jew" could possibly accept a religion containing so many "false and unfounded statements regarding Judaism."[27]

Moreover, it was Alfred Moses' conviction that no Jew needed to become a Christian Scientist in order to discover the healing power of prayer, for he believed that Christian Science offered "nothing new to the Jewish Mind. It is simply Judaism, veneered with Christology or the belief in the divinity of Jesus."[28] In order to prove this thesis, he sought to reveal the biblical basis of Eddy's belief in God as healer, citing passages from every part of the Hebrew scriptures that attests to God's healing power. Unlike Morris Lichtenstein and Clifton Harby Levy, Moses did not focus on Psalms and Proverbs, although several were cited. Rather, by also quoting from the first five books of the Bible, I and II Kings, Samuel, and numerous books of the prophets, he attempted to underscore the pervasiveness of this theme throughout scripture and, by quoting from the daily prayer book, throughout later Jewish literature as well.

He also attempted to describe specific historical expressions of this belief in God. Focusing most fully, although selectively, on eighteenth-century Hasidism, he maintained that Hasidism as envisioned by its founder, the Baal Shem Tov, was an early expression of Jewish Science, "inspired by a sincere and genuine effort to afford a living faith, and to improve the individual in conduct and character." Recognizing that true religion did not lie in Talmudic learning but in the love of God, he claimed that Hasidism sought to change the believer rather than the ceremonies and dogmas of traditional Jewish life. Thus, "by suggestion, it created a new type of religious man, who placed emotion above ritual, and religious excitement above knowledge."[29] Moses omitted mention of Hasidism in the second edition of his work, after Rabbi Max Heller, whom he greatly respected, convinced him that his characterization of Hasidism as a historical expression of Jewish Science was unfounded. As Heller pointed out, Hasidism was not a protest against legalism, as Moses had claimed. Nor could one equate the Hasidic reliance on divine providence with simple faith healing.[30]

There are no extant records attesting to the financial success or failure of

Moses' work or to how many copies were printed. By 1919, however, in writing back both to men and women interested in purchasing the book and to rabbis congratulating him on the important task he had undertaken, Alfred Moses maintained that all printed copies of *Jewish Science* had been sold. He planned to publish a second edition, he continued, yet had decided to substantially revise his work before doing so. In part, this decision must have been in response to such critics as Max Heller. In part too, however, his decision to substantially change the content of his work reflected his own newfound interest in applied psychology and in the broadly based Protestant alliance known as New Thought, thanks to readers of *Jewish Science* who brought both to his attention. Consequently, the greatly expanded and largely rewritten second edition, published in 1920, devoted less attention to the broader historical and religious Jewish context out of which Jewish Science emerged. Rather, it tried to create what Moses identified as an "applied psychology of Judaism."

As he had not done in the earlier edition, in which he had argued that Jews need not abandon Judaism for Christian Science because the fundamental teachings of Christian Science were Jewish in origin, he here argued that Christian Science's fundamental beliefs were in fact antithetical to what Jews and, for that matter, most Christians believed. Revealing a better understanding of Christian Science than he had in the 1916 edition, in which he simply equated Christian Science with belief in God as healer, Moses now focused on Eddy's denial of matter, including her denial of the body's organs and functions. Asserting that the body was real, just as sickness was real to the sufferer, he maintained that the sufferer "may dissolve the abnormal state by suggestion and spiritual realization, but he must recognize the temporary reality of his malady, in order to understand and deal with it."[31] Insisting that Christian Science was a false conception, unsupported by reasoning, logic, "or any modern system of idealistic thought," he faulted Mary Baker Eddy for not recognizing that healing and indeed, all mental ends could be attained without denying either the body or the reality of nature. Thus, he concluded, Jews must reject Eddy's teachings, for "all philosophies that minimize or deny the sensuous are rejected by the practical genius of Israel," whose scriptures in no way share the "strange, mystical claim of Christian Science that 'mind being all, matter is nothing.' "[32]

In voicing these beliefs, Alfred Moses revealed the growing influence of the so-called new psychology on him. He did not identify specific psychologists or schools of thought to whom he was indebted. Yet, as he understood it, the "central feature of the new and applied Psychology is the rediscovery of the truth that man has in himself the power to create health, happiness and success, by direction of the Sub-conscious mind and by conscious relation with the Super-mind of God."[33] Affirming the reality of the material world, Moses maintained that Jewish Science, unlike Christian Science, recognized the "psychological truth" that individuals possess the mental power to modify and mold the material elements of creation. Viewing the body as an extension of the mind, Moses labeled disease a "dis-ease," that is, a "lack of ease or harmony" that can be overcome by directing the conscious, reasoning self to the subconscious mind, the agency that converts thought into action. It is thus the subconscious mind, he wrote, that directs the breathing, the blood circulation, "the creation of lymph, secretions, depositions, [and] in fact, every iota of bodily functions." While medicine may prove beneficial, its efficacy depends on the extent to which it succeeds in assisting the subconscious mind by "removing certain obstructions that impede its free flow." Yet ultimately, Moses continued, it is neither the conscious nor the subconscious mind but the superconscious mind, or God, that is responsible for healing. It is this force, he maintained, that impels the conscious self to direct the subconscious mind into developing those habits, methods, and "moral ways" that ensure creativity and accomplishment.[34]

Between 1917 and 1920, Moses corresponded with a number of Jews who regularly attended New Thought lectures and were inspired by the messages they contained. Enthusiastic about the possibility of harmonizing Jewish and New Thought teachings, they encouraged him to learn more about New Thought and possibly to consider forming a group of his own.[35] During the summer of 1919, while in New York City, Moses studied both the methods and teachings of New Thought and Christian Science. Among the New Thought leaders to whom he was particularly drawn were Harry Gaze, the minister of the First Church of Life and Joy, and Eugene Del Mar, a founder and leader of the League of the Higher Life in New York City. Moses attended their lectures and classes, met with them privately, and discussed with them at length his own desire to religiously revitalize the American Jewish community. Later, Moses thanked Gaze, Del Mar, and other New Thought leaders whom he had met for helping him broaden his concept of Jewish Science from a focus on negative states of being such as sin, sickness, and poverty to a focus on the positive act "of assisting in the creation of the normal and God-given states of consciousness, as strengthen character, holiness, power, poise etc. by means of the understanding and application of certain Jewish standards."[36]

By 1920, Alfred Moses began to speak of God as a divine mind existing within the soul, the "pure and perfect standard of right" within us that makes the human achievement of absolute goodness possible. Although in content this description of God—or, as he more frequently wrote, of the God-consciousness—did not substantially differ from the nonsupernatural concept of divinity, that is, classical Reform's God-idea, which he wrote about in 1916, the terminology he began to use, as well as the healing techniques he adopted, clearly revealed the influence of New Thought. Like Mary Baker Eddy, New Thought preachers advocated religious psychotherapy. Yet not all believed, as did both Eddy and Emma Curtis Hopkins (1849–1925), "the primary founder of the New Thought movement,"[37] that matter was not real. Perhaps following the lead of the late nineteenth-century healer, popular writer, and New Thought pioneer Warren Felt Evans (1817–1889), many viewed medical science as "an auxiliary to the mental system of cure"[38] and thus did not refuse, and indeed at times welcomed, medical treatment. Like Eddy, however, they emphasized the power of the mind, employing techniques such as silence, affirmation, visualization, and denial to bring about divine healing.

Along with other more secular advocates of psychotherapy, members of New Thought sought to advertise and promote the benefits of what they identified as peace of mind. Maintaining that peace of mind was the key to both happiness and health, they emphasized the aforementioned methods, which one might employ to prevent mental disorders. While most did not deny the reality of either physical illness or death, they focused their attention on those functional diseases that modern middle-class men and women were prone to suffer from, such as nervous tension, sleeplessness, excessive worry, and depression. It was their belief that such illnesses could be cured through right thinking and moderate living. Beginning with the presupposition that happiness is normal and that we possess the power within us to retain or achieve this normal state, leaders of New Thought, again like secular psychotherapists, emphasized the power of suggestion in conquering disease and attaining health. While, as previously mentioned, some may have advocated the use of modern medicine in helping to fight such diseases, they believed, as did Christian Scientists, that ultimately it is the mind that governs the body.

Acknowledging their indebtedness to Ralph Waldo Emerson and other nineteenth-century Transcendentalists, who spoke of the world as the product of a mind that is active everywhere, practitioners of New Thought placed special emphasis on ways one could become receptive and responsive to the activity of the divine mind within one. Like Emerson, they believed in beginning with a posture of silence, for, as Emerson wrote, "real power is in silent moments." It is then that we become most aware of our own internal power. New Thought advocates viewed silence as a spiritual state. Thus, as Lilian Whiting wrote in 1895, it was through silence alone that one discovered that, "like the kingdom of heaven, the World Beautiful is within."[39] Leaders of New Thought (again, like Emerson) maintained that self-perfection—what Emerson called self-reliance—was similarly attainable through silence. Echoing Emerson's sense of optimism, they insisted that self-perfection was not a privilege but an absolute duty, attainable once we recognize "through the channel of our minds" that the "Infinite Divine life force" and our own life force are one and the same. Many within New Thought, including the prolific popular writer Ralph Waldo Trine, identified this divine force as Christ. Consequently each maintained, as Trine often did, quoting Emerson, that he or she believed in the " 'still, small voice, and that voice is the Christ within me.' "[40]

Sharing this belief in the importance of silence was Ernest Shurtleff Holmes (1887–1960), who began publishing books on what he called Mental

Science in 1919, and later founded and led what eventually became known as the Church of Religious Science.[41] In his writings, Holmes frequently pointed to the biblical proverb " 'As a man thinketh in his heart, so is he,' " a proverb that, according to Alfred Geiger Moses, crystallized Jewish Science.[42] This verse, Holmes later maintained, reveals the truth that what we are and what we become depends on what we are thinking. This is so, he continued, because the infinite mind that surrounds us reacts to our thoughts and to our mental state rather than to our words. Mind, in other words, reacts to mind, and thus, according to Holmes and others more closely identified with New Thought, it is through contemplative silence that one is best able to stir the divine mind within oneself into action.[43]

Without explicitly acknowledging his indebtedness to New Thought, although elsewhere in the book he did quote Emerson, Alfred Geiger Moses devoted an entire chapter of his revised *Jewish Science* to what he identified as "the Silence." "Silence," he wrote,

> is the divine manner of manifestation. God reveals Himself to the listening ear of faith in complete stillness. In Silence, we find God and commune with the Spirit of all flesh. Be still and in the holy awe know that God exists. To know God means to cast off the coils of sensuous life and to enter the realm of spiritual thought. Casting off the bonds of mortal mind, we enter the Silence of the inner soul and dwell on the thought of the Infinite and Eternal.[44]

Although not denying the reality of matter, Moses insisted that only the spirit, the universal creative energy or power that we identify as God, was permanently real. Invisible and unchanging, this spirit could be heard as "the still, small voice of Conscience, the immutable law of right that has worked inexorably in world history." To Moses, the power of silence lay in its ability to strip away all distractions, leading people to focus their thoughts on God. He therefore advised his readers to school themselves in the practice of silence so that they could enter into "the Silence at any time or place," finding moments within everyday life to enter into the state of spiritual quietude.

While his description of silence as both a spiritual state and a mental technique may have been borrowed from New Thought, Moses' understanding of why such a state was important unmistakably bore the imprint of classical Reform Judaism. When Moses discussed the importance of recognizing the God-consciousness within, his emphasis was not on the realization of one's own internal power, as it was for members of New Thought. Rather, his emphasis was on the importance of becoming aware of God's presence, or, echoing Reform's concept of mission, on bearing witness to the reality of God. The identification of the divine with one's conscience, the "still, small voice" within, was a belief Alfred Moses shared with many Reform rabbis of his day. Moreover, Moses' insistence that communion with the divine led one to seek

righteousness and truth, since God is not just the source but the law of morality, reflected Moses' concept of Judaism as ethical monotheism, the heart
and soul of classical Reform.

In describing the power of silence, Moses sought to apply the teachings
of Reform Judaism as he understood them to every day life. In so doing, he
found himself indebted to the insights of applied psychology. By controlling
the conscious mind through silence, the subconscious self, he maintained, is
able to respond to the mental suggestions or demands of the superconscious
mind, or God. Thus, through solitude, one can invigorate one's spiritual powers, establishing "a direct communion with Divinity" that makes possible the
realization of one's higher aims, particularly the carrying out of God's moral
law. Combining the teachings of Reform Judaism with those of New Thought,
Moses included as part of this law the law of self-perfection. Through silence,
he asserted, one discovers the God consciousness within, a belief shared by
Reform Jews and advocates of New Thought. This discovery, he continued,
brought about by inaction, that is, meditative silence, leads one to action; that
is, to the pursuit of justice and the attainment of happiness and health. Without
denying the centrality of God's moral teachings, Alfred Geiger Moses thus
sought to incorporate within Reform's ideological understanding of ethical
monotheism the more personal goals espoused by leaders of New Thought
and Christian Science of health, joy, and inner peace. To achieve these aims,
he offered practical suggestions, all of which had already been articulated by
New Thought practitioners.

First, he suggested finding a quiet place where one could relax completely.
He next advised breathing deeply, letting "the body be in repose so as to render
the mind receptive." Shutting out all external stimuli and suggestions, the
individual should then concentrate intensely on an appropriate biblical verse,
to be selected from among those he offered in chapter 14 of his book, or on
thoughts of petition, affirmation, or denial, taken from chapter 15, or from any
text wherein one found a theme of particular spiritual meaning. Moses advised
reading this text repeatedly until one's minds was filled with its central thought.
Photograph that thought, he instructed, and try to recall it continuously until
the art of concentration has been mastered. Only after having done so, he
asserted, could one begin to affirm one's own beliefs and desires, thanking
and praising God for their fulfillment.

Moses viewed personal affirmation as a central method of Jewish Science.
Like petition and denial, it might be practiced either through words or through
silence. In describing this method, Moses wrote: "The Affirmation is the dwell-
ing on or affirming of the principle of Good . . . a positive statement made in
full faith that our desires and prayers are established by the power of God."[45]
Distinguishing between the great affirmation that God is One (Judaism's
"Shema": "Hear O Israel, the Lord Our God, the Lord is One," taken from
Deuteronomy 6) and the lesser affirmations that stress conditions like health,

joy, strength, and courage, Moses believed that such affirmations were important in bringing "absolute conviction to the Sub-conscious mind . . . command[ing] it to exercise its imperial power." Moses advised his readers to enter
the silence with a particular affirmation in mind. One might focus, for example,
on a particular biblical verse that expressed in a positive manner an ideal one
desired to embody, like courage, joy, success, justice, kindness, love, or faith.
Thus if one sought the power to better deal with life's difficulties, one might
enter the silence with the pervading idea, taken from Psalms, that one should
"be strong and of good courage." Hold this idea in your mind, Moses wrote,
and say it repeatedly, letting it "flood your being and fill your soul with its
dynamic message." Once the subconscious mind has absorbed the message,
retain it as a mental image that one can revitalize, or, in New Thought terminology, visualize, at any time. Think of this message constantly, when awakening, during the day, and before retiring at night. If you do so, he asserted,

> by the exact law of God, written in the human spirit, you will find
> that you have actually incarnated "courage" into your being. You will
> feel a new interest in your life-tasks, a new enthusiasm for work and
> ambition. Fear and sensitiveness will be dissolved. You will actually
> demonstrate power, fearlessness, directness, determination. You will
> lose your self-consciousness and feel at one with [yourself and with]
> God.[46]

Moses used the method of affirmation both to attain self-realization (again,
a goal he shared with New Thought and Christian Science) and to attain Reform Judaism's goal of bearing witness. Beginning with the biblical text "God
is my strength and my salvation," he encouraged his readers to enter the silence
with this "God-cognition" and to affirm it at all times. Think of it at every
opportunity, he continued, until your soul, indeed "every cell, nerve and fiber
of your being," is filled with the presence of God. Having done so, you will be
changed into a believer, and faith in the unseen will become a tangible reality.
God, he concluded, combining the ideas of Reform Judaism and New Thought,
"will be no longer a formula, expressed in particular form, rite, prayer or ceremony but a vital principle. You will realize the three great attributes of Godhead: Omnipresence, Omniscience, Omnipotence. God will appeal to you in
constant revelations of your higher and better self."[47]

Moses' chapter on the affirmation clearly reveals the ways he attempted to
combine the concerns of Reform Judaism with the techniques, language, and
insights of both applied psychology and New Thought. The notion of God as
a superconscious mind and the identification of the subconscious as "the real
agency of all healing" reveal the influence of applied psychology, while the
identification of God as a life-giving principle, a universal mind, and a divine
current, his call to "discover the God-mind in you," and the very techniques
of silence and affirmation reveal the influence of New Thought. Perhaps Moses

was able to draw on New Thought and applied psychology so successfully because classical Reform Judaism's understanding of Judaism and religion in general easily lent itself to the incorporation of these ideas. Reform's God-idea, as opposed to belief in a supernatural God with its subsequent emphasis on divine immanence, rejection of most rabbinic ceremonies and observances, and overriding emphasis on Judaism as a religion that seeks to stimulate inner faith made Reform Judaism, as understood by Alfred Geiger Moses and other classical Reformers, particularly receptive to new ways in which one's spiritual nature might best be awakened. What's more, Reform's universal vision of true religion enabled its adherents to borrow freely not just from Jewish sources but from non-Jewish sources as well. Believing, then, that it was his duty, as a Reform rabbi and as a Jew, to bring others to an awareness of God's presence, and unafraid to use the techniques and aims of either applied psychology or New Thought in order to do so, Moses enjoined his readers to

> take religion from its cold-storage and vivify it by your understand-
> ing of the laws of mind. Cease to make God a phrase. Realize Him
> as a vital principle. Feel the stirring of the Infinite in your soul, even
> as a tidal wave in the depths of your being. Apply the truths of God
> to health, happiness, and all real problems. Affirm your faith in the
> One, only God, with full understanding of the spiritual truth. Say to
> yourself the central truth of the Jewish dispensation at all times and
> places: " 'Hear, O Israel, the Lord our God, the Lord is one.' "[48]

To Alfred Geiger Moses, the biblical text that best conveyed the reality of human-divine kinship, an idea shared by members of New Thought, as Christians, and Reform Jews, as Jews, was the revelation of God's name to Moses at Sinai as " 'I Am That I Am.' " Moses encouraged his readers to say this text repeatedly, dwelling on its all-embracing concept of the almighty. As one repeats these words, either out loud or in silence, one must remember, Moses wrote, that God, as immanent, is within us and that we, therefore, share in God's nature. Thus say to oneself that one is the child of God and therefore " 'I am well. I am strong. I am happy. I am serene and joyful.' " Affirm, in other words, one's spiritual nature, the realization that ultimately we are one, or, taking the Jewish concept of atonement as at-one-ment, that we are at one with God.

For Moses, as for those in New Thought and, for that matter, in Christian Science, denial was another effective method through which one could affirm one's true spiritual nature. By denying the reality of fear, worry, anger, and other negative emotions, one was able to free oneself of negative states of being (the disease or dis-ease to which we are prone) and to affirm instead one's essential oneness with God. "To deny," Moses wrote, "means first to recognize the wrong reality or condition in order to remove it from the mind." Or, in psychological terms, "to deny is to inhibit or dissolve the abnormal state that has been built up by conscious or unconscious cause. It means that we direct the Sub-conscious mind to destroy the undesirable condition."[49]

Like leaders of New Thought and Mary Baker Eddy, Alfred Moses paradoxically viewed denial as a positive method of healing. By denying the reality of sin, sickness, and sorrow, one is best able, he maintained, to affirm health, joy, and well-being. Once one reveals that evil thoughts are only illusions, the product of imagination or of an unnatural obsession, one is able to dissolve them, replacing them with thoughts that are wholesome and healthy. Moses claimed that to do so through the method of denial ultimately leads one to affirm that God, as the source of good (a central focus of New Thought and Christian Science teachings), is ever present. It is this affirmation, Moses insisted, that gives one the strength and courage to overcome those negative ideas that continue to plague one's temperament or body.

In emphasizing the power of both denial and affirmation in removing what he identified as abnormal states of being, Moses, like most of those involved in New Thought, did not mean to claim, as Mary Baker Eddy did, that physical suffering was an illusion. Rather his point, again like most advocates of New Thought, was that *mental* suffering is an illusion and that all suffering is abnormal. In discussing the nature of evil, however, Moses seemed to vacillate between New Thought's denial of its reality and the more Jewish belief that evil exists but one should deny oneself or refrain from doing evil actions. In order to overcome what even Moses recognized as an apparent contradiction in his thinking, he maintained that although God is good, God is also the source of both good and evil. Similarly, while human beings possess good and evil impulses, their inherent goodness enables them to resist evil by denying or shutting out thoughts that lack ethical judgment. Again, combining New Thought's understanding of evil as illusion with Reform Jewish emphasis on morality, Moses acknowledged the presence of evil in the world but, at the same time, insisted that such moral evils as violence, sin, and injustice could indeed be overcome through human effort. Harmonizing the essential vision of Jewish Science with that of classical Reform, New Thought, and Christian Science, Moses thus maintained that Jewish Science "sounds the note of optimism—the principle that, by conscious realization, we can make to-day better than yesterday and each day watch for the rising sun of a grander tomorrow. Optimism is not a sentimental mood but a definite state of mind, arising only from thought and achievement."[50]

Finally, although he did not discuss it at length, Moses advocated seeking God through the use of petition, a method revealing greater indebtedness to Judaism than to New Thought. He continued to maintain that traditional prayers asking God for strength, courage, health, and so on often were effective means of vitalizing one's spiritual power. By turning the mind toward God, both private and public devotions could stimulate faith, and thus lead one to trust in God (from the Hebrew *emunah*) as the source of healing and inspiration. Although he placed greatest emphasis on silence and affirmation, Moses sought to encourage any method that helped to keep one's mind on God.

In describing Jewish Science, Alfred Geiger Moses often maintained that it was simply applied Judaism—that is, the application of Jewish teachings to everyday life. Although Moses explicitly identified applied Judaism with applied psychology, his understanding of Judaism did not significantly differ from that of most nineteenth- and early twentieth-century Jewish Reformers. Indeed, many within the Reform movement, both in America and England, shared Moses' belief that only by revealing the practical application of its teachings could Judaism hope to remain a living religion. Viewing the spiritual revitalization of contemporary Jewry as part of their religious mission, many leaders of classical Reform, including Moses, sought to discover ways in which religiously apathetic Jews could begin to take seriously the concept of bearing witness.[51] What Alfred Moses also attempted to do, primarily through his writings, was to underscore the belief that bearing witness was a Jewish concept and that therefore one need not turn to other religious faiths in search of the one true God.

In sum, Alfred Geiger Moses attempted to harmonize the teachings of Reform Judaism with New Thought and applied psychology and, to some extent, Christian Science, by maintaining that: (1) it was the responsibility of every Jew to bear witness to the reality of God and to spread God's moral teachings throughout the world (Reform's idea of religious mission), and (2) included in these moral teachings were the imperatives to be happy and healthy.

Citing the Israelites' promise at Sinai to hear and do God's commandments, Alfred Moses maintained that the aim of Jewish Science similarly was to hear God's message of truth and bring that truth to others. Faith, he contended, was pragmatic, and thus brought concrete results such as greater joy, life, and harmony, which in and of themselves made faith possible. Put succinctly, Moses both claimed that faith brought one peace of mind and that peace of mind was a precondition of faith. One could only keep one's mind on God if one were calm, happy, and cheerful, while keeping one's mind on God helped create these positive mental states. "Faith," he wrote, "leads to life more abundant, and life, rightly understood, leads to ever-increasing faith."[52]

For Alfred Geiger Moses, one could not understand life correctly if one did not acknowledge the importance of mental and physical health. First of all, one could not love God with all of one's heart, soul, and might, as Deuteronomy enjoins one to do, unless one were healthy; and second, health was in and of itself a visible sign of God's immanent power. Moses asserted that suffering was rooted in a disregard for God's laws, leaving one open to weakness and disorder. On the other hand, he claimed, health "is God's gift to those who recognize and realize His laws of Being."[53] As in the 1916 edition of his book,

Moses drew on numerous Jewish sources to underscore his belief in God as healer. If God is one, he maintained, God must indeed be "the Power that makes for life and well-being." Faith healing, then, is possible because it recognizes and utilizes this power. In psychological terms, it is through mental suggestion, the belief in God as healer, that the subconscious acts on the superconscious to direct the conscious mind toward greater health and perfection, which, in religious terms, Moses identified as the salvation of mind and body. Thus, he insisted, Jewish Science does not deny the benefits of modern medicine but, like Judaism itself, maintains that it is not the surgeon who heals. Rather, all healing is from God acting "through the soul of man." Identifying God with mind, Moses concluded that mind or thought is more important in the healing process than people imagine. Medicine alone cannot make one well; it is the attitude that one has and the thoughts that one thinks that have greatest affect on one's mental and physical condition.[54]

Moses' attempt to create an applied psychology of Judaism was to some extent successful. The 1920 edition of his work, more so than the 1916 edition, is difficult to read, in no small measure because of its lack of clear organization and its endless repetition of ideas. Yet, set within a context that by the standards of classical Reform was explicitly Jewish, Moses' major thesis, namely, that peace of mind leads to faith and vice versa, appealed to several hundred if not thousands of Jewish men and women. While the letters of praise found among Moses' private papers, written by fellow rabbis and members of the laity, are insufficient in number to determine the true extent of positive interest in his work, there are several indications that as early as 1917, Moses' concept of Jewish Science received serious attention.

First, between 1917 and 1922, Moses received a number of letters from both traditional and Reform rabbis who praised his work and promised to share his ideas with others. For example, Moses Gaster, the chief rabbi of the Spanish and Portuguese Jews of Great Britain, maintained that he would not fail to bring Moses' "excellent little book" to the attention of a wider circle of friends,[55] while Emil Leipziger, leader of the (Reform) Touro Synagogue in New Orleans, wrote that he hoped to organize a group of congregants who would meet with him on a regular basis to discuss the subject of religious psychology in general. "If I succeed," he wrote, "I shall be glad to have you come over to address them."[56] In 1917, Martin A. Meyer, the rabbi of Temple Emanuel in San Francisco, asserted that he hoped to one day get together a group that would discuss (the 1916 edition of) Moses' book page by page, and Rabbi Louis Mann of Congregation Mis(h)kan Israel in New Haven, Connecticut, notified Moses that the study circle of the local Council of Jewish Women was about to discuss his book at their next Monday afternoon meeting.[57]

Among the most enthusiastic letters Moses received were those written by Jews who were attracted to the ideas of New Thought. Some, including Marcel Krauss, a New Orleans manufacturer with whom Moses carried on an extended correspondence, regularly attended New Thought lectures and classes. It was Krauss, in fact, who suggested that Moses attend the 1921 Conference of the International New Thought Alliance, confiding that he himself received "great inspiration" in annually attending.[58] Many of the letters that Moses received described his book as a "revelation," satisfying a deep, spiritual hunger. "Since childhood," wrote one woman from New York City,

> I have yearned for a more complete definition of Judaism or I might say a spiritual explanation that I always felt was lacking in the average Jewish congregation. . . . Rather than leave my faith I remained at home. A few years ago that urge was somewhat soothed by my attendance at [the lectures sponsored by the] League for [the] Larger Life . . . [and] later the "Harry Gaze" lectures. . . . The New Thought Movement appealed to me intensely and how I wished that it could be spread amongst our people, in a Jewish sense, of course. I used to think to myself—will I ever be satisfied? Now my hope is realized in . . . "Jewish Science."[59]

Throughout the 1920s, Moses traveled and lectured extensively, sharing his religious ideas in synagogues and auditoriums throughout the United States. On occasion, he participated in conferences that focused on spiritual healing. In addition, he lectured to New Thought groups, emphasizing both the similarities and differences between the teachings of New Thought and what he called Jewish Science. Christians who heard Moses lecture often expressed their appreciation of the work he was trying to accomplish, suggesting books he might find useful in developing his ideas further. One man, for example, after attending a lecture Moses delivered in New York City to members of the League for the Larger Life, sent him a copy of *Primary Lessons in Christian Living and Healing*, by the New Thought leader Annie Rix Militz (1856–1924).[60] This work, he wrote, will "more nearly coincide with and corroborate your message than anything else you will find in the teachings of the liberal or the orthodox world today."[61]

Of the thousands of Jewish men and women who heard Moses lecture, many were already familiar with his work and came wanting to know more about the ways in which one might incorporate the teachings of Jewish Science into every day life. Some began to conceive of ways in which groups might be formed to study and attempt to live by Jewish Science teachings. Marcel Krauss, for example, after listening to Alfred Moses' lecture at the Atheneum in New Orleans in early 1920, suggested that Moses form Jewish Science groups in Mobile and New Orleans, adding that he himself would provide the necessary finances.[62] Della H. Bloomstein, a Nashville woman who wrote to Moses on several occasions and who apparently had written a number of papers on Jewish spiritual healing, expressed the hope that when Moses next came to Nashville she might be able to talk to him about the "possibility of spreading the belief in Jewish Science"[63] further. It is unclear whether Krauss, Bloomstein, or most of the other men and women who expressed interest in forming local Jewish Science groups ever did so. Moses himself apparently decided against forming such groups himself. At least one group, however, was formed as a result of Moses' work. This group, which identified itself as both the First Society of Jewish New Thought and the Jewish New Thought Center, was founded in New York City by Lucia Nola Levy and Bertha Strauss, two Jewish women who sought to spread the message of happiness and health, as articulated by New Thought preachers and by Alfred Geiger Moses, throughout the American Jewish community.

Lucia Nola Levy and Bertha Strauss first met Alfred Moses during the summer of 1919. They may have met him first at one of Harry Gaze's Sunday lectures, which Moses regularly attended during his stay in New York, or at one of the numerous lectures sponsored by the League for the Larger Life, some of which Moses attended as well. Undoubtedly, they attended Moses' lecture series on Jewish Science at the League for the Larger Life that August. Before the summer had ended, they, along with Hattie Seidenbaum, S. S. Rosen, and other "Jewish New Thoughters," began to consider the possibility of establishing a Jewish New Thought group with Alfred Moses as their leader. Lucia Nola Levy approached Moses with this idea; apparently, he agreed to give it serious consideration, for early that fall, Hattie Seidenbaum wrote to Moses asking him whether he was still considering coming back to New York City. Having recently seen one another at one of Harry Gaze's lectures, she and Lucia Nola Levy, she explained, had begun to talk about the work that Moses had contemplated doing. They were eager to help him form a local Jewish New Thought group and thus decided to write in order to ascertain his present intentions. Expressing the hope that he still planned to return to New York, she wrote:

> I am afraid that if some big Jewish [New Thought] centers are not started in the East soon, a great many of our people are likely to discard their religion for some other, just because they can get a good lecture on healing outside of their own synagogues. I myself was drifting when you came along, and I thank the dear Lord that He has shown me the way through you. And so it must be with many people. . . . We need you and your fine interpretations of the Old Testament to make us feel that our own religion holds all that we really need.[64]

While Alfred Moses may indeed have contemplated moving to New York City and establishing a Jewish New Thought group, the only remaining record of these intentions is Hattie Seidenbaum's letter. There is no indication that Moses ever approached his congregation with these plans. Indeed, the minute books of Sha'arai Shomayim's Board of Trustees reveal Moses' apparent satisfaction with his work as rabbi of the congregation and his hope for remaining its spiritual leader. Whatever thoughts Alfred Geiger Moses may have had about leaving Mobile and forming a Jewish New Thought group in New York were thus temporary and not made public, at least to members of his own congregation. Although it's unclear when he informed Hattie Seidenbaum and Lucia Nola Levy of his decision not to leave Mobile, by the fall of 1920, Lucia Levy and Bertha Strauss, in light of Moses' decision, decided to organize a Jewish New Thought group of their own.

In September of that year, Alfred Moses received a letter from Lucia Nola Levy, indicating that preparations for the organization that she and Mrs. Strauss hoped to form were very much under way. They had worked very hard, she told him, to set forth their objects and plans, and hoped that in the future he would agree to speak at some of their meetings. In light of his having served as a "prime mover" in their deciding to form a Jewish New Thought group of their own, they hoped that he would agree to lend his name as honorary president of their organization. Its formal name was to be the First Society of Jewish New Thought, and Jewish New Thought would be described in the society's publicity folder as applied Judaism.[65]

Jewish New Thought, as defined by Bertha Strauss and Lucia Nola Levy, rested on twelve basic principles, all of which, they maintained, sought to teach the practical application of Jewish teachings. The first four principles focused on God's omnipotence, omnipresence, omniscience, and justice. The next maintained the inherent righteousness of every individual; the "responsibility of every human soul for its heritage"; and the importance of serving humanity, revealing both a universal belief in divine-human kinship (or, as put succinctly in principle number 8, "The Fatherhood of God—The Brotherhood of Man") and the importance of serving God by remaining faithful to one's own religious heritage. Principles 9 through 12, which the society shared in common with other New Thought groups and which, according to Levy and Strauss, were new in their practical focus, were love for others and for oneself (that is, affirming oneself as well as affirming others); heaven as within us here and now (i.e., salvation as self-realization); spiritual healing as an important part of conscious individual development; and spiritual perfection (i.e., self-actualization) as the "goal of man."

On Sunday afternoon, October 3, 1920, the Society held its first meeting in Genealogical Hall on West 58th Street. Lucia Nola Levy gave a lecture on "Common Denominators," the first of over twenty-five lectures she delivered before the society between October 1920 and May of the following year. Determined to form a Jewish New Thought group even without the active involvement of Alfred Geiger Moses, Strauss and Levy became the group's actual leaders, with Strauss assuming the major organizational responsibilities and Levy delivering weekly (and sometimes biweekly) lectures. The focus of Levy's talks did not differ significantly from that of other New Thought leaders. The titles of her lectures, which included "A Hymn of Love vs. a Hymn of Hate," "How to Build a Consciousness," "Creating Environment," "The Joy of Life," and "How to Demonstrate Success," sounded very much like titles of lectures that were delivered by Maud Pratt Messner, Mary Chapin, Richard Lynch, Villa Faulkner Page, Eugene Del Mar, Anna C. Nolle, Addalyne Menzel, and others identified with New Thought during those years. Levy, in fact, initially sought to attract Jewish New Thoughters to the society by listing its meetings in the Saturday edition of the *New York Times* (which regularly featured a listing of "church services") under the heading "New Thought" rather than under the heading "Jewish."

Like other New Thought lectures, those delivered by Lucia Nola Levy promised to put joy into the lives of the listeners, and promised that their teachings, if practiced daily, would bring one health, happiness, and prosperity. Like New Thought lectures, too, those delivered by Levy were often followed by a healing meeting, in which participants, through silence, affirmation, and visualization, would get in touch with God's (or the mind's) healing powers. Those interested in private healing sessions were encouraged to contact Miss A. Joseph, whose function in the society remains unclear from existing materials, though in all likelihood she functioned as the society's secretary, either by mail or by phone. The society also met on Wednesday evenings, in a studio located in Carnegie Hall. Occasionally, Lucia Nola Levy gave a talk, but more frequently, she and Bertha Strauss informally answered questions about Jewish New Thought or studied, with those in attendance, their "textbook": Alfred Geiger Moses' 1920 edition of *Jewish Science*. While on at least one occasion, Alfred Moses addressed the society[66] and remained honorary president during Lucia Nola Levy's tenure as lecturer, his involvement was largely confined to an ongoing correspondence with Strauss and Levy, who referred to him as her rabbi. They kept him informed of the society's activities and occasionally asked him for advice, though it remains unclear how much advice, if any, he actually gave them.

In February 1921, Levy and Strauss seriously considered applying for formal membership in the International New Thought Alliance (INTA). To this end, Lucia Levy, as "local leader," and Bertha Strauss, as "organization officer," of the First Society of Jewish New Thought, attended a New Thought local leadership meeting at the Hotel McAlpin. Apparently a friend from the League for the Larger Life, of which Levy remained a member, had invited them to attend. At the meeting, Levy requested and readily received permission from James Edgerton, president of INTA, to join the alliance. However, Levy made it clear to Edgerton that, while "living in the principles of New Thought," their center, as a Jewish organization, did not "teach the Christ-Consciousness." Therefore, she continued, she needed to know whether in joining the alliance they would be presumed to be assenting to specific theological propositions. Was belief in Christ-consciousness, for example, considered to be an essential component of New Thought? Were there in fact particular beliefs that all New Thought members shared?

Edgerton's apparent response was that if they were "in the Divine Mind," that is, if they believed in the power of the mind and saw that power as divine in nature, they were welcome to join the alliance. Another leader indicated that there was in fact a New Thought platform to which Levy's society would be expected to adhere. While at that point Levy decided that she and other members of the society's executive board needed to examine the platform carefully before deciding whether they actually wanted to become alliance members, the subsequent address by Edgerton to those present convinced Lucia Nola Levy that, as Jews, she and the other members of the First Society of Jewish New Thought were not welcome. In his address, Edgerton spoke about the importance of the gospel of Jesus, concluding his remarks by saying that the only way to salvation was through "Jesus, the Christ." Although Edgerton later assured Lucia Levy that these remarks expressed his own sentiments and were not necessarily shared by all New Thought members, Edgerton's insensitivity to her presence, or what she later referred to as his "stand of exclusion," led her to recognize that the New Thought Alliance was indeed a Christian organization. As she wrote in an open letter to Edgerton, her own "delightful" experiences with the League for the Larger Life and its teachers had led her to expect "the greatest breadth of view from any New Thought organization leader." Instead, she maintained, she found Edgerton's statement to be an expression of both "narrowness and orthodoxy," different in nature and in content from her own understanding of the truth as "that of a glorious, illumined jewel, with many facets, each one exquisite yet individual; no one more beautiful than the other, and all equally near to the great Heart and Source of All."[67] Edgerton's views, she concluded, made it impossible for the Society of Jewish New Thought to become a member of INTA.

Edgerton's reply to Levy's letter, meant to assure her that there was room in the alliance for Jewish members, only served to underscore Levy's conviction that Jews, as Jews, were not welcome. Attempting to clarify his views, he maintained that his address had referred to "the Christ in all of us" rather than to the historical figure of Jesus Christ. Given the opportunity, he concluded, he was certain that he could get Miss Levy to realize that New Thought did not exclude her or any other Jews, since its understanding of Christ was not that which had "caused division between Christians and Jews" in the past but rather of a universal Christ consciousness that Jews and Christians shared.[68] Sending a copy of this letter to Alfred Moses, Lucia Nola Levy tersely scribbled on the bottom of the page: "Have not answered this yet but have several methods of procedure under advisement."

By mid-March, Levy still had not answered Edgerton's letter. "I wish," she wrote to Alfred Moses, "you were here to advise me." Though she expressed the hope that her open letter to Edgerton, dated February 21, 1921, in which she repeated his exclusionary statements, would bring others to publicly offer a more inclusive understanding of New Thought teachings, there is no indication that such offers were ever forthcoming. By April, Levy's initial hope that the Jewish New Thought Center might join INTA was firmly abandoned, and notices in the *New York Times* of the society's weekly meetings were placed in the church services listings under the "Jewish" rather than the "New Thought" heading. They included the dates and places of the week's meetings, the topic of Lucia Nola Levy's Sunday lecture, and the newly given assurance that Jewish New Thought was "the golden link to Judaism."

By June, the society began to talk of ways its membership might be increased. One plan was to offer membership for one dollar a year, a plan that Bertha Strauss hoped might attract as many as ten thousand members. As of that June, as Strauss indicated in a letter written to Alfred Geiger Moses, there were only about fifty "regular members." Yet of even greater concern than membership figures was finding someone who could serve as the group's religious leader, as Lucia Nola Levy recently had announced that she was leaving the society to spread the teachings of Jewish New Thought through "field work." Without going into further detail, Strauss stressed the necessity of finding someone, hopefully a man, to replace her. "If you hear of someone who would be fit to do this work," she concluded, "kindly tell us."[69] Though Bertha Strauss mentioned in her letter how glad she was to have heard that Rabbi Moses was thinking of starting a Jewish Science magazine, she apparently had abandoned her earlier hope that he might eventually agree to leave Mobile and become the society's leader.

It is unlikely that Alfred Geiger Moses offered Bertha Strauss any concrete suggestions. He, like Lucia Nola Levy and Bertha Strauss, had interested several rabbis in the teachings of Jewish New Thought, but none seemed willing to take what Bertha Strauss described as "an active part" in their efforts. Consequently, throughout the fall, the society stopped holding its weekly meetings. By December, however, Bertha Strauss had finally found someone to replace Lucia Levy. On December 10, 1921, the first of many listings in the *New York Times* proclaimed: "Society of Applied Judaism (formerly known as Jewish New Thought) announces lectures and classes to start in January [with] Rabbi Morris Lichtenstein [as] lecturer and teacher."[70] By the end of January 1922, Lichtenstein had become far more than Lucia Nola Levy's replacement. Explicitly identifying himself as the society's leader, he began to reevaluate and redefine the teachings of the society, hoping to create a movement that was less indebted to the teachings of Alfred Geiger Moses than to his own.

There is no evidence to suggest that Moses or Lichtenstein were ever in direct contact with one another. While Alfred Geiger Moses apparently retained a great interest in Jewish Science, participating in both Jewish and New Thought discussions concerning Jewish Science teachings and the benefits of spiritual healing in general, it seems that he never attended any meetings of the society once Morris Lichtenstein became its leader. Indeed, throughout the 1920s, as the so-called Jewish defection to Christian Science continued, Moses took few concrete steps to bring Jews back to Judaism. While at least hundreds of Jews still read and were inspired by his earlier writings on Jewish Science, Moses himself focused on his daily responsibilities as rabbi of Sha'arai Shomayim. At the same time, he continued to fight what by the 1940s had become a losing battle against his own slowly deteriorating mental health. Ironically, despite his belief that mental illness was an illusion, Moses spent the last years of his life in a mental institution. For over twenty years, the teachings of Jewish Science may have helped him cope with his mental problems, but, in the end, struggling to retain his sanity, he found that optimism could not defeat the mental "illusions" from which he suffered.

Despite the interest that Moses' work generated within the American Jewish community, his disinterest in creating a Jewish Science group, even within his own congregation, limited his influence on both Reform Judaism and American Jewry as a whole. Yet the term *Jewish Science*, which he created, succeeded in attracting the attention of Jews already interested in Christian Science. Believing that it was his duty as a Reform rabbi and as a Jew to bring others to an awareness of God's presence, and unafraid to use the techniques and aims of Christian Science, applied psychology, and New Thought in order to do so, Moses encouraged his readers, as well as those, like Rabbis Morris Lichtenstein and Clifton Harby Levy, who later developed Jewish Science further, to incorporate within Reform's ideological understanding of ethical monotheism the more personal goals of health, success, and happiness.

3

The Creation of a Movement

In many ways, the newly named Society of Applied Judaism was Morris Lichtenstein's creation. Although its earliest adherents were those who had previously attended meetings and lectures sponsored by Levy and Strauss's Society of Jewish New Thought, and while it was Bertha Strauss herself who initially hired Lichtenstein to assume leadership of the society that she and Lucia Nola Levy had founded, Lichtenstein quickly transformed the society into a movement that promulgated his own ideas. He did so not only through numerous lectures and publications but also by creating an organizational base that firmly ensured his lifetime tenure as the society's religious leader.

Lichtenstein (1888–1938)[1] assumed leadership of the Society of Jewish New Thought after briefly serving as rabbi of the Congregation of the Children of Israel in Athens, Georgia. A small Reform congregation numbering no more than a few hundred families, it was in fact the only Jewish congregation in Athens, a city of twenty-five thousand people and home to the University of Georgia. Having been without a rabbi for several months, the congregation, which the *Athens Daily Banner* regularly identified simply as "the local synagogue," first hired Morris Lichtenstein to lead both Sabbath and high holy day services in September 1920. Identifying him as "Morris Lichtenstein of New York," the *Athens Daily Banner* announced that Rabbi Lichtenstein would be preaching on such topics as "Progress and Regress," "Assimilation," and "Souls of the Departed." It further announced that following services, he would be available to meet members of the congregation and the teachers, pupils, and friends of the congregation's Sunday school, presumably because, should Lichtenstein become the synagogue's rabbi, he would become principal of the Sunday school as well.

Lichtenstein apparently made a favorable impression on members of the congregation. Though not physically imposing, he was gifted with a quick mind and a deep, powerful voice that helped to make him a dynamic, inspirational speaker. His demeanor was calm yet intense, and he must have struck members of the congregation, as he later did his followers in New York, as a sympathetic listener who was genuinely interested in helping them. In brief, he seemed to be deeply spiritual yet at the same time capable and interested in offering practical advice. By the end of September 1920, a year after he had received his master of arts degree from Columbia University,[2] Morris Lichten-

FIGURE 3.1. Rabbi Morris Lichtenstein. Courtesy of the Society of Jewish Science.

stein accepted the call to become Children of Israel's spiritual leader. Within a week, he and his wife, Tehilla, had moved to Athens, with Lichtenstein immediately assuming his congregational duties.[3] While by his own account Morris Lichtenstein occupied a pulpit in Troy, New York, sometime before his call to Athens, there is no evidence to suggest that this was a full-time position. He simply may have led services on the high holy days and weekends. Indeed, from the few records that remain, it seems that Lichtenstein's position as rabbi of the Congregation of the Children of Israel was his first and last full-time position as rabbi of a Reform congregation. Throughout his lifetime, he remained a member of the CCAR and on occasion attended its annual convention. Yet from December 1921, when he accepted Bertha Strauss's invitation to lead the Jewish New Thought Center in New York City, until his untimely death from colon cancer in November 1938, Morris Lichtenstein devoted almost all of his time and effort to formulating and disseminating the teachings of Jewish Science.

Like Alfred Geiger Moses, Morris Lichtenstein viewed Jewish Science as a means of turning Jews away from Christian Science while at the same time revivifying American Jewry's spiritual life. The aim of Jewish Science, he wrote, is "to intensify the spiritual consciousness of the Jew . . . [by] show[ing] him the way to health and happiness through the channels of his own faith."[4] While Lichtenstein later maintained that he had first begun to think of ways of combating the spread of Christian Science among Jews during his student days at HUC—the years immediately preceding and following the 1912 CCAR Conference at which the relationship between Judaism and Christian Science was first discussed—he took no concrete steps in this direction until he assumed leadership of the Society of Jewish New Thought in December 1921. While he was in Athens, Lichtenstein may well have heard of Alfred Geiger Moses' theories about mental healing, yet he never acknowledged any indebtedness to him either in his sermons or his writings. It does not seem that they ever corresponded with one another, and in fact it is unclear whether they ever met.

Eleven years his senior, Alfred Moses attended HUC in Cincinnati almost fifteen years earlier than Morris Lichtenstein. With the exception of his years in Cincinnati, Moses spent his lifetime in the South. In contrast, Morris Lichtenstein, the son of Eliezer (Ozer) and Hannah Surasky Lichtenstein, was born in Bialystock, Lithuania. Arriving in the United States in 1907, at the age of nineteen, he spent three and a half years in Columbus, Ohio, living with and/or supported by relatives of the five-year-old cousin whom he'd brought to America with him. From 1911 to 1916 he lived in Cincinnati, receiving a bachelor of arts degree from the University of Cincinnati and rabbinic ordination from HUC. He briefly moved to New York City, then to Athens, Georgia, before returning with his wife, Tehilla, to Manhattan. His parents remained in Europe, both of them dying before the outbreak of World War II. His two brothers also remained in Europe, but apparently they, like the rest of Lichtenstein's family, did not survive the war. Though he rarely, if ever, spoke about it, almost all of his family, including his brothers, were victims of Nazi oppression.

If Alfred Moses and Morris Lichtenstein met one another it was most likely at an annual meeting of the CCAR. Yet, again, since they did not serve on any of the same committees or share a platform either at a CCAR conference or any other publicized event, if they did meet, they may only have engaged in a brief conversation. Perhaps Morris Lichtenstein failed to acknowledge Alfred Moses' books on Jewish Science because he was not familiar with them. It seems unlikely, however, that neither Bertha Strauss nor other "Jewish New Thoughters" who joined the Society of Applied Judaism would have failed to mention Alfred Moses' work. Indeed, it is entirely conceivable that Bertha Strauss gave Lichtenstein a copy of the 1920 edition of *Jewish Science*, if he didn't already own one. If so, perhaps Lichtenstein felt that acknowledging Moses' work was either unnecessary, because his own ideas of Jewish Science differed so greatly, or undesirable, since to do so might diminish his own achievements.

Given the fact that Lichtenstein's first active involvement in spreading the ideas of Jewish Science was as leader of Bertha Strauss and Lucia Nola Levy's Jewish New Thought Center, the group that claimed Alfred Moses as their inspiration and honorary president and his *Jewish Science* as their textbook, it is highly unlikely that Morris Lichtenstein did not read Alfred Moses' work sometime before 1925, when his own book on Jewish Science was published. It is true that Lichtenstein's vision of Jewish Science differed in many respects from that of Moses. Yet the identification of Jewish Science with applied Judaism, which Lichtenstein repeatedly made, was first articulated by Alfred Moses. Indeed, when Lichtenstein assumed leadership of the New York City group, he immediately renamed it the Society of Applied Judaism. Thus, it is likely that Lichtenstein's failure to acknowledge Alfred Geiger Moses reflected his desire to found a movement that, in terms of its leadership and teachings, would be recognized as his alone.

Perhaps what was most attractive about Bertha Strauss's invitation to lead the Society of Jewish New Thought was the opportunity it afforded Morris Lichtenstein to serve as leader of his own spiritual movement. According to some who knew him, Lichtenstein disliked having his work directed by or subject to the approval of others.[5] At the Congregation of the Children of Israel, his work was constantly under the scrutiny of the synagogue board and its president, M. G. Michael, one of the wealthiest and most prominent Jews in Athens. In New York, he would have free rein to create and direct a movement that would truly be his own. While the *Athens Banner* maintained that during his brief stay in Athens, Rabbi Lichtenstein had formed a "host of friends who [would] regret to see him leave,"[6] his sudden departure in mid-December, after giving the congregation little more than a week's notice, suggests that Lichten-

stein was less than satisfied with his position. Indeed, he left before a replacement for him could be found, leaving Colonel Michael, as president of the
congregation, with the responsibility of leading services for the remainder of
the Jewish year.[7]

However great the allure of leading his own movement may have been,
Morris Lichtenstein's desire to help combat the inroads that Christian Science
had made in the American Jewish community obviously was sincere. In finding
a means of doing so, he received inspiration and encouragement from his new
father-in-law, the well-known and greatly respected rabbi and scholar Chaim
Hirschensohn. Through both his writings and role as leader of the Orthodox
Jewish community in Hoboken, New Jersey, Hirschensohn attempted to apply
the teachings of traditional Judaism to the realities of modern-day life. While,
unlike Hirschensohn, Lichtenstein equated Jewish teachings with the teachings of American Reform, he, like his father-in-law, sought to discover ways in
which Judaism could be applied to the realities of modern existence.

Lichtenstein and Hirschensohn retained a close friendship with one another. Indeed, Lichtenstein saw himself as one of his father-in-law's disciples
and went so far as to request that when he died, he be buried next to him, a
wish that was subsequently granted.[8] Morris Lichtenstein and Chaim Hirschensohn shared much in common, including their religious backgrounds.
Though ordained as a Reform rabbi in 1916, Lichtenstein came from a traditional Jewish home in eastern Europe. He studied both privately and in yeshivot
in Bialystock and Lomza. While, as some biographical references have claimed,
he may have received *semikha* (rabbinic ordination) before coming to the
United States,[9] there does not appear to be any extant statement to this effect
by Morris Lichtenstein. Chaim Hirschensohn also came from a traditionally
religious family. Spending half of his life in Palestine, he immigrated to the
United States, again, like Morris Lichtenstein, in the early twentieth century.
Both were gifted with a quick mind and a deep spiritual nature. Both devoted
their lives to discovering ways in which Judaism could meet the needs of every
generation and sought to address those concerns through personal leadership
and scholarly writings. Indeed, before coming to the United States, Lichtenstein had received not just an extensive Hebrew education but a *gymnasium*
(modern, secular) education as well.[10] Moreover, Jewish Science, as Lichtenstein understood it, was not an alternative to Orthodoxy, or to any other branch
of Judaism for that matter, but rather a supplement. It was, quite simply, a
philosophy that sought to reveal the ways Jewish teachings could become a
powerful influence in daily life.

Within a month of his assuming leadership of the renamed Society of
Applied Judaism, Morris Lichtenstein had become more than the society's lecturer, the title previously accorded Lucia Nola Levy, and one widely used in
New Thought circles. Formally recognized as the society's leader, he led services and delivered a formal lecture each Sunday morning at the Hotel McAlpin.

His first lecture, delivered on January 8, 1922, was entitled "A Spiritual Rebirth."[11] In the months that followed, he gave talks on such topics as "Optimism and Pessimism," "The Jewish Soul," "In the Image of God," "Religion and Medicine," "The Power of Thought," and "The Conquest of Fear." In March of that year, he delivered a special series of lectures on "The Road to Happiness," "The Road to Peace," and "The Road to Health." In addition, he began to hold "healing meetings" after each service, and on Wednesday evenings he offered classes and informal discussion on the teachings of Jewish Science.

Each Saturday, Sunday services and classes were advertised in the "Church Services" section of the *New York Times*, sometimes under the heading "New Thought," more frequently under the heading "Jewish." The time and place of services was announced, as was the topic of the week's lecture, followed by the promise that "we offer happiness and health to the Jew through his own religion." One week's listing, announcing that Rabbi Lichtenstein's Sunday lecture would be on "Applied Judaism vs. Christian Science," went on to maintain that "we accomplish through Judaism what Christian Science accomplishes through Christianity."[12] Staunchly insisting that Jewish Science was not a Jewish counterpart to Christian Science, since the theological differences between them were significant, but rather an alternative, explicitly Jewish way for the Jew to discover happiness and health, Morris Lichtenstein spent most of 1922 establishing himself as leader of the society and forming an organizational base that would support and actively assist him in his efforts.

In May 1922, at Lichtenstein's instigation, the group changed its name from the Society of Applied Judaism to the Society of Jewish Science. Presumably, this change was made to make the nature of the society clearer and to appeal more directly to those Jews who already were attracted to Christian Science teachings. Three months later, the society officially became incorporated as a religious organization, with Morris Lichtenstein as its leader and rabbi. Nine men and seven women were listed as members. Hattie Seidenbaum, one of the early members of the Society of Jewish New Thought, was among them. Noticeably absent was the name of Bertha Strauss. Strauss's departure from the Society was apparently triggered by a personal disagreement with Lichtenstein, perhaps over his insistence that in the future he alone would formulate and develop the teachings of Jewish Science. Indeed, once Morris Lichtenstein became leader of the society, Alfred Geiger Moses' *Jewish Science* no longer served as its textbook, and in 1925 Lichtenstein's own *Jewish Science and Health* replaced it.[13]

In March 1925, with the drafting of a constitution and bylaws, Morris Lichtenstein was formally granted lifetime leadership of the society. He was empowered with formulating, expounding, and teaching the principles of Jewish Science to others. The bylaws clearly said that no interpretation of Jewish Science could be accepted by members of the society unless sanctioned by Rabbi Lichtenstein. Members who lectured publicly on Jewish Science needed to be authorized by him, and he had the power to revoke an individual's membership at any time and, presumably, for any reason. A board of directors was established; yet its stated function was to cooperate with Lichtenstein, not to oversee or approve of his activities.[14] The board was to consist of six elected members (by 1929 the number was expanded to twelve) plus Lichtenstein in an ex officio position. Each member was to serve a three-year term, with the exception of those first elected, two of whom would serve for one year, two for two years, and two for three, so that in any given year no more than two (later four) new board members would be selected. While in theory any member of the society was eligible to serve, the 1925 bylaws and later revised versions clearly said that "in order that the board and the leader shall work in perfect harmony for the advancement of Jewish Science, the board shall first secure the approval of the leader for its candidates to the vacancies created by the retiring [board] members."[15]

Officers of the society, elected from among themselves by the Board of Directors, consisted of a chairman, vice-chairman, treasurer, financial secretary, and recording secretary, each of whom was to serve a one-year term. The chairman's chief function was to preside at Board of Directors meetings, with the vice-chairman doing so in his absence. The treasurer was placed in charge of the society's money, signing all checks, along with either the chairman or vice-chairman. The financial secretary oversaw the society's monetary affairs, while the recording secretary took minutes of board and membership meetings. While the officers assisted Lichtenstein in running the society, the constitution and bylaws made it clear that he alone was the society's leader. His book *Jewish Science and Health* became the society's textbook, and, echoing the practice of Christian Science in relation to Mary Baker Eddy's *Science and Health with Key to the Scriptures*, a portion was assigned each week for home study and recitation at the weekly Jewish Science service. The society sought to encourage the establishment of Jewish Science groups, or branches, throughout the American Jewish community. However, as its bylaws clearly said, all branches had to "follow the precepts, rules, regulations and doctrines" of the society, identified as the "home center," as set forth in the constitution and in Morris Lichtenstein's writings. As leader of the society, Lichtenstein was to receive a "salary, commensurate with [its] financial resources." Consequently, his salary varied from year to year. In the 1920s, for example, it ranged from a comfortable $7,420 in 1928 to a low of $2,240 in 1929 (the year of the stock market crash, when only $360 was collected in membership). While Lichtenstein did not control the society's finances, his salary was a generous one, usually exceeding half of the money received by the society in any given year.[16]

By 1926, apparently in response to numerous individual requests and what Morris Lichtenstein and members of the board believed to be a "generally felt need," a branch of the society was created in Brooklyn. Wednesday evening discussions in Manhattan were replaced with a service and lecture held at the Jewish Community Center in Flatbush at least through that spring, after which no further announcements concerning the Brooklyn branch appeared in the *Jewish Science Interpreter*. In addition, also by 1926, the society began to hold Friday evening Sabbath services, led by Morris Lichtenstein. They were initially held at the Heights Club in Washington Heights, then at Morris and Tehilla Lichtenstein's apartment on West 72nd Street, and beginning in late 1928, at the True Sisters' Building on West 85th Street, soon considered to be the society's headquarters. Services were also held on the Jewish high holy days, for which a fee was charged, and on other Jewish holidays as well.

During the early years of the society's existence, Lichtenstein devoted most of his efforts to articulating the teachings of Jewish Science and revealing the efficacy of his teachings through daily healing sessions. From 1922 to 1929, these sessions were held from 2:00 to 6:00 p.m. and from 1930 to 1935 from 2:00 to 5:00 p.m., with reduced hours during the summer. They were held in Manhattan at his home, which for a brief period was located at 610 West 163rd Street, then at 166 West 73rd Street, and from September 1926 until his death in November 1938, at 100 West 72nd Street. By the end of 1935, healing sessions were moved to the True Sisters' Building, where they were held from 2:00 to 5:00 p.m. every afternoon except Saturday and Sunday. These regularly scheduled sessions with Rabbi Lichtenstein continued through 1937, apparently coming to an end by the beginning of 1938, approximately ten months before his death. By then, however, there were over twenty men and women in New York and New Jersey, trained by him as spiritual practitioners, who were "actively engaged in the practice of Jewish Science healing."[17]

By February 1923, Morris Lichtenstein began to publish the monthly periodical the *Jewish Science Interpreter*, which helped spread his ideas further. Every issue included at least one, and usually two or three, essays by Lichtenstein, most of which were edited versions of previously delivered sermons. Focusing on such topics as "The Sin of Worry," "The Power of Kindness," "Spiritual Religion and Practical Religion," "Perpetual Youth," and "The Secret of Courage," these essays attempted, as Lichtenstein himself maintained, to offer readers "a way-finger to the solution of life's problems and perplexities, an answer to spiritual questionings and disquietudes, and a practical guide to happiness and peace of mind."[18] The *Interpreter* also included a list of Bible readings for the month, divided into weekly selections; daily meditations; personal testimonials from countless men and women who had found health and happiness through Jewish Science teachings; an invitation to the reader to attend the society's services, classes, and other activities; and a list of practitioners who, along with Morris Lichtenstein, could assist the reader in attaining spiritual and physical health.

Beginning with its second issue, published in March 1923, the *Jewish Science Interpreter* also included two affirmations that articulated what Morris Lichtenstein considered to be the fundamental principles of Jewish Science. These affirmations were to be repeated silently by the reader every morning and every evening. Lichtenstein instructed the reader first to relax completely for approximately fifteen minutes, releasing every muscle from any possible tension. "Take an easy comfortable position," he said, "and dismiss all strain both from mind and body. Then repeat [the following] affirmations." First:

> "I am calm and cheerful; I hate no one; I envy no one; there is no worry or fear in me; I trust in God all the time."

And second:

> "The God consciousness in me expresses itself in health, in calmness, in peace, in power and in happiness."

Morris Lichtenstein encouraged meditating on the significance of every phrase and letting each thought engrave itself on one's consciousness. Those who did so, he maintained, would begin to feel a deep change within the innermost recesses of their being. Their suffering would cease, and their depression would vanish. In describing the significance of these affirmations, Lichtenstein wrote:

> [An affirmation] is a prayer offered to the divine within man. We must bear in mind that we understand God as dwelling in every form of reality; in fact, without God's presence, reality is impossible. God's presence within man is manifested by the very life that is in him, by the presence of thought, feeling, emotions. For while it is ours to utilize those powers within us, it is not we who have brought them into existence. Their existence is due to the divine within us. It is this divine in us that we call on to express itself in its perfection, when we offer these prayers or affirmations. And these prayers are always answered.[19]

As a means of explaining the affirmations further, Morris Lichtenstein pointed to various biblical psalms that used affirmation as a form of prayer. One noteworthy example was Psalm 23. The psalmist, he wrote, intentionally says: "The Lord *is* my shepherd," rather than "Oh, Lord, *be* my shepherd," and "The Lord *is* my Light and my Salvation," rather than "Oh, Lord, *be* my Light and my Salvation" because he knows that God's presence is already within him. Thus, we attain courage, strength, and joy not by imploring an outside presence to bestow such attributes on us but by getting in touch with or tapping into an inner divine energy that is in fact the source of all that we most desire. It is, then, through affirmations directed to this inner divine energy or mind that courage, strength, and joy, among other positive attributes, can best be attained.

The *Jewish Science Interpreter*, which, with the exception of one brief period in the 1970s, has continuously been published since 1923, helped to bring, and still brings, the teachings of Jewish Science as expounded by Morris Lichtenstein to thousands of men and women. Today, as in the 1920s, most of its subscribers do not live in New York City and are not members of the society, although today, again as in the 1920s, local branches in a number of American cities do exist. Thus, in attempting to evaluate Jewish Science's appeal, membership statistics are misleading. Even at its peak during the late 1920s and early 1930s, membership remained fairly small. While Lichtenstein claimed that at one time membership rose as high as five hundred men and women, the few early membership lists still in existence suggest that membership did not substantially exceed two hundred.[20] Even so, it probably is true, as Morris Lichtenstein claimed, that at one time or another thousands of men and women literally passed through the doors of Jewish Science, attending services, reading its literature, and/or seeking help from a spiritual practitioner. If we are to believe testimonials published in the *Interpreter*, many of those who subscribed attempted to incorporate Lichtenstein's teachings into their everyday lives, faithfully reading the weekly selections from the Bible and *Jewish Science and Health* and reciting Lichtenstein's two affirmations every morning and night.

While Morris Lichtenstein came to be seen as both the leader and founder of the Society of Jewish Science, he was greatly assisted, financially and personally, by members of the society's Women's League. Indeed, existing records indicate that during its initial period of growth, the society was financially dependent on funds raised and contributions given by league members. It was particularly dependent on the generous contributions made by the league's president, Rebecca Dreyfuss (1871–1942), life member of the society and the first woman to serve on its Board of Directors. The role of Rebecca Dreyfuss in the development of the society cannot be overestimated. Born in England, she eventually made the United States her home. She was deeply religious and, according to those who knew her, saintly in nature. A convert to Judaism, she later discovered Morris Lichtenstein's Society of Jewish Science. From that moment on, she devoted her life to the propagation of his teachings, becoming his foremost disciple and the "spiritual mother" of the society. Throughout Morris Lichtenstein's tenure as the society's leader, Rebecca Dreyfuss served as his right hand: leading services in his absence, often leading members in the recitation of the affirmations at general membership and Board of Directors meetings, actively working to increase subscriptions to the *Jewish Science Interpreter*, serving as a practitioner, and, as president of the Women's League, organizing countless social and fundraising activities.

The Women's League, as conceived by both Morris Lichtenstein and Rebecca Dreyfuss in 1923, was founded as an auxiliary organization dedicated to furthering the ideals and teachings of the Society of Jewish Science. In order to do so, it pledged to assist the society financially, spiritually, and through various activities organized by Women's League members. Membership was "open to all women whose qualifications would entitle them to membership in the Society of Jewish Science," namely, Jewish women who were not members of Christian Science or of any other non-Jewish religious organization.[21] Though most league members eventually became members of the society, membership in one group was not a prerequisite for membership in the other. The league had its own slate of officers, board of directors, and set of committees.

As its constitution and bylaws clearly said, every member of the league was expected to be an active member, "feel[ing] equally with every other member the duty and responsibility of advancing the cause of Jewish Science among the Jewish people."[22] In order to do so, each member was required to make a personal effort to increase attendance at Jewish Science services by bringing friends and sending invitations. More specifically, each member was to bring at least one friend with her to Sunday morning services. Members were also required to personally spread authorized Jewish Science literature, that is, the works of Morris Lichtenstein, and to actively participate in affairs given by the league and the society that would increase the society's funds. They were to attend league meetings frequently, if not regularly, and "speak of Jewish Science to . . . [their] friends at every appropriate occasion." According to its bylaws, the primary purpose of the Women's League, at least in its earliest years, was twofold. Its members were, first, to help spread the teachings of Morris Lichtenstein throughout the American Jewish community, and, second, through a number of regular and special funds established by the league, to raise money that would "further the advancement and growth of Jewish Science" and would be readily available to the society should funds be needed. As financial statements show, most of the society's early income came directly from the Women's League. By the late 1920s, with the establishment of a life member category, Rebecca Dreyfuss, the first and for a while the only life member, singlehandedly contributed a major percentage of the society's income.

Sometime before her death in November 1942, Rebecca Dreyfuss wrote a poem entitled "Jewish Science" that reveals the centrality of Jewish Science in her life. Written out in ink and mounted on a cardboard placard, her poem may well have been intended both as a personal record of her faith and as an inspiration to others. It read:

> Jewish Science is to me
>   the law of love God gave to be
> The great creative power in man
>   imagination, deepest calm.
>
> Its "textbook" is the key to find
>   the inner workings of the mind

FIGURE 3.2. Rebecca Dreyfuss, "spiritual mother" of the Society of Jewish Science. Courtesy of the Society of Jewish Science.

>The secret of each living thing
>   the presence of God within.
>
>In this book of God so good
>   much is found for mental food
>Much that "bible writ" conceals
>   *Jewish Science and Health* reveals.
>
>It teaches "how in truth" to pray
>   how to study day by day
>How to live a life of calm
>   and cheer—the wealth of that I am.
>
>Then thank the Lord my soul each day
>   that Jewish Science leads the way

> To richest treasures of all wealth
> contentment, happiness and health.[23]

While to a large extent the early growth of the Society of Jewish Science was made possible by the efforts of Rebecca Dreyfuss and other members of the Women's League, one should not conclude that the league was the only group that actively sought to spread the ideals of Jewish Science. By 1927, for example, at Lichtenstein's urging, the society established a Propaganda Committee, composed of six members of the Women's League and six male members of the society. Holding monthly meetings at Lichtenstein's home, the committee saw as its goal the devising of new ways and means of propagating the teachings of Jewish Science.[24] By the mid-1930s a Junior League, open to young men between the ages of eighteen and twenty-five and young women between sixteen and twenty-one, was created by Morris and Tehilla Lichtenstein with the help of Rebecca Dreyfuss and William Fried, chairman of the society.[25] Its goal was both social and spiritual. It not only offered young men and women of post–Sunday school age the opportunity to meet and socialize with one another but also provided them with the opportunity and means of studying and eventually spreading the teachings of Jewish Science. A great number of its members presumably were already familiar with Jewish Science, since many, if not most, had previously attended the Society's Sunday school, established by the Lichtensteins in 1923.

Initially consisting of a single class offered by Tehilla Lichtenstein on Sunday mornings at the Hotel McAlpin, the school met at 11:00 a.m., the same time as the society's Sunday morning services, also held at the McAlpin. They were later held at the Leslie Hotel, at the Hotel Astor, and, by 1928, at the True Sisters Building on West 85th Street, where they continued to be held for almost thirty years. While the adults were in one room, reciting the affirmations and listening to the teachings of Morris Lichtenstein, their children were in another, learning about Judaism and Jewish Science from Tehilla Lichtenstein, the school's principal and teacher. By 1927, the school boasted an enrollment of thirty-nine, plus an additional eight who were members of the school's special Confirmation Class.[26] The following year, Tehilla and Morris Lichtenstein's sons, six-year-old Emanuel (later spelled Immanuel) and four-year-old Michael Jonathan, joined the list of Sunday school members. By 1935, the society's Sunday school had grown to include eighty-six enrolled students and a teaching staff of seven under Tehilla Lichtenstein's direction. Maintaining that "the Jewish Science Sunday School teaches its children, from their earliest years, to live a happy, fearless, healthy life," giving them "a foundation in faith and right living,"[27] it was open to all Jewish children between the ages of six and thirteen, whether or not their parents were members of the society. Through 1935, if not later, the Sunday school did not charge tuition.

It wasn't until 1950 that a separate Men's League of Jewish Science was established. It never reached the level of membership or active involvement of the Women's League and, in fact, ceased to function as an independent auxiliary organization by 1954. Some men were members of both the society's Membership Committee and the Year Book Committee, which, by the late 1920s, helped raise a significant amount of money. A small but active group of men were involved in the socially oriented Men's Club, as well as in the Business and Professional Group of Jewish Science, a group initially formed as an auxiliary women's organization. Nonetheless, despite a significant male membership, the majority of those who actively participated in the society were women. Most were middle-aged, middle-class, married women, with minimal religious education. Most, including those who were not born in the United States, were highly acculturated and most, but by no means all, had no other affiliation within the American Jewish community. Though on the whole the women and men who joined Jewish Science were not intellectuals, many could boast of a good secular education. While most of its early female members went no further than high school, and some only through grade school, some were college graduates, and a few had advanced degrees as well.

In examining the development of Jewish Science, it is important not to minimize the role women played both as members and as lay leaders. In an era in which the participation of women in the synagogue was not equal to that of men, even in the Reform movement, and when pronouncements of women's equality were more theoretical than real, it is noteworthy that from its inception in 1922, Morris Lichtenstein's Society of Jewish Science afforded women spiritual opportunities that were unique within the American Jewish community. From the beginning, women like Rebecca Dreyfuss helped lead worship services and were encouraged to become practitioners of spiritual healing. In 1938, with the death of Morris Lichtenstein, Tehilla Lichtenstein succeeded her husband as leader of the society, becoming the first woman to serve as leader of an American Jewish congregation.

Yet along with the opportunities that Jewish Science afforded women, it must also be noted that Jewish Science offered a number of similar opportunities to men. Those from traditional backgrounds whose knowledge of Hebrew was not sufficient to enable them to lead services in an Orthodox congregation or even to participate fully in a *minyan* (a quorum of ten necessary for public worship), as well as those from backgrounds that were either secular or Reform, were given the opportunity to assist in leading the worship service and were encouraged to become practitioners and to form local Jewish Science groups of their own. Indeed, since its inception, the Society of Jewish Science has relied on the dedication and efforts, and in some cases the financial contributions, of men every bit as much as it has relied on its female members. Clearly, there were a number of women who played important roles during the earliest years of the society's growth. These women included Rebecca Dreyfuss, Ruth Fauer, and Sarah Fellerman of the Women's League; Anna Moser,

FIGURE 3.3. Tehilla Lichtenstein. Courtesy of the Society of Jewish Science.

Rebecca Dreyfuss's successor as chair of the Women's League and later chair of the Business and Professional Group, who, like Dreyfuss, Fauer, and Fellerman served as one of the society's spiritual practitioners; and last, but certainly not least, Tehilla Lichtenstein, principal of the Sunday school from its inception and editor of the *Jewish Science Interpreter*. Yet despite their important contributions and despite the fact that throughout its existence, approximately two-thirds of the society's membership has been made up of women, it would be a mistake to characterize the Society of Jewish Science as a "women's movement."

From its inception in 1922, there were a number of men who, with or without the participation of their wives, became active and devoted members. Like the women who joined the society in its earliest years, most male members were middle-aged and middle-class. Most were acculturated, even those who were immigrants, possessed at least a high school education, often more, and again, like their female counterparts, came from both eastern European and German Jewish backgrounds. While most of the men had some religious education, and many had studied through bar mitzvah, few if any possessed great knowledge of Hebrew or of the Jewish tradition. Unlike most of the women, who previously had considered themselves to be unaffiliated Jews, many of the men had considered themselves to be either Orthodox or Reform before joining Jewish Science, and some retained their synagogue membership even after they had joined the society. Yet, like their female counterparts, the men who became part of the society found in Jewish Science something they had not previously discovered, namely, a Jewish movement that actively sought to tap the spiritual potential of its members. Among the men who were drawn to the society during the 1920s and 1930s were Jacob Ansbacher, one of the society's first practitioners and author of several essays on Jewish Science that appeared in the earliest issues of the *Jewish Science Interpreter*; Sidney Morgenstern, a founding member of the society, one of its first practitioners, and treasurer; and Monroe Flegenheimer, who was a chairman of the society, practitioner, and active member of several committees. Other early male members, whose involvement grew under Tehilla Lichtenstein's leadership, were Harry Hartman, Sam Moser, and Abraham Goldstein, who served as chairman of the society from 1943 until his death in 1998, in 1973 succeeding Tehilla Lichtenstein as leader.

In attempting to understand the early appeal of Jewish Science, as well as the great devotion it inspired, one only need turn to the *Jewish Science Interpreter*. In almost every issue, one can find testimonials by men and women praising the work of Morris Lichtenstein, the society's practitioners, and later, the work of Lichtenstein's wife, Tehilla, for curing specific illnesses from which they suffered, relieving them of depression, helping them attain a more positive outlook toward life, providing with a Jewish alternative to Christian Science, or, as was frequently the case, simply helping them to discover God. One woman, for example, expressed thanks to Morris Lichtenstein and his teachings for showing her how to remain calm, even in the face of illness. "Since my husband and I began to understand Jewish Science," she wrote, "we have had no need for doctors nor nurses. We have had very little sickness in the family since we joined Jewish Science; and when any of us did feel sick during the last winter we were healed through the channels of Jewish Science, without worry of any kind."[28] Another woman wrote to thank Etta Naftal, the Jewish Science practitioner to whom she had gone after her baby daughter took ill, for giving her the "encouragement, peace of mind, and strength to fight mental fears" that she needed but had not received from any of her daughter's three attending physicians.[29] One woman reported, that armed with a newfound faith in God, she had thrown away the medicines that she had been taking for rheumatism, which had "ruined [her] stomach," and since then had been steadily improving,[30] while another claimed that the "happy disposition" and "optimistic outlook" she gained from Jewish Science cured her of the sleeping problems she had had for years.[31]

One early issue of the *Jewish Science Interpreter* featured the personal testimony of Julius Schwartzwald of New York City, who remained an active and devoted member of the society throughout the 1920s. In his letter, he described in detail the "wonderful help" he had received from Jewish Science. For twenty-four years, he wrote, he had been afflicted with diabetes. His doctors had told him that unless he kept to a strict diet, he might go blind, get blood poisoning, or even go insane. The fears that these doctors had instilled in him adversely affected his eating habits. He ate so little that he became extremely weak and nervous and consequently ceased to function well at work. This went on for eighteen years. Then, "about six years ago," he wrote,

> I attended for the first time a Sunday morning service of Jewish Science, conducted by Rabbi Lichtenstein. While listening to his sermon, I had the feeling that he was addressing me alone, so well did his words fit my case. But what impressed me most were the affirmations. I repeated over and over: I am calm and cheerful; and when I left the Hall, I felt calm and serene, and was looking toward the future with hope, and thanked God all the way home. Where physicians had inculcated fear in me for years, Dr. Lichtenstein showed me in one hour how to throw off fear, and to look to God for help and guidance.[32]

Many of the testimonials that appeared in early issues of the *Jewish Science Interpreter* were from men and women, though usually the latter, who previously had been drawn to Christian Science. One writer, S. V. Rosenblum, who claimed that he or she had gone to Christian Science because of poor health but had never felt that he or she belonged there, spoke of Jewish Science as what first revealed to him (or her) the "beauty and blessings" of Judaism.[33] Another writer, who had been a member of the Christian Science Church for five years, described Jewish Science as a new hope, enabling her to discover in her own faith what she had previously thought possible only through the teachings of Christian Science.[34]

Numerous testimonials expressed appreciation to Morris Lichtenstein for helping the authors recognize the power of God within. "In these days," wrote one man, "when I find that more and more Jews are wandering far away from their religion, and though they bear the name 'Jew,' are Jews in name only, and not in faith, Jewish Science is calculated to awaken the spark of Judaism, as no other movement has done."[35] Another writer, who suffered both physical pain and mental anguish as a result of a serious accident that had occurred eight years before, described years of misery in which she medicated herself continually and went from one physician's office to another. Medical aid, she said, brought her some relief, but it did not cure her. Finally, on the advice of a physician, she tried Jewish Science. "I remember well," she wrote Morris Lichtenstein,

> what confidence and hope I derived from my first visit to your office. I felt suddenly that there was one Source I could turn to for

help, when all other help failed me. I wondered that in all the years that I was seeking for help, I had never thought of turning to God.[36]

In a testimonial that appeared in the *Jewish Science Interpreter* in May 1932, Sam Moser described Jewish Science as having given him powerful reasons for believing in God, as well as a wonderful understanding of the nature of religion. Though he was raised in a strictly observant, Orthodox home and for many years after his bar mitzvah found himself donning *tallis* (prayer shawl) and *tefillin* (phylacteries) each morning and fervently praying to God, he wrote,

> I never suspected before [I joined Jewish Science] that God was so near to me. What an awakening. What a reality God became. What an answer to all my questioning. And it came all at once, from a set of wonderful teachings, full of logic and reason; and the philosophy it carried with it made things so clear that there was no room for doubt. The teachings expounded a great many self-evident truths and it was not necessary to carry a person into the realm of heaven but instead made one search for God in himself.[37]

In a talk entitled "What Does Jewish Science Mean to Me," written by Harry Hartman and apparently delivered in May 1939, Hartman maintained that above all else, Jewish Science provided him with a conception of God different from that which he had been taught in his youth. "Then," he said, "I pictured God as a king on a throne meting out rewards for good deeds and punishing for misdeeds. Now I know that God is everywhere, not material, but spiritual, permeating everything, a part of you and me, but with good attributes only." God, he continued, is a loving father who emanates love and kindness, "someone on whom you can always depend for help when you have done all you can," answering all prayers that are earnestly offered.[38] Similarly, Jeannette Mayer, a practitioner and early member of the society, described Jewish Science as a "Magic Mirror in which I see reflected the Divine Mind," enabling her to behold Divinity in herself, in others, in action, and in nature. "Jewish Science," she asserted,

> has made me Rich for it has brought me the Priceless Gift of Peace, which in turn has brought Poise and Serenity. . . . It has given me a new God-conception—that of a Loving Merciful Father—who showers blessings on us, if we but open the windows of our Soul to receive and express His Divine Love. It has brought me the full realization that all things work together for good to those who love God and keep His commandments.[39]

In countless interviews, men and women described to me the importance of Jewish Science in their lives. Older members of the society who knew Morris Lichtenstein, reverentially referred to as "the Rabbi," recalled friends and relatives, primarily women, with whom they had gone to Christian Science services before learning about Jewish Science. While they were often unsuccessful in convincing others to leave Christian Science with them, Morris Lichtenstein's teachings helped them to discover happiness and health within Judaism itself. Most of the testimonials printed in early issues of the *Jewish Science Interpreter* emphasized the extent to which Jewish Science provided both a Jewish alternative to Christian Science and a means of discovering God. Personal interviews have revealed a further, equally important, source of Jewish Science's early appeal. As one woman succinctly put it, Jewish Science "shows you how to live."[40]

A good many of those who came to Jewish Science in its earliest years were from Orthodox backgrounds. Yet all had long since rejected what they considered to be Orthodoxy's narrow and, to some, outdated understanding of the ways one should live one's life. No longer observant, or only nominally so (e.g., they may have kept a kosher home and/or lit Sabbath candles), those from Orthodox backgrounds were actively seeking an understanding of Judaism that would be as all-encompassing as Orthodoxy but would address modern problems more directly. Those from Reform backgrounds, as well as the considerable number of early Jewish Science members who were attracted to Reform, liked Reform's understanding of God as universal, the source of morality, and so on but found that aside from its broad notion of social justice, that is, the notion that one serves God best by serving others, Reform provided little practical guidance in terms of how to live. In short, Jewish Science as applied Judaism held great appeal to Jews from a variety of religious and nonreligious backgrounds. It provided a satisfying, personally meaningful concept of God and, stemming from this concept, revealed a means of approaching life that promised its adherents the attainment of happiness and health. Unlike Orthodox Judaism, whose system of *mitzvot* (commandments) dictated specific forms of behavior, Jewish Science placed greatest emphasis on cultivating a particular psychological and spiritual attitude that would then lead one to act in a specific, internally directed way that might or might not be in conflict with Orthodoxy's externally imposed commandments. Unlike Reform Judaism, Jewish Science as promulgated by Morris Lichtenstein did not place great emphasis on social action. Yet it wasn't, as critics like Rabbi Stephen Wise falsely maintained, that Lichtenstein felt that social action was unimportant. Rather, he saw the attainment of personal happiness and health as necessary preconditions for such behavior.

It is not difficult to understand why Wise and other Reform rabbis of the day who devoted great time and effort to fighting poverty, anti-Semitism, and other forms of injustice were angered over Lichtenstein's seeming disregard of these problems. What they failed to understand, however, was that by and large the Jews who came to Jewish Science came precisely because they were looking for something that they felt other synagogues, whether Orthodox or liberal, did not offer. It wasn't that the men and women who came to Jewish Science were uninterested in hearing about or fighting poverty, anti-Semitism, and so on. Indeed, as previously mentioned, several remained active members of other Jewish congregations and organizations. Yet what they had hoped to find in the synagogue but had not found until they discovered Jewish Science was, quite simply, how to pray.

Jewish Science provided them with a concept of God to whom, as modern men and women, they felt they could pray. It further offered a guide as to how God is best addressed (primarily through silence) and an understanding of self-identity that was what William James in his *Varieties of Religious Experience* had described as "healthy-minded." According to Abraham Goldstein, it was through Morris Lichtenstein and his teachings that he first began to discover his spiritual potential. "I became interested in Jewish Science," he once told me,

> about the year 1937. I had been working very hard [in the successful paper container business he and his brother owned] and apparently it had affected me unknowingly because I found myself mentally distressed on many occasions. In those days we didn't go to psychiatrists—that was a dirty word—but both my wife [Mildred] and I began visiting different synagogues in the area [of the Bronx where they lived] and also in Manhattan. I remember one particular night. . . . We had been to Rodeph Sholom, which is a large [Reform] Temple on [West] 83rd Street near Central Park West, and Rabbi Louis Newman, who was a very distinguished personality and well known in the rabbinate at that time, gave us a lecture, a book review as I remember, which was not what I was looking for. And that's what I found as I went from Temple to Temple. I wasn't getting what I should have from my faith, my religion. One Friday night after attending Rodeph Sholom, my wife and I were walking down Amsterdam Avenue and we saw a placard in the window. It said: SERVICES, JEWISH SCIENCE. TRUE SISTERS BUILDING, 150 W. 85th St. 8:30 p.m. So we decided to have dinner and then go to services. We got to the True Sisters' Building about a quarter after eight, and there was a man standing there in his shirt-sleeves, and I said, "Where are Jewish Science services?" and he pointed down to the cellar. So we went down and there was a room, probably twenty feet by fifteen feet, with a raised dais of maybe eight to ten inches, and sitting on this dais was a little man, slightly bald, wearing one of the old Prince Albert high collars, a white collar with a colored shirt, which is now the vogue. He started to speak, and I listened for about ten minutes, and I said to my wife, "This is what I want." That was 1937, and I'm still here, and I'm still reading his works

and listening to all the words he told me. . . . He taught me how to pray.[41]

Morris Lichtenstein placed great emphasis on the power of prayer. When he spoke of prayer as efficacious, he meant its ability to lead one to God and to provide one with a guide to right living. In answer to the question "How does one learn to pray?" his answer was practical and simple: one learns to pray by praying, that is, by reciting the affirmations, visualizing that which one most desires, or using any other method that will lead one to actually feel the presence and power of God. "Pray to God," wrote Morris Lichtenstein,

> and then you will come to know Him. Those who stand at a dis-
> tance and just debate as to whether or not religion is in harmony
> with science, whether or not the Biblical statement of the creation is
> to be credited . . . even those who are engaged in theological discus-
> sions as to whether God spoke to this prophet or to that, whether he
> selected this one or that one as His messenger, these people are al-
> together far from grasping God's presence. But he who prays to God
> whole-heartedly never fails to arrive at a knowledge of God. . . .
> Through frequent and earnest prayer . . . new powers of conscious-
> ness come into action; new layers of mind come into being; we at-
> tune ourselves to God and powerfully feel God's Presence.[42]

Lichtenstein flatly denied that only mystics or "men of particular [spiritual] endowments" could realize God. Through prayer, he maintained, everyone could arrive at the same realization. For Lichtenstein, this was so because one attained a knowledge of God not through study, a path long emphasized by rabbinic Judaism, but rather through feeling and inspiration. When Morris Lichtenstein spoke of prayer, he primarily spoke of personal prayer, "prayer in its simplest form, in the most earnest manner, offered with deep devotion and concentration."[43] To him, prayers of appeal, thanksgiving, adoration, and re-alization offered "not only in moments of need, but daily and more than once each day," helped purify one's emotions, annihilating "animosities, jealousies, and mean feelings" and giving full sway to such qualities as kindness, tender-ness, and gentleness. Through prayer, he insisted, we discover all that is fine and noble within us. Through this process of spiritualization, each of us "be-comes a spiritual being."[44]

Yet for Lichtenstein, as for other Reform rabbis of his day, to become a spiritual being not only meant that one became aware of God's presence but also that one succeeded in walking in God's ways. To be spiritual, then, nec-essarily meant that one was ethical. However, when Lichtenstein spoke about morality as part of the essence of Judaism, the language that he used was not that of classical Reform. Unlike Alfred Geiger Moses, he did not emphasize the importance of the Jewish mission. Indeed, he faulted contemporary Reform rabbis for emphasizing communal and global concerns, including the hope for universal brotherhood and peace, at the expense of individual hopes and longings. When he spoke of love, justice, and mercy, he primarily spoke of one-to-one human relationships, of doing unto others as you would have them do unto you. He criticized both Orthodox and Reform Judaism for being more concerned about the group, whether that group be the Jewish people or humanity as a whole, than with the individual. Our prayers, he maintained, referring to the liturgies of both Orthodoxy and Reform, are group prayers. In using these liturgies, "we do not pray, in fact we are not taught to pray, for our individual well-being . . . hope, and peace of mind."[45]

While Morris Lichtenstein retained membership in the CCAR and, in terms of training and sympathies, continued to identify himself with Reform, he saw Jewish Science as a separate movement, critical in many ways of both Reform and Orthodox Judaism. In offering his critique of American Jewish life, he spoke as one who stood outside both. His major critique of Orthodoxy was that it mistook traditional ceremonies for the essence of Judaism and thus failed to recognize that Judaism's essence consisted of "the realization of One Divine Presence, the adherence to its ethical law, and the pursuance of personal virtues." His major criticism of Reform was that despite its recognition of the ideals of ethics, virtue, and the realization of God as Judaism's essence, it had made little attempt to inculcate its followers with these ideals. "If Reform Judaism," he wrote,

> had, as a result of its teachings, produced Jews of a more upright, more honest, more just, more pure, more God-conscious character, we would regard Reform Judaism as a true expression of prophetic Judaism [as classical Reform claimed to be]. But to such a far-reaching effect on the life of the Jew, even the leaders of Reform lay no claim. The contributions of this movement so far can not therefore be regarded as significant to the preservation of Judaism.[46]

Armed with these critiques, Morris Lichtenstein thus set out to form a new movement that would offer the Jew that which he felt neither Reform nor Orthodoxy provided, namely, a real concern for the individual's own spiritual needs. To satisfy these needs, he sought to bring Jews to an awareness of the reality of God. By emphasizing the centrality of private prayer, and by creating a brief liturgy highlighted by personal affirmations and silent meditations, he sought to help individuals recognize their own hopes and aspirations. By suggesting specific material that one read each day, he hoped to inspire greater religious feeling. Through healing sessions that he conducted and through the ministrations of spiritual practitioners whom he himself trained, he hoped to demonstrate the power of faith. Finally, through his lectures and writings, he sought to provide American Jews with what he felt they not only needed but wanted, namely, a satisfying concept of God and practical advice on how to make that concept, and spirituality in general, a central part of one's daily existence. The organizational base that he established was meant to support and help spread his teachings. Lichtenstein's expressed intent was not just to lead Jews away from Christian Science, but also to lead them toward an understanding of Judaism as a personal and practical religion concerned with the physical and spiritual well-being of American Jews.

4

Morris Lichtenstein

The Man and the Message

Of the thousands of Jews who at one time or another met Morris Lichtenstein, it seems that a great many found appealing the great fervor with which he embraced the teachings of Jewish Science. Inspired by his enthusiasm and dedication as well as by his message, many eagerly read the *Jewish Science Interpreter*, with its personal testimonials and affirmations of faith, selections from Morris Lichtenstein's sermons and writings, and suggestions for daily readings from both the Bible and Lichtenstein's *Jewish Science and Health*. Hundreds of those who lived in or near New York City unfailingly attended his services and lectures and frequently went to see him, if not for healing, at least for some friendly advice. More often than not, the advice they sought related to matters of personal happiness or health. How, some wanted to know, could they best free themselves of stress, incessant worries, fear, or insecurity? How could they rid themselves of debilitating headaches or constipation or problems with their kidneys? How could they get over the incredible sorrow caused by the death of a son or daughter or spouse? How might they deal with a nagging wife or husband who claimed that she or he had little time for the family? How could they gain the kind of faith and trust in God that Lichtenstein himself seemed to have in his possession? How could they learn to pray?

Some who came to see him, particularly among the men, asked his advice on business matters. Those who were unhappy in their current jobs or occupations sought his guidance and encouragement in seeking new ones. Some shared with him ideas for new business ventures, seeking his opinion as to their practicality and promise.

One man apparently approached Morris Lichtenstein with the idea of forming a soft drink company to compete with Coca-Cola that he intended to call Pepsi-Cola. What, he wanted to know, did Rabbi Lichtenstein think of the idea? "Go ahead with the idea," Lichtenstein advised him. "Such a company should be a great success!"[1]

From 1922 until his death in 1938, Morris Lichtenstein completely devoted himself to Jewish Science, forgoing vacations, even during the summer, and taking little time out to simply enjoy the company of his sons and his wife. Perhaps it seems paradoxical, if not inconsistent, that a man who enjoined others not to be consumed by their work was apparently consumed by his. Once he embraced Jewish Science, Morris Lichtenstein could think about or talk of little else. Like many other founders of modern movements, including, on the Jewish scene, Theodor Herzl, the founder of modern Zionism, and Lily Montagu, the founder of the Liberal Jewish movement in England, Lichtenstein was driven by a personal vision that he hoped to make a reality. Just as Herzl sacrificed his health, marriage, and money to ensure that his dream of creating a Jewish state would become a reality, and just as Lily Montagu sacrificed marriage and motherhood, as well as the close relationship that she previously had maintained with her father, in order to advance the Liberal Jewish "cause," so Morris Lichtenstein refused to be distracted by anything that might prevent him from single-handedly revitalizing the spiritual life of American Jewry.

With the exception of an occasional game of chess, he and his wife, Tehilla, spent most of their time together either working on the *Jewish Science Interpreter*, for which she served as editor, or on his numerous essays and sermons, which he carefully wrote out in longhand and which she typed and often edited. Daily, Morris Lichtenstein would sit at home and write. If his young sons were at home playing, they played around him, not with him, for they quickly discovered that nothing was to distract their father from his own important work. Almost every day, from 2:00 to 6:00 in the afternoon (and after 1930, from 2:00 to 5:00, as mentioned in the previous chapter), Morris Lichtenstein made himself available to those in need of spiritual guidance. Inviting them either to call or visit, he carefully listened to their problems and offered specific suggestions as to how they might best be solved. Those who came to discuss either business or domestic problems found Morris Lichtenstein to be an exceptionally good listener who dispensed advice and guidance gently yet firmly, insisting on the importance of courage, patience, cheerfulness, and optimism even in the face of adversity. He encouraged the men and women who came to see him to take risks, though not blindly, and spoke to them of the importance of making one's life successful. As he envisioned it, a successful life was one of self-realization, a life in which "all the powers and faculties find full expression, in which the whole of the man [or woman] lives and creates."[2] Voicing sentiments that extolled the virtues of the Protestant work ethic and the values of the American middle class, he told the men who came to see him that ultimately happiness was dependent on work. "It is only the work for which a man is not fitted, for which he is not born," he once wrote,

> that makes him miserable, kills his ambition, makes him lazy and unprogressive. If your work does not make you happy, if you do not put forth, joyously and willingly, all your efforts and energies, if the hours drag while at your task, then you have not found the field for which you were destined.[3]

Encouraging them to "commune with their hearts" and to give free rein to their longings and desires, he maintained that only by working in a field in which he sincerely wanted to participate and achieving something that gave him personal satisfaction could a man realize the "zest of life and vital happiness."

The women who came to see him received other advice. Believing that men and women were fundamentally different by nature and that men were to be the builders of life while women the preservers,[4] he maintained that in order to be happy women needed to be loved. He claimed that women's interests in life were primarily emotional, based on their own God-given spirit of love and tenderness, which contrasted to men's innate ambition, hardness, and perseverance, He thus encouraged the women who sought his advice to find happiness by creating a loving, peaceful, and joyful environment within their homes through self-sacrifice and spiritual influence. It was primarily as wives and mothers, he believed, that women were able to find personal fulfillment and to make their greatest contribution to Jewish life.

For men to achieve and women to maintain satisfying personal relationships, that is, for men and women to be happy, he insisted that both needed to free themselves of fear and worry. Over and over again, he admonished those who came to see him, just as he admonished his listeners from the pulpit, to free themselves of unnecessary fears and worries, to remain calm and in control of their emotions. He advised them to develop a positive attitude toward life, for, he maintained, "the more one utilizes his energies constructively, the more one brings his vision, his judgment, [and] his creative ability into action, the more may he be rest assured that he will receive his share of God's supply."[5] Over twenty years before the publication of Norman Vincent Peale's enormously popular book *The Power of Positive Thinking*, Morris Lichtenstein reiterated the importance of right thinking as the key to health and success. It is essential, he wrote, that one free oneself from all that is petty and insignificant in order to see things with "unblurred vision and unfettered imagination."[6]

Lichtenstein encouraged both men and women to develop greater self-confidence and belief in their own potential. Rather than dwelling on the past, he urged them to look toward the future. While acknowledging that at times feelings of regret about past thoughts and actions might be signs of personal growth, he maintained that simply bemoaning one's errors was morbid. Rather than dwelling on the past, he said, one needed to possess the courage and the wisdom to uproot one's weaknesses, recognizing, as he wrote in one of his essays, that "every new conquest is a new joy, every new day is a new life and a new aspiration; every undertaking is a new birth and a new hope, and every effort means a new . . . goal" and purpose.[7] To the many elderly men and women who came to see him, Lichtenstein offered particular advice about accepting and enjoying old age. Emphasizing that growth and aging were laws of nature, he insisted that they view advanced age not as a period of rest but as a period in which to enjoy new and varied activities. Your energies, he said, follow the law of supply and demand. If you don't call on them, they recede; if you use them, they become replenished. He wrote in one of his earliest essays (published in 1923):

> Keep your interests in life constantly alive and you will ever be young; keep your aspirations constantly in action, your enthusiasms ever aflame, your hopes always awake, your mind always at work either for yourself or for others, and perpetual youth will dwell in your soul and in your body.[8]

Many of those who came to see him sought his advice on interpersonal matters. How, for example, might they attain a happier marriage? How might they get along better with their children? How might they gain more friends? In response to these questions, Morris Lichtenstein continually emphasized the importance of ridding oneself of anger, hatred, and envy and cultivating instead an attitude of serenity and love. In emphasizing the importance of friendship, Morris Lichtenstein enjoined the men and women who came to see him not to be overly critical of others, for what one gives to others, he said, one soon receives in return. Elaborating on this idea in one of his essays, he wrote:

> When one gives kindliness, he receives kindliness; when he gives devotion, he receives devotion; when he offers courtesy, he receives courtesy; when he gives love, he is rewarded with love; but when he offers carping criticism, when he finds that those with whom he is associated are full of failings, when he harps constantly on their weaknesses, they may not repay him with criticism, but they will surely fall away from him, they will hide from his presence, they will refuse to be found within reach of his barbed words, they will avoid him as they do all else that is disagreeable, and he will soon discover that "he who findeth fault, findeth loneliness."[9]

Lichtenstein emphasized the importance of sharing one's joy, hopefulness, and wealth. He talked of sharing one's feelings, but at the same time he spoke of moments in which one should be silent. "When we are irritable and irascible, when calmness vanishes, when our better judgment retires and our whole inner being is in turmoil," at these times, he maintained, "it would be well for us to see before us in huge letters the word *silence*. For whatever we will utter at such a moment will hurt others and also ourselves."[10]

Morris Lichtenstein counseled at least hundreds of men and women to cultivate the virtue of patience. Yet patience, he insisted, did not mean indifference or resignation but hope in the future, even in the face of great hardship and calamity. One needed to recognize that while life might be full of setbacks and depressions, we, as human beings, are equipped with the capacity to meet and overcome them. Thus, even in the face of illness, one ought not to be dismayed but rather view one's illness as transient and place confidence in God's healing power.[11] Finally, in discussing ways in which one could banish anxiety, relieve sorrow, and fight off depression, Morris Lichtenstein spoke about the importance of laughter. He emphasized the social aspects of laughter, that is, its ability to make people feel close to one another by demolishing all barriers, formalities, and conventions. He described a home that is filled with laughter as a blessed home, "a home which God himself has built . . . a place of refuge from which [its members] may draw inspiration and cheer."[12] And, like increasing numbers of physicians and laypeople today, Morris Lichtenstein recognized the value of laughter in healing mental and physical illness. To him, it was a divine medicine, a "tonic," as he called it, that was well worth taking.

From 1923 through 1938, the *Jewish Science Interpreter* published letters and lengthy testimonials attesting to the great influence and guidance exerted by Morris Lichtenstein. Writers would thank him for advice he had given, for passages they had read in *Jewish Science and Health* that were particularly meaningful, or for sermons he had given that had touched them in some deeply personal way. One man, who had gone to Rabbi Lichtenstein suffering from a nervous breakdown, maintained that after several visits almost all the symptoms of his breakdown had vanished and he now felt able to return to work. Promising not to forget what the rabbi had taught him, he wrote: "I shall try to live serenely and work seren[e]ly and avoid, under all circumstances, the excitement which I had been in the habit of stirring up in myself and in others, and which was greatly responsible for my shattered nerves."[13] Another writer, who apparently came to see Rabbi Lichtenstein with problems of insomnia, claimed that he had changed her "entire trend of thought." "I have gained such composure," she continued,

> that I am able to meet with fortitude and patience the petty annoy-
> ances which formerly upset me and caused many a sleepless night.
> . . . I now have a serene state of mind, my heart and soul abound
> with joy, and these are priceless possessions which I hope will be
> mine for the rest of my life.[14]

Another woman, again writing in the *Interpreter*, thanked Rabbi Lichtenstein for freeing her from the "prison house of terror and fear" that had been destroying her. Your teachings, she told him, have taken "out from my system terror, fear, intolerance, excitement, nervousness, worry, hatred, and ever so many negative and destructive elements," replacing these with "faith, courage, hope, cheer, calmness, tolerance and love for the whole of humanity."[15]

Most of the letters Lichtenstein received described specific health problems the writers suffered from. Each writer would describe in detail a nervous condition or physical illness with which he or she had been afflicted and which subsequently had been healed through Rabbi Lichtenstein's ministrations. To these men and women, Morris Lichtenstein was more than a helpful listener. He was a spiritual healer, who through a series of "treatments" had been able to cure them. One woman, after describing the agonizing physical pain she had been in during a prolonged stay in the hospital, maintained that it was through the teachings of Jewish Science that she was able to overcome her "dreadful ordeal." Never once, she wrote, did "I [lose] my faith in God's goodness and mercy. In fact, I believe my faith was firmer [than it had ever been]; my mind was serene, my heart tranquil; I surrendered myself to God."[16] Another woman, writing to Lichtenstein from Baltimore, thanked him for praying on behalf of her mother, who had fallen down a flight of steps and had become quite feverish, and was now on the road to recovery.[17] A (Mrs. J.) P.S.C., writing in the summer of 1934, reminded Dr. Lichtenstein of his previously having healed her son from a neuritic condition that prevented him from walking about freely and pursuing his daily activities,[18] and asked if he could similarly heal a friend of hers "who for years has been suffering from an inner condition which has baffled the efforts of physicians who have tried to help her."[19]

One woman, who apparently had suffered from a serious heart condition, gave Morris Lichtenstein full credit for the recovery of her health. "I attribute it all to Jewish Science," she wrote; "to the wonderful healings you gave me, and to the wonderful teachings of Jewish Science which I have tried to practice."[20] Another woman, a Mrs. Sadie Feinberg, writing from Kingston, New York, similarly attributed her regained health to Rabbi Lichtenstein's teachings and to the treatments she had received from a Jewish Science practitioner. Bent over in pain as the result of a local anesthetic she had been given for a particular spinal operation five years earlier, she had gone to see three doctors, none of whom were able to help her. Though the pain apparently had subsided on its own two years previously, it recently had returned, and this time, rather than seeking out new doctors, she decided to go to a Jewish Science practitioner. After two weeks of treatment, she reported, the pain disappeared, and for the first time in five years, she felt completely better.[21]

Many of the letters were lengthy, personal documents testifying to the efficacy of Jewish Science teachings. One such letter, written by a woman living in St. Paul, Minnesota, began with a description of the mental and physical problems she previously had suffered. "Three years ago," she began,

> I was employed as an executive secretary for a large concern in my town. . . . I worked very hard—much too hard, I now realize—and did not let up on my social engagements, so that I sometimes came to the office in the morning weary from lack of sleep. My right arm began to pain me occasionally, but I gave no heed to the warning, and kept up the same intense pace in and out of the office. One day, soon after, as I was seated at the typewriter, I found that my right arm suddenly went numb and I was unable to use it. It had become completely paralyzed.

The doctors whom she went to see informed her that her condition was a permanent one and she became inconsolable, refusing to eat, sleep, or see her friends. She became hysterical and, frightened by the prospect of never being able to move her right arm again, spent most of her time crying in bed. A few weeks later a friend gave her a copy of *Jewish Science and Health* and read aloud to her the section on healing. After the friend had left, she became calm enough to read the entire book and subsequently wrote to Rabbi Lichtenstein, who gave her further suggestions about using the power of prayer to obtain both courage and healing. Almost immediately after applying Jewish Science teachings, she ceased to be hysterical. "I began to reconstruct my life," she wrote, "taking calmly into account my new handicap." Recognizing that she could no longer type but possessing newfound courage, she went to see her employer and asked him if it would be possible for her to return to work and assume at least some of her former duties. To her delight, he agreed, and in time she once again became "really happy and cheerful."

"Now," she continued, "I come to the best part of my experience." After reading and studying *Jewish Science and Health*, she began to apply Morris Lichtenstein's directions for healing. For months there was no progress, but her faith remained steadfast, and she never gave up hope. "God," she maintained,

> was with me, for after the first slow months of waiting and believing, I began to feel some sensation in my arm. . . . The feeling in my arm became more and more evident, until finally, thank God, I recovered its use completely. I am typewriting this letter—something I thought I would never be able to achieve. Can I tell you how grateful I am to God for this recovery, and to Jewish Science for helping me in my great distress? My experience, though at one time I looked on it as the greatest calamity, has enriched my life; it has

made me realize the blessings that are mine through God's great
goodness.[22]

As these and other letters show, at least hundreds of men and women,
probably more, found in Jewish Science the key not only to happiness but also
to health. While the power of positive thinking remained an important component of Lichtenstein's teachings, it would be a mistake simply to equate
Jewish Science, as he understood it, with applied psychology. While Lichtenstein acknowledged the usefulness of modern psychology, the heart and soul
of Jewish Science remained, for him, belief in the efficacy of prayer. What made
Morris Lichtenstein's movement a Jewish movement was ultimately his belief
in and reliance on God. Like other Reform rabbis of his day, he viewed Judaism
primarily as a religion, based not on the observance of particular laws and
customs but on faith in the reality of God and in the universal import of God's
teachings.

In his essays, sermons, and other major writings, Morris Lichtenstein developed his understanding of divinity at length. As early as March 1923, he
published an essay in the *Jewish Science Interpreter* entitled "The Jewish Science-
God Conception," in which he maintained that God was not a supernatural
deity, a "Being in some remote space beyond the world He created," but a
vitalizing force within us and around us. God, he insisted, was "the life principle of all that exists," He whose essence fills the world and is manifested in
all forms of reality. "There is no life," he wrote, "no particle of existence that
is not impregnated with His divine essence. All forms of beings are like rays
of light radiating from one powerful luminary, each of them reflecting the
essence of its source." Believing, then, that all things were essentially divine,
he maintained that one could not draw a line of demarcation between spirit
and matter. Matter, he said, was "only the visible aspect of spirit . . . the visible
expression of God," divinity made manifest in creation.[23]

Like many other Reform rabbis of his day, Lichtenstein spoke of the God-
idea in referring to human conceptions, or ideas, of the divine. In rejecting the
supernaturalism of traditional Judaism, he, again, like many other early
twentieth-century Reform rabbis, rejected the traditional belief in God as miracle worker. God, he insisted, did not reveal himself through the disruption of
nature but through the harmony and unity of nature itself. Thus, while Morris
Lichtenstein continually spoke of the God-idea, at the same time, he firmly
believed in the reality of God. "God," he wrote,

> is not an abstraction, not a hypothesis, not a mere philosophic ne-
> cessity, but an ever-living, ever-present Reality. God . . . saturates all
> existence; He is the life-force in everything that is and grows and
> flourishes. . . . He is the creator of the immutable laws of nature; He
> dwells in everything that exists; He is the very soul of everything
> that exists, and therefore, also the very soul of man.[24]

Most frequently, the theological language Lichtenstein employed was that of religious naturalism. Forsaking belief in the omnipotent, transcendent, and providential God of traditional theism, Lichtenstein, like the Reform rabbi Emil Hirsch (1851–1923), the Conservative rabbi Mordecai Kaplan (1881–1983), and a number of other liberal thinkers, Christians as well as Jews, envisioned God as a power rather than as a Being, a force residing in the individual as well as in nature. While throughout the 1920s and 1930s, religious naturalists like Lichtenstein remained a distinct minority within the American Reform rabbinate, Lichtenstein was by no means alone in describing God as an intelligence creating and sustaining the world, "the soul, the essence of all the universe," the "Source of all life," and the "Fountain of all reality." Abba Hillel Silver (1893–1963), for example, a contemporary of Lichtenstein and one of the most prominent Reform rabbis of his generation, described God, in a sermon delivered in 1926, as the "creative energy of the universe, the source of all that is and is to be, the substance and the form and the purpose of everything."[25] In Chicago, Rabbi Felix A. Levy, president of the CCAR from 1935 to 1937, who as incoming president appointed a commission to draft a new ideological platform for the Reform movement, later known as the Columbus Platform of 1937, similarly equated God with energy and spoke of harmonizing scientific views with those of religion.

Younger rabbis—for example, Maurice Eisendrath (1902–1973), the spiritual leader of Holy Blossom Temple in Toronto from 1929 until the early 1940s, when he left the pulpit rabbinate to become director of the Reform movement's Union of American Hebrew Congregations—delivered powerful, impassioned sermons describing science as having demolished traditional faith and science's concept of God as person apart from the universe and all creation. In its place, he later wrote, stood a new, more modern concept of divinity as "that power, force, spirit which is not apart *from* but a part *of* both the universe and oneself, as well as of everything that lives and breathes and whose being derives from the primal and pulsating energy suffusing the whole of life."[26] Similarly, Joshua Loth Liebman (1907–1948) and Roland Gittelsohn (1910–1995), both ordained from HUC in the 1930s, preached and wrote about religious naturalism. Drawing on his own belief in God as "the power of love and creation, the source of human fulfillment and salvation," as well as insights gleaned from modern psychology, Liebman later gained national prominence with the publication in 1946 of his enormously popular book *Peace of Mind*. Gittelsohn, an author and congregational rabbi, first, at Central Synagogue of Nassau County in Rockville Centre, New York, and later as Liebman's successor at Temple Israel in Boston, articulated a theology that reflected belief in God as energy, power, force, and intelligence rather than as person or being. Reflecting on his religious views, Gittelsohn wrote that his concept of God was one that needed to be in accord with the knowledge of reality given to the individual by science. "God," he maintained, "is a creative, pervasive Spirit—

within me as He is within all existence." Thus, the will of God is nothing more
nor less than the nature of the universe and of humanity, and prayer is an
appeal to our highest selves, "that part of the ineffable Creative Mind of the
universe" that is the shared possession of all human beings.[27]

In many ways, Morris Lichtenstein's understanding of God seems to have
resembled that of Mordecai Kaplan. By the 1920s, Kaplan had long shared his
theological views with students and colleagues at the Conservative movement's
Jewish Theological Seminary in Manhattan. By then, he had begun to articulate
his vision of a reconstructed Judaism, most notably at the Society for the Advancement of Judaism, where he served as rabbi. He had also begun to share
his views in writing. Indeed, as early as 1915, Kaplan began to publish a series
of essays in the *Menorah Journal* articulating his views on Judaism, including
his understanding of divinity. These ideas would be developed further by Kaplan in scores of books, including *Judaism as a Civilization* (1934), *The Meaning
of God in Modern Jewish Religion* (1937), *The Future of the American Jew* (1948),
and *Judaism without Supernaturalism* (1958).

Both Lichtenstein and Kaplan spoke of finding the supernatural, which
they defined as the miraculous or wondrous, in the natural, and both placed
great emphasis on the functional value of faith. Kaplan spoke of God as a
"power that makes for salvation," that is, as a power or process that makes self-
fulfillment possible. Lichtenstein similarly spoke of God as a power, a divine
mind whose existence makes possible the attainment of happiness and health.
Moreover, like Kaplan, Lichtenstein rejected the traditional concept of Jewish
chosenness. Unlike most of his colleagues in the CCAR, he did not attempt to
replace this concept either with the classical Reform notion of a Jewish mission
or with what Samuel Cohon (1888–1959), professor of Jewish Theology at HUC
and chief architect of the Columbus Platform, described as "prophetism," an
ethical universalism rooted in the teaching of the prophets whose moral outlook was of value to the entire world. Rather, like Kaplan, Morris Lichtenstein
simply viewed the notion of election as outmoded, based on previous, less
enlightened concepts of God. Despite these similarities, however, it would be
a mistake to draw too great a theological connection between Lichtenstein and
Kaplan. Although, as I have indicated, the theological language that each employed often resembled the other's, a more careful examination of their writings reveals a number of fundamental differences between them. Indeed, a
comparison of Kaplan's and Lichtenstein's religious thought is particularly
instructive because it serves to highlight the ways in which Lichtenstein's theological vision was in many respects unique.

In expounding on God and the function of religion in general, Mordecai
Kaplan began with the Jews as an ethnic unit, a group of people who had
created and continue to create their own civilization. Judaism exists, he maintained, because the Jewish people created it. Its teachings were not revealed by
God; rather, the Jewish people, as a collective group, formed and continue to

form teachings that are important to them. Its religious beliefs are the primary, but not sole, component of a larger civilization that includes a particular music, literature, language, land, customs, and art. In short, following the French sociologist Emile Durkheim and his understanding of community, Kaplan focused on the importance of religion in the development of a group's own collective consciousness. For him, as for Durkheim, by reflecting those interests that a group deems most important through symbols and rites that they themselves have created, religion becomes significant to the personal growth of the individual as member of a specific social unit and helps to advance the self-consciousness of the group as a whole.

Beginning, then, with the assertion that Jews are members of a particular ethnic group and that Jews, a priori, have a rational will-to-live as part of that group, Kaplan's theology was firmly rooted in sociology. Indeed, since he limited his theological discussions to the ways in which belief in God functions for the individual and for the group, one can question, as have some scholars, whether Kaplan's theology was really a theology at all. Kaplan himself insisted that

> Judaism, to be significant to modern man or woman, can no longer afford to speak in the language of theology. Psychology and social science, history and human experience, have revealed new worlds in the domain of the spirit. The language of theology might have a certain quaintness and charm to the ears of those to whom religion is a kind of dreamy romanticism. But to those who want to find in Judaism a way of life and a higher ambition, it must address itself in the language of concrete and verifiable experience.[28]

In a similar vein, Kaplan insisted that one cannot "abstract Jewish religion from the rest of Jewish civilization and treat it as if it consisted merely in a particular concept of God, one that differs from the conception held by other religions." What differentiates Judaism from other religions is not so much the uniqueness of its God concept but rather the uniqueness of its sancta— those institutions, places, heroes, popular events, and other objects of popular reverence to which sanctity is ascribed. "We are faithful to [the] Jewish religion," he wrote, "not because we have chosen it as the best of all religions, but because it is ours, the only religion we have, an inseparable part of our collective personality as a people."[29]

At the same time, however, Kaplan acknowledged that belief in God is important in helping one to face death and suffering. It gives one faith in the possibility of human achievement and ethical living. In brief, he wrote, expressing what he took to be a functional rather than an ontological claim, "the God idea . . . expresses itself pragmatically in those fundamental beliefs by which a people tries to work out its life in a consistent pattern and rid itself of those frustrations which result from the distracting confusions of ideals and aims." In our day, he insisted, belief in God can function in the same way it has always functioned, namely, "as an affirmation that life has value" and that "reality is so constituted as to endorse and guarantee the realization in man of that which is of greatest value to him."[30]

In developing his theology, Morris Lichtenstein began not with the Jews as an ethnic group but rather with the individual in search of happiness and health. Like most Reform rabbis of his day, he took exception to Kaplan's claim that Judaism was primarily a social heritage, "the sum of characteristic usages, ideas, standards, and codes by which the Jewish people is differentiated and individualized in character from the other peoples."[31] Indeed, for Lichtenstein, as for most of his colleagues within the CCAR, Judaism was primarily, if not solely, a religious heritage. Jews, he maintained, were members of a specific "religious brotherhood" rather than of a particular ethnic group. As such, they, like other religious people, were to recognize within the universe the all-pervading presence of God.

By the late 1920s and 1930s, most Reform rabbis began to take the concept of Jewish peoplehood more seriously than had the generation of Reformers that had preceded them. Yet Morris Lichtenstein, unlike most of his CCAR colleagues, continued to focus his theology almost exclusively on the individual's one-on-one relationship with God. What's more, he explicitly critiqued what he took to be the outward thrust of Reform—its emphasis, in other words, on social justice often at the expense of cultivating one's inner spiritual soul. "Social justice," he insisted, is not

> the all-embracing problem of existence. The prophets accentuated
> vehemently the need for social justice and righteousness among
> men not because they were the only vital phases of existence, but
> because they lived in that early era in which these emphatic teach-
> ings were essential for the elevation of the people. They were en-
> deavoring to aid the people to lift themselves from a stage of barba-
> rism to one of civilization, from chaos into order, from laxity into
> morality.[32]

While acknowledging that "civilizing" the Jewish people took time and that identifying God's will with the demands of righteousness and justice was a great service to Jews and to the entire world, Lichtenstein firmly maintained that religion was far more than prophetism. Serving God, he wrote, is important, but just as the prophets were called on to elicit divine powers within us that would make for righteousness and justice, so we today are called on to reveal another aspect of divinity, namely, the divine power within us that makes for happiness and health. "Our era, more than any previous age in history," he continued, "is stricken with worry, depression and nervousness. The on-slaught of the times, the rush, the struggle, the competition, has drained man's vitality, has blocked the reservoir of health within him." Medicine alone cannot cope with these ailments, since medicine is a physical science, while these problems are spiritual in nature, the result of an overburdened mind, an anxious heart, and a sick soul. Thus, he concluded, to secure health we must

> realize with heart and soul God's presence, His immanence, in this universe and in us, to feel Him, to invoke Him, to trust Him as the source of all good, all joy and all well-being. The application of the God-consciousness to the attainment of individual happiness; that is the contribution of Jewish Science to the definition of religion.[33]

Certainly, Morris Lichtenstein was not alone in describing Judaism, as he often did, as personal religion. Reform leaders in the United States and England continually emphasized, again in marked contrast to Mordecai Kaplan's understanding of Judaism as a social heritage, the importance of individually bearing witness to or becoming conscious of the eternal presence of God. Yet for Lichtenstein, unlike most Reform rabbis, including such proponents of Jewish Science as Alfred Geiger Moses and, later, Clifton Harby Levy, awareness of God's reality did not necessarily lead one to a greater mission, stimulating an ethical consciousness in which one served God by serving others, but rather to individual creative achievement. No matter where our creative abilities lie, he wrote,

> whether in art or artisanship, in the realm of intellectual endeavor or of manual effort, when we realize and express the Divine creativeness in us, we are actually sharing an experience with God; the joy that accompanies creativeness is palpably above that which any mundane experience can give.

All of Lichtenstein's books, like his sermons, focused on the Jew as individual spiritual being rather than as member of a particular religious group. In *Jewish Science and Health,* the textbook of the society, he spoke of the divine as manifested within each human being and offered advice on how to live a life of love, faith, joy, courage, serenity, and domestic happiness. Discussing ways in which worry, fear, grief, envy, and anger serve as hindrances to such a life, he included passages from the Hebrew scriptures that might be used by the individual in prayer. While he included a number of passages under the subsection "Israel," the biblical selections he chose did not place great emphasis on Jewish peoplehood. Rather, they focused on divine commands to the individual, individual responses to divine reality, and assurances that faith in God would be rewarded. At the end of the book, he included four brief biblical passages, under the subsection "Zion," that spoke of a love for Jerusalem. Yet these passages, containing ideas not included either explicitly or implicitly elsewhere in the book, appear almost as an afterthought or as a concession to those, like his wife, Tehilla, in whose understanding of Jewish self-identity love of Zion played a central role.

None of Lichtenstein's other books advocated a love for Zion, though they did not oppose it either. Indeed, most of his books, focusing exclusively on the individual's inner religious needs, did not speak of Zion at all. In *Judaism*, published in 1934, in a chapter that probes the question "Why do we remain Jews?" Lichtenstein made his position on Zionism clearer. Zionists, he wrote, remain Jews because they believe in the national future of the Jewish people, with Jews, again established in Palestine, taking their place among the nations of the world "unhampered and unmolested." This, he conceded, is a beautiful hope. Nevertheless, by focusing on the future of Israel and life in Palestine, Zionism "holds out little to the Jew of the present here and in all the other lands." Moreover, while Zionism attempts to satisfy certain vital needs of the Jewish people and, as such, deserves the cooperation of all Jews, it fails to account for the existence of Jews as a separate people. What Zionists fail to realize, he maintained, is that Jews remain a distinct people not because they are members of a particular national group or because others continue to hate them. Rather, Jews remain a distinct people because "it is our function to live a distinct life, a life that must represent the embodiment of the teachings of Judaism. It must be a life of deep religious devotion, of scrupulous ethics and of absolute virtue."[34]

In *Peace of Mind* (1927), *How To Live* (1929), and *Joy of Life* (1938), Lichtenstein explored in detail ways in which such a life could be attained. Again, his emphasis lay with the realization of inner harmony and personal growth rather than with the creation of either a just society or a dynamic, continually evolving Jewish civilization. This does not mean that Morris Lichtenstein only saw Jews as individuals. He staunchly maintained that Jews were members of a particular religious "brotherhood" and firmly advocated the continuance of the Jewish people and Jewish life. He recognized why some Jews found sociological if not religious value in traditional observances, customs, and so on. He himself continued to observe Jewish holidays and based Jewish Science worship services on the Reform movement's *Union Prayer Book*. Indeed, on some occasions, presumably, for example, on the high holy days, the *Union Prayer Book* itself was used. Yet, as Lichtenstein himself insisted, the major thrust of Jewish Science, as a philosophy and as a movement, lay with the inner spiritual needs of each and every Jew.

In Lichtenstein's view, what distinguished Jewish Science from other Jewish movements was its emphasis rather than its content. Other movements, such as Reform Judaism and Zionism, sought to solve the problem of religious apathy either through sociological or political solutions. Thus Reform enjoined its adherents to help create a more just society, while Zionism advocated rebuilding the Jewish state. At the same time, he believed, by viewing ceremonialism as important in and of itself, Orthodoxy espoused a solution to religious apathy that often lost sight of the essence of Judaism, namely, "the realization of One divine Presence, the adherence to its ethical law, and the pursuance of personal virtues."[35] Jewish Science attempted to awaken within each Jew an awareness of God's eternal presence and to apply this consciousness of God to the attainment of individual happiness. We have taken this focus, he insisted, not because we have no interest in Judaism as an entity belonging to, supported by, and supporting a particular group; on the contrary, he maintained, Judaism is the chief interest of Jewish Science. Yet, just as in other ages other aspects of Judaism have needed greatest emphasis, so in this age it is essential that individual Judaism be stressed. Having already given to the world a lofty and true concept of God, as well as patterns of ethical living, it is time for Jews to make use of their spiritual heritage and to feel God's presence within them.

To Lichtenstein, spiritual apathy could only be cured by acknowledging that (1) Judaism is no longer a powerful influence among Jews because its teachings no longer seem meaningful or relevant; (2) most Jewish children are growing up ignorant of their faith; and (3) we have spent so much time emphasizing the communal aspect of Judaism that we have neglected those aspects that pertain to the life of the individual Jew. Our prayers, he asserted, are primarily group prayers, expressing the longing, hopes, and aspirations of the group but not of the individual.

> We pray for the health, for the uplift of the people; we pray for the restoration of Zion (in the Orthodox ritual), for God's return to Jerusalem, for universal peace and brotherhood; but we do not pray, in fact we are not taught to pray, for our individual well-being, for individual help and hope and peace of mind.[36]

Yet it is precisely this aspect of religion, he insisted, that we need today. In this whirlpool of hurry, strain, and personal difficulties, "there is nothing more soothing, more helpful to an individual than to be able to appeal to his Maker for guidance and aid."[37] It is for that reason that so many Jews had gone to Christian Science churches, seeking the individual spiritual help that they had not found in the synagogue. In order to preserve Judaism and to ensure that its teachings wield a deep influence on Jews today, we need, he maintained, to emphasize the application of Judaism's ethical and devotional principles to every day life.

As the foregoing discussion reveals, Morris Lichtenstein's belief in the primacy of individual Judaism led him to assume a position of either non-Zionism or pro-Zionism. That is, he advocated support of efforts to rebuild Palestine as the homeland of the Jewish people, although he did not view such efforts as central either to American Jewish life or to that which he identified as the essence of Judaism. This position also led him to emphasize personal morality and devotion to God as more essential to Jewish life than ceremonials or folkways. For these reasons alone, the theological connections between Morris Lichtenstein and Mordecai Kaplan are superficial at best. Indeed, while

Lichtenstein employed the theological language of religious naturalism, he was not, as Kaplan and most naturalists within the Reform movement were, a religious humanist. Rather than focusing on Jewish civilization or on the creation of a more just world, Lichtenstein focused on God. While emphasizing the functional value of faith, he did not view happiness and health as ends in and of themselves. For him, the attainment of happiness and health were proofs of God's existence and of his goodness. Finally, while Lichtenstein acknowledged the importance of ethical conduct, he placed greatest emphasis on personal prayer as a means of realizing God's presence. Unlike Kaplan and other naturalists, for whom prayer was either problematic or at least not a major concern, Lichtenstein saw prayer as central both to pure religion in general and to Judaism in particular.

In grappling with the question "If God is not a Being, to whom does one pray?"—in other words, "How can one pray to a process or power?"—Lichtenstein attempted to separate the God of belief from the God of faith. While the God in whom he believed was a naturalistic power, the God to whom he prayed, and, he suspected, the God to whom most people prayed, was indeed a providential and transcendent being. Belief, he asserted, is dependent on intellectual assent; faith is dependent on feeling. Unlike belief, faith rests on something that can neither be seen nor experienced through one's senses. We cannot perceive God's presence, he maintained, because God is "too closely intertwined with the very essence of our life," yet we can and do experience or intuit God's presence. Faith, he maintained, is more than belief. While belief is usually established "either as a sequence to logical deductions or as the outcome of trust in authority," faith rests neither on authority nor logic. Thus, the man of faith

> does not rationalize, he feels that there is an overwhelming Presence filling the universe and interested in the destiny of each of His beings, also in him who is one of His creations. In a sense, faith is like love which, when it surges in the heart, has no interest in argument or in proof, but strives only to identify itself with its object.[38]

Unlike the man of philosophy, then, who may believe in God either as a philosophical necessity or as a "remote First Cause," the man of faith, he insisted, "knows God as a living reality; he *feels* His presence and turns to Him for aid knowing that [God] will never fail him."[39]

Given his understanding of faith as originating in the spiritual, nonrational, and nonintellectual nature of the individual, Lichtenstein insisted that faith was inseparably connected to prayer. Belief, he asserted, does not impel an individual to pray, while faith, as trust in God, evokes a yearning to actually feel or know the divine presence. Moreover, since prayer is neither rational nor based on logical proofs, the individual who prays does so intuitively knowing or feeling that his or her prayer will be answered. One need not, and in fact, cannot, prove that prayer is efficacious. Yet the individual who seeks divine aid does so without vacillation and doubt, knowing that his or her supplication will be heeded. In describing God as the object of one's devotion, Lichtenstein used traditional, theistic language. The reality of God is known to us, he wrote, for we perpetually witness God's work, see expressions of God's infinite wisdom, experience God's goodness, and continually feel God's power. Using personal images of God as a means of visualizing and thus tapping the divine energy or power within us and within the world, Lichtenstein spoke of God as creator of the universe and of all human beings, a father who loves his children, a shepherd who faithfully looks after his flock. He described God as sustainer of the universe, placing great emphasis on God's righteousness and sense of justice. Finally, he talked of God as the almighty, the source of life and the giver of health.

Sensing God's presence as benevolent, Lichtenstein vigorously denied that God was the source of sickness, evil, or vengeance. Indeed, he maintained that to view God as punishing the wicked and sending suffering and misery to his creations was superstition, not faith. Men and women of faith, he maintained, love God; they don't fear God. They realize that it isn't God who punishes human beings but we who bring misery on ourselves. While one who is superstitious

> finds a barrier between himself and God, the man of faith finds
> himself very near to God, he finds himself identified with God. He
> realizes that life without God is impossible, that thought without
> God is impossible, that feelings, aspirations, hopes without God are
> impossible. . . . [Unlike the superstitious], the man of faith is never
> fearful, he is free and joyous and optimistic, and has full confidence
> both in the world and in himself.[40]

Scriptural references to God's wrath and vengeance, he maintained, are only human conceptions and forms of expression. They occur when some historical or natural upheaval occurs that the individual seeks to explain. They cannot come from God because God only works "in a well of serenity." Men and women may know of "tumult and fervid excitement," but the heart of the universe is tranquil and calm, "for serenity is the concomitant of creation."[41] According to Lichtenstein, then, one could only be like God if one were good, loving, caring, and serene. To work with God, he asserted, one must work in perfect serenity, throwing off excitement, never permitting oneself to be overtaken by agitation or recklessness, becoming self-possessed and calm. "Only from a background of serenity," he insisted, "can man's creativeness flow with fullness; only by achieving with serenity can man perfectly express the Godly quality of creativeness within him."[42]

Lichtenstein acknowledged that there are many forms of prayer through which one can seek God. He recognized that within the Jewish tradition, great importance is placed on petitionary prayer. The individual asks God for something, hoping to receive a positive answer. Closely connected to this type of prayer are prayers of thanksgiving, offered either when one finds that one's petition has been answered or when something good unexpectedly happens in one's life. There are also prayers of adoration, expressing awe, wonder, and admiration at all that God has done, as well as prayers of confession, in which one asks God to forgive one's misdeeds. He recognized that all of these types of prayers have merit. Yet superior to them all, he believed, and the one he therefore described and utilized most, was the type of prayer most frequently used in New Thought, namely that of affirmation. Morris Lichtenstein described an affirmation as "a prayer offered to the divine within man." By affirming God's presence, he maintained, we actually begin to feel God's presence, and in so doing begin to experience divinity in action. When we affirm that we are strong, we begin to feel strong, when we affirm that we unafraid, courage wells up within us, and when we affirm that we are cheerful, we actually feel cheerful.

Perhaps what drew Lichtenstein most to prayers of affirmation was that, for him, at least, affirmative prayer did not require one to suspend belief. While in petitionary prayer, for example, the individual either explicitly or implicitly addresses a supernatural God deemed capable of suspending the laws of nature and granting the petitioner's request, no matter what that request might be, affirmations draw belief and faith together. Logically, we believe that there must be an eternal power at work within creation while intuitively we feel that that power, imaged in personal terms, cares about us and the ways we live our lives. Through affirmative prayer, we invoke the inner power that we rationally believe and confidently feel will set the divine mind within us into motion.

This type of prayer, he insisted, is Jewish in origin, rooted in the teachings of the biblical Psalmist. In his books and sermons, Lichtenstein continually described the God of the Psalmist as both a naturalistic life force and an immanent and providential power. To him, of all Jewish texts, the Psalms best spoke to the spiritual needs of the modern Jew. By simply affirming that which is most needed, the Psalmist, he wrote, utilizes a religious language that appeals, or can appeal, to the modern individual who rationally and instinctively is unable to petition God as he or she would a human king. As a man of faith, the Psalmist is confident of God's nearness, turning to God as a helper and sustainer of all existence, certain that his prayers will be answered. Just as the God in whom one believes is not supernatural, so the God in whom one places one's faith, or trust, is capable of setting into action those internal, natural powers that make it possible for what one has affirmed to actually be attained.

Lichtenstein maintained that, like other types of prayers, affirmations are best offered in silence. It is in silence that our best thoughts are born, our talents and powers formed, our deepest feelings generated and perfected. In silence we make our clearest judgments and our most carefully formulated plans and are best able to formulate our aspirations and ideals. Silence, he wrote, is important because it enables the mind to concentrate. In silence, "the heart can speak, the soul can take its highest flight. God, too, answers man's petition in silence; no voice is heard, no hand is visible, but the wounds are closed up, pain is erased, and well-being is restored. For God works only in silence."[43] The method of communication that silent prayers employ is that of visualization. By visually imagining oneself to be strong, healthy, cheerful, and so on, one is best able to become strong, healthy, or cheerful. Visualizations employ the power of positive thinking and in so doing overcome such negative feelings as worry, fear, or doubt that might hinder the realization of one's desires. To be happy, for example, one needs to affirm that one *is* happy and to then picture oneself as happy. Having done so, one finds not only that one is happy but also that one has attained the kind of serenity, or peace of mind, that is a precondition for the attainment of all positive states of being.

Morris Lichtenstein viewed spiritual healing as "essentially a belief in the efficacy of prayer." All of us, he maintained, possess a power that has been given to us on which we can draw when we find ourselves in distress, a power that "has not only made all things" but also preserves them. "While illness is essentially a human creation," that is, while the individual

> through excess, rashness or worry, makes himself ill, health is a Divine creation. And healing rests with the one who created health. . . .
> A physician may . . . bandage a wound and set a broken bone, yet it is not the physician who injects new vitality into the body, or changes the helplessness to strength, or knits a bone together, or weaves a new skin over an open wound; all these are achieved by a Power far superior to that of the physician, it was achieved by the Power that made and makes everything good. . . . The physician may indeed fully comprehend the process of healing, yet he will admit that he is not the healer himself.[44]

Prayer, then, is the human means by which one invokes divine help in moments of great difficulty or despair. It is an instrument used by the individual when "his own powers are too limited or feeble to meet his needs." This concept of prayer, Lichtenstein added, is not new to Judaism. Indeed, from the time of the biblical patriarchs through the rabbinic era, prayer for the "distressed and the ailing" has been an essential element of Jewish faith.

Clearly, he added, prayer is much more than a form of religious expression or an articulation of human desire. Had our ancestors discovered that prayer does not invoke a response, surely they would have abandoned it long ago. Yet at the same time, he continued, we in Jewish Science believe in prayer not because of any historic testimony to its efficacy but because we experience its effectiveness in our everyday lives. "To us," he maintained,

prayer is a power—a power that can change and transform and restore. We prove it by the testimony of hundreds and hundreds of
our people, who have sought and found physical as well as spiritual
relief through prayer. Such testimony is, after all, the only testimony
by which any science can establish and confirm a truth. We know
from experience that when an appeal is thus made for help, someone actually helps, someone actually heals, someone actually causes
a change in the flesh or in the mind of the ailing, and from our Jewish viewpoint, this Someone is God. He acts in answer to our
prayer.[45]

Unlike those in Christian Science, Morris Lichtenstein firmly believed that
both matter and spirit exist. "Matter," he wrote, "is the visible manifestation of
the divine, spirit is the invisible; matter is tangible, spirit intangible; matter is
receptive, spirit is creative; but both are real, both express the nature and the
will of God."[46] Since human beings are made up of both matter and spirit—
flesh and bone as well as a "spark of divinity encased in terrestrial vestures"—
medical science cannot in and of itself be sufficient for healing. Were men and
women purely physical creatures, medicine would be sufficient. Yet because
we are essentially spiritual beings, our higher centers cannot be reached
through physical channels. To reach those centers, even in cases of physical
ailments, it is best to employ the dual spiritual methods of concentration and
prayer.

We do not wish, he insisted, to minimize or deprecate either modern
medicine or the medical profession. Indeed, he asserted, we recognize that it
has its own place and sphere of efficacy. Medicine, for example, can help prevent disease by teaching sanitary and helpful modes of living. Yet "when it
comes to actual restoration, medical authorities, even the greatest of them, can
[like laypeople] only wait and see, watch for progress made, made by another
power not themselves," for human beings are God's creations, and when an
individual's "system becomes impaired, only his Maker can restore and
strengthen him."[47]

Much of Morris Lichtenstein's understanding of God, humanity, spiritual
healing, the efficacy of prayer, and the nature of Jewish Science as a movement
were summed up in what he identified as the ten fundamentals of Jewish
Science. First: "The Jewish faith is the only faith we acknowledge. Jewish Science is the application of the Jewish Faith to the practices of life." Second: "We
believe wholeheartedly in the efficacy of prayer. We believe that no prayer, when
properly offered, goes unanswered." Third: "We shall endeavor every day of
our lives to keep serene; to check all tendencies to violence and anger; to keep
calm even in the fact of unpleasant and discouraging circumstances." Fourth:
"We shall strive to be cheerful every day of our lives . . . [for as the Talmud

insists,] it is God's design that man should find joy and cheer in his existence on this earth."

The fifth fundamental expressed the desire of the Jewish Scientist to eliminate hatred from his or her heart and "to cultivate an attitude of love and goodwill toward everyone," while the sixth pledged to "cultivate a disposition to contentment, envying no one, and praising God for the good he has already bestowed on us." In the seventh fundamental, Lichtenstein declared that Jewish Scientists should "make a conscious effort to banish worry and fear from our lives," and in the seventh, should promise to "trust in God's goodness in every circumstance of our life." Ninth, Lichtenstein asserted that "we believe that death is an elevation to eternal life, and not a cessation of existence," and he concluded, in the tenth fundamental, that "we believe that God is the Source of Health and the Restorer of Health." First outlining these fundamentals in 1924, Lichtenstein continued to expound on their significance in subsequent sermons, books, and essays. The two affirmations that he created and that served, from the inception of the society in 1922, as a central feature of both its public worship services and members' personal prayers, contain most of the ideas that Lichtenstein later identified as the fundamentals of Jewish Science.

The earliest editions of the *Jewish Science Interpreter* included instructions on how these affirmations should be recited. "Relax completely for about fifteen minutes," Lichtenstein advised, and

> release every muscle from any possible tension. Take an easy comfortable position, and dismiss all strain from mind and body. Then repeat your affirmations. Meditate on the significance of every phrase, and let each thought engrave itself on your consciousness. Meditate in this manner daily, morning and evening, and you will begin to feel a deep change taking place in the innermost recesses of your being; you will grow calm, and cheerful, and hopeful. All suffering will pass away, and all depression will vanish.[48]

Though less time was allotted for the initial period of relaxation, the method of visualization was more explicitly employed, and the affirmations were recited together, many of these instructions were repeated, and continue to be repeated today, during the healing portion of the Jewish Science worship service, that is, the section in which the worshiper sets the healing forces within himself or herself into motion through the methods of visualization and affirmative prayer. They were also repeated, and again, continue to be repeated, by spiritual practitioners during individual healing sessions.

Recognizing that many people have difficulty entering into the modes of contemplation and prayer, Morris Lichtenstein, drawing on methods used by Christian Science, trained a number of his followers to become spiritual practitioners. Lecture notes taken by Harry Hartman, trained as a practitioner in 1927, indicate that the practitioners' course that Lichtenstein developed, and that continued to be offered through the mid-1990s, consisted of twenty-nine weekly lectures, later expanded to thirty, on such topics as matter and spirit, the divine and human minds, specific physical and nervous ailments with which the practitioner needed to be familiar, and the power of positive prayer.

In order to become a practitioner, one needed to be serene and "have perfect faith in the treatment." One also needed to be a good listener, capable of giving the patient both confidence and hope. Begin the treatment, Lichtenstein maintained, by seating the patient in a comfortable chair. Never argue or disagree with the patient, and let the patient do the talking, though some will hesitate to talk. For those patients who have difficulty relaxing, walk them around the room slowly, "slower and slower each time, passing back and forth three times," until they feel more relaxed. Then, begin to suggest the help that Jewish Science can provide through the process of spiritual healing. For instance, he said, remind the patient that

> if by accident a piece of flesh is cut, you can do many things for this, but the one thing you must do is to bandage it and leave it alone. You may use peroxide but this is only a preventative. In a few days the nerves reunite and the skin heals. [Then ask the patient:] Who does it? [And answer him:] I do not do it but someone in me does it. It is the divine mind. . . . After this talk [about the nature of the divine mind], ask the patient to relax and close his eyes. Then you realize and visualize a stream of health entering the organ affected. This is scientific prayer, using the highest faculty of the imagination.[49]

Thus, for example, one helps a patient experiencing stomach pain to visualize a stream of health entering into his or her mouth, passing through the esophagus, entering the stomach, and flowing abundantly through it. Similarly,

> if the heart is affected, see the stream of health flowing from above, entering the mouth and filling the heart with substance, making it perfect. Likewise with liver or kidneys or any organ in the body or the limb or any exposed part of the body. Always see the divine stream of health flowing strongly and [the] more strongly the better. Mentally picture a waterfall. This may be helpful. If you see the stream clearly and do it earnestly, the wound will begin to respond, pain will be assuaged and in time the wound will heal.[50]

For those patients who had difficulty visualizing a divine stream, a method of healing he called method B, Lichtenstein offered a substitute technique, called method A, which called for visualizing "a perfect organ or limb descending on high and superimposing itself on the defective organ." Thus, if one seemed to have heart trouble, one might "visualize a perfect heart entering from on high superimposing itself over the defective heart, absorbing it, thus beating with new life and new vitality." Lichtenstein particularly recommended the use of this technique in treating problems of sight or other senses. Finally, Lichtenstein recommended employing another method in conjunction with either of the previous two, called method C, which involved visualizing the "whole individual in perfect health." Though only one organ might be in pain, "while one organ is defective the whole body is suffering," for "the whole body," he insisted, "is in pain through the nerves carrying pain throughout the system."[51] Lichtenstein recommended that the entire treatment last for approximately fifteen minutes; ten minutes for methods A or B, concluding with five minutes for method C.

In subsequent lectures, Lichtenstein identified other methods that might also be employed. Method D, a less effective but possible alternative to method B, involved speaking directly to those organs that were weak or malfunctioning. Maintaining that every organ in the body possessed both intelligence and individuality, Lichtenstein suggested utilizing a method of direct address through which silently, with full voice, or in a whisper, one would command or ask a particular organ to "discharge its duty faithfully without stop [and] without weakness." Believing that this method was particularly helpful in treating oneself, he nonetheless felt that it could successfully be used in treating others, and should be used if a practitioner felt that his or her imaginative faculty was "inactive or obscure." As in a classroom of children, some of the organs, he said, were brighter or more obedient than others. Thus, for example, one might be able to calm an overexcited heart by saying: "Heart do not beat so violently, beat normally and not so rapidly." After repeating this statement several times but more slowly, one should add: "God made you to function properly. Follow this law, function properly." With other, less intelligent organs, however, one needed to be more persistent and assume a more urgent tone. Thus, for example, one should say to a malfunctioning liver: "Liver of [the person to be healed], cast out all pain, function properly, thou art created to function properly." In all cases, he advised, tell the organ when to function and the patient exactly when you expect him or her to "give the organ a chance." Then, as with methods A and B, end with method C, envisioning the patient's entire body as healthy.

Lichtenstein also discussed the efficacy of absent treatment. Utilizing this method, one would appeal not to the patient but to the force of healing that exists everywhere in everything. Beginning by visualizing the patient, or at least conjuring up an image of the patient based on detailed information concerning his or her age, size, appearance, and whereabouts, one would then relax, close one's eyes, and visualize the patient sitting in an opposite chair, as though he or she were actually present. The practitioner would use method A, B, or D and finish with method C. Finally, one would call the patient by name several times and call out the name of the city where the patient lived, along with as many details of his or her life as possible. The image would slowly fade from the practitioner's consciousness, while the powers of healing set into motion would continue to work, helping to restore the patient to health.

Practitioners were also instructed in ways of healing themselves. While Lichtenstein admitted that self-healing is more difficult than being healed by another, as one tends to be more conscientious in following the ministrations of another, he believed that methods B and C, that is, "visualizing a divine stream of health entering and filling up the defective organ" and then "seeing oneself in a perfect state" of health, could be extremely efficacious. "Always relax," he advised. "Close the eyes in all healings and let your vision do the work. Closely allied with the system of direct address is the affirmation which is an appeal to the divine mind for help. Every being has a divine mind which sustains and has charges over all inner processes." Thus, he counseled, address your prayers in the form of affirmations to the divine mind within yourself, for God is not a supernatural being in heaven but rather a power "extending throughout the universe." If you are unable to visualize and lack the patience to try and do so, affirm that which you most desire simply and straightforwardly. For example, if one desires strength, one might say: "God is giving me new strength and new vigor every day"; if suffering from depression, one might affirm: "I am filled with divine health, calmness and cheer." Reading selections from *Jewish Science and Health* and the Book of Psalms was also recommended.[52]

The remainder of the practitioners' course was far-reaching in scope. Among those subjects addressed were the restorative power of sleep and how to cure insomnia; causes and cures for habitual constipation; mind cures for asthma and hay fever; and detailed discussions of both causes of and cures for epilepsy, hysteria, depression, diabetes, ulcers, and various contagious diseases. While most involved drawing on healing methods A through D, several necessitated the using of additional methods as well. The first, method E, involved visualizing "rays of serenity, energy, and cheer" and was particularly helpful in curing insomnia, overcoming worry, and relieving periods of mental depression. The second, method F, was recommended in curing ulcers, mild forms of melancholia, and certain cases of epilepsy. Utilizing this method, the practitioner was to visualize "a burning fire, narrow and concentrated, descending from on high, entering the afflicted part and working in a circle around the walls of the wound, burning out the infectious element" or malignancy. The third, method G, the visualization of freezing rays or crystals of ice entering and filling one's brain, was offered as a preliminary to method E in treating certain cases of mental disorders, while the fourth, method H, the visualization of rays of strength, was particularly recommended in the treatment of hysteria. The fifth, method I, was offered in conjunction with method C as a means of treating diseases that were the result of blood impurities, including diabetes.

Using this method, one was instructed to visualize an opening under the heart through which all of the blood impurities, and in the case of diabetes, blood sugar, could pass. "Always see the blood," he advised, "coming more and more freely from the opening. Always see this wound closed up when finished. In addition to this see a sugarless blood stream coming from above entering [the] top [of the] heart and uniting with the rest of the blood stream in the body."[53] Finally, method J, the visualization of rays of clearness, often visualized as silver rays, was recommended, along with method F, in curing mental delusions.

While Lichtenstein never advised his practitioners to discourage patients from seeking medical attention, and in the case of diabetes, advocated letting the patient continue the diet prescribed by a physician, he believed that spiritual healing was most effective independent of drugs, pills, or any other kind of medication. Indeed, he said, one should not treat an individual currently on medication but rather suggest that he or she return for treatment if the medicine prescribed by a physician proved to be ineffective.[54] At the same time, Lichtenstein made it clear that despite the efficacy of spiritual healing, there were some diseases for which such healing could offer only relief and comfort. In the case of diabetes, for example, Lichtenstein acknowledged that although spiritual healing could do a great deal to reduce the amount of sugar in the blood, not all cases of diabetes could be cured. Severe cases of mental disorders, he maintained, were sometimes "beyond recovery." He advised practitioners not to treat children born with limited mental capacities (i.e., those whose minds never developed beyond the age of seven) though he thought one might be effective in consoling the child's parents. Similarly, Lichtenstein maintained that while method F, the visualization of a fire burning out a malignant growth, could be effective in treating cancer in its earliest stages, all that one could do for a patient suffering in its last stages was to relieve, or calm, the mind.[55]

In a few instances, Lichtenstein advocated seeking medical help instead of spiritual healing. While over time, the ministrations of a practitioner could help one afflicted with a contagious disease, it is better, he said, to advise such an individual to go to a physician, for medicine can stop the contagion more quickly. Similarly, he counseled, while an inflamed appendix can be spiritually healed, immediate surgery performed by a competent physician is often preferable to the more protracted ministrations of a practitioner. All forms of healing, he insisted, are "God's creation," and thus it makes no difference whether one is treated by a practitioner or a physician. All that matters is that one utilize the most effective form of treatment.[56]

While Morris Lichtenstein firmly believed that "the problem of the preservation of Judaism will be solved when the Jew learns again to think in terms of spirituality, to conduct himself in accordance with the ethical laws of Judaism, and practice the virtues stressed in his faith,"[57] he also believed that communal institutions, including the synagogue, were of vital importance in helping to make Jewish teachings a central part of the Jew's everyday life. Yet to

succeed in doing so, he insisted, such institutions needed to concern themselves with both the Jewish people and the God of Israel. "Judaism without the
Jew," he wrote, "can only be an abstraction; the Jew without Judaism must
gradually dissolve as a people."[58] He thus castigated religious schools that did
little if anything to foster the religious consciousness of Jewish children. He
applauded those schools that sought to transmit to their students Jewish teachings and traditions and gave credit to those that rightly understood the importance of teaching Hebrew, engaged in the study of sacred texts, and offered
their students a knowledge of and personal sense of connectedness to Jewish
history. Indeed, he believed that all were essential elements of Jewish education. Yet he also believed that such schools needed to teach their students how
to pray. In addition to familiarizing them with liturgical prayers, religious
schools needed to foster within Jewish children "the habit of appealing to God
silently in moments of difficulty and distress," helping them to feel "God's
nearness and love," gaining spiritual fortification "against the onslaughts of
life." God, he insisted, must not be presented to the child only as

> an historic Reality, as the God of the past, as the God of our fathers;
> He must be given to the child also as a present Reality, as the child's
> God, as our God today, who sustains and loves and guides today as
> He did in the days of the remote past, a God to whom every one
> today, and the child, too, may have access no less than did our fore-
> fathers.[59]

Similarly, he maintained, if most American Jews rarely, if ever, attended synagogue, perhaps the fault lay with rabbinic leaders who possessed intellectual
but not spiritual training, and worship services that possessed little more than
aesthetic appeal. If most of American Jewry found that synagogue services
lacked religious significance, it was because they themselves did not believe
that God listens to their prayers and thus "experience[d] no inspiring effect
from them." Indeed, he observed, "it appears that sanctity has fled from the
sanctuary or from the heart of the people; religious zeal has vanished, hence
the house of God is deserted."[60]

The answer, he maintained, implicitly criticizing the efforts of Mordecai
Kaplan and others, was not to build multifunctional Jewish centers in the hope
that Jews who were attracted to their swimming pools and gymnasiums would
eventually be attracted to their religious services as well. Indeed, in already
existing centers, "the synagogue in the heart of all this hubbub still stands
melancholy and deserted, attended at its services by the same few old men and
women." Thus, he concluded, "it becomes more and more evident that in order
to make the synagogue once more a center of spiritual gravity, more than mere
'attractions' must be offered to the people." Firmly believing that both the
survival of the Jewish people and the preservation of Judaism depended on the
restoration of religious consciousness, Lichtenstein's own suggestion was that

the synagogue again emphasize the immanence of God, "preaching the truth" of God's nearness, goodness, and responsiveness to prayer. "If the synagogue," he said, "cannot reinstate religion in the consciousness of our people, then the synagogue should be altogether abandoned as an institution which cannot function in this land and in our generation."[61] To Morris Lichtenstein, what the American Jewish community most needed were institutions that taught Jews how to practice the teachings of Judaism. Only through such institutions, he believed, could Jewish teachings successfully be transmitted from parent to child by word and by example.

5

Clifton Harby Levy and the Spiritual Reeducation of American Jews

Had the Reform rabbi Clifton Harby Levy attended Morris Lichtenstein's lectures or regularly read the *Jewish Science Interpreter*, he undoubtedly would have agreed with much of Lichtenstein's critique of the contemporary synagogue. Like Lichtenstein, Clifton Harby Levy believed that rabbis possessed insufficient spiritual training and therefore did little if anything to revitalize the religious consciousness of American Jewry. He too insisted that worship services needed to emphasize God's immanence and the importance and efficacy of personal prayer. Indeed, like Morris Lichtenstein, Clifton Harby Levy continually spoke of God as healer and viewed happiness and health as important human and religious goals. Yet Levy, unlike Lichtenstein, did not advocate abandoning the synagogue if it were unable to "reinstate religion in the consciousness of our people." Rather, he sought to spiritually reeducate both rabbis and laity through a system and method that he identified as Jewish Science.

Like Morris Lichtenstein, Clifton Harby Levy frequently equated Jewish Science with the application of Jewish teachings to everyday life. Yet to Levy, it was essential that the principles of faith be used "in the light of the laws which science has read through its investigations."[1] As he said in a 1927 address delivered at the annual meeting of the CCAR, the term *Jewish Science* represented the conjunction of Judaism and Science, thus aiming "to utilize all of the tested results of the surgeon, the physician, the psychologist, and the psychiatrist, in cooperation with the highest spiritual teachings of Judaism."[2] Moreover, Levy understood the goals of Jewish Science to be individual and social. He viewed the attainment of personal happiness and health as essential to one's spiritual development. At the same time, however, like other classical Reform rabbis, Levy firmly believed that one served God best by serving others.

Morris Lichtenstein's understanding of the term *Jewish Science* was very different from that of Levy. He did not see the term as a reflection of Jewish attitudes toward modern science or scientists. While he recognized that at certain times medical treatment was a necessary precondition to one's physical recovery, he did not view cooperating with physicians as Jewish Science's primary goal. Nor, for that matter, did he view social service as one of Jewish Science's chief objectives. While Morris Lichtenstein certainly advocated helping others, he saw the primary goal of Jewish Science as personal in nature. More specifically, it was to help the individual attain happiness and health within the context of his or her own religion. To Lichtenstein, *Jewish Science* was a term that invoked yet clearly delineated itself from Christian Science. Both Christian Science, as taught by Mary Baker Eddy, and Jewish Science, as understood by Morris Lichtenstein, equated the term *science* with true principles or knowledge. Their emphasis, for example, on God as an inner power or process, as opposed to an external, supernatural being was on that which made sense or was in some way demonstrable to modern men and women. It was, in other words, a rational idea in which they could believe. To Lichtenstein, unlike Eddy, it was equally rational to believe that matter was real, as was disease and death. Yet Lichtenstein, like Eddy, viewed spirit as the basis of all existence. Consequently he believed, as she did, that human beings have within them recuperative powers that are divine in origin, which unfailingly can be made to function through the appeal of personal faith. Thus, as Lichtenstein wrote in the first issue of the *Jewish Science Interpreter*,

> Christian Science has indeed a vital appeal to Christians in that it
> lays emphasis on the Christ consciousness. But for the Jew, to
> whose soul the Christ consciousness is entirely alien, Jewish Sci-
> ence, which is based on a religion to which his soul has been at-
> tuned [sic] for centuries, is the only channel by which he may attain
> lasting health and happiness.[3]

In December 1924, Clifton Harby Levy began to work with a group of laypeople to create what became known as the Centre of Jewish Science. Soon after, he initiated publication of the monthly *Jewish Life*, "the official organ of Jewish Science, Inc.," edited and largely written by Levy himself. The first issue included a lengthy article by Levy entitled "Why the Jew Cannot Accept Christianity." In it he maintained that while it was the Jewish attraction to Christian Science that had prompted him to include the article in *Jewish Life*, its more general intent was to offer reasons that would "bar any real Jews from accepting Christianity in any guise whatever."[4] As Levy continued to explain, the article previously had appeared in a periodical called *Christian Work* and excerpted in

Literary Digest. It was part of a debate between John Stuart Conning, superintendent of the Jewish evangelization work of the Presbyterian Church, and Levy himself.

In this debate, Levy acknowledged that Christian proselytizing efforts undoubtedly reflected the genuine desire to save Jews from eternal damnation. Yet he insisted that for Jews no such efforts were needed, as they did not believe that only through faith in Christ and his martyrdom on the cross was salvation possible. Levy went on to maintain that if Christian thought was so superior, how could one explain "this last war" (World War I) between Christian nations? More specifically, he asked his Christian audience: "Have you converted your own sons and daughters, your own governments to the principles of love, right and peace?" Further, he insisted, if the Christian missionary came to either Jews or Christians, insisting that the miracles performed by Jesus were proofs of his divinity, we would require him "to prove the truth of the account of the miracles," and even if he duly authenticated each of them, there would still be too much room for doubt for us to accept the miracles as evidence of his having been supernaturally divine.[5] With all of Levy's points Mary Baker Eddy undoubtedly would have concurred.

The inner Christ-consciousness of Christian Science was not the inward manifestation of a supernatural son of God but of "Truth, Life, and Love." Non-Christians were not relegated to eternal damnation. Indeed, in Eddy's view no one was, as she denied the reality of death. For Eddy, the crucifixion was not what overcame human sin, since she believed that sin too was an illusion. What she meant by Jesus' death as atonement was an at-one-ment, that is, something that provided men and women with evidence not only of God's love but also of the unity that exists between God and humanity. When Mary Baker Eddy asserted that human beings are "saved through Christ," what she meant was that "in healing the sick and overcoming sin and death," Jesus showed the way all human beings might discover the healing powers, or mind, within themselves. Salvation was thus a this-worldly attainment of happiness and health, best achieved through Christian Science teachings.[6]

It therefore is not surprising that Clifton Harby Levy's reprinted article did not specifically refer to Christian Science. While he, like Morris Lichtenstein, emphatically rejected Eddy's belief in the illusory nature of the body, illness, and death as both unscientific and un-Jewish, Levy's critique of Christianity primarily focused on specific theological teachings promulgated by most mainstream Christian denominations, not by Christian Science. Levy's intent, therefore, was not to create a Jewish countermovement to Christian Science but rather to educate or reeducate the modern Jew to the spiritual possibilities of Judaism. This interest was one Levy shared with other leaders of Reform, not only in the United States but also in Great Britain. A few years later, with the establishment of the World Union for Progressive Judaism, discovering Judaism's spiritual possibilities came to be an idea articulated by Reform rabbis throughout the world. It was also an idea long held by many of Levy's ancestors, prominent Jews who first settled in Charleston, South Carolina, around 1740. Indeed, as far as Levy could recall, all of his relatives on his mother's side were Reform Jews. Several of his ancestors had been among the earliest members of the Reform Society of Israelites, established in Charleston in 1825 as the first organized Jewish Reform congregation in America. Among them was the well-known journalist, playwright, drama critic, and educator Isaac Harby (1788–1828), one of the society's founders. According to his biographer, Gary Zola, Harby soon became its most prominent intellectual, with his "widely circulated discourse, delivered before the society on November 21, 1825, re-main[ing] a compelling statement of the group's goals and aspirations." Isaac Harby helped compile the society's prayer book and by 1827 became its president.[7]

Clifton Harby Levy was born on June 21, 1867, to Almeria Emma Moses and Eugene Henry Levy in New Orleans, Louisiana. He received his early Jewish education in Mobile, Alabama, and was confirmed in 1880 by Adolph Moses, the rabbi of Congregation Sha'arei Shomayim.[8] Moses' son, Alfred Geiger Moses, who would become the congregation's rabbi, was then only two years old. By the time Alfred Geiger Moses had reached his teens, Clifton Harby Levy had studied with the Reform rabbi James Gutheim of New Orleans in preparation for admission to HUC and had spent eight years in Cincinnati, receiving his bachelor of arts degree from the University of Cincinnati in 1887 and rabbinic ordination from HUC in 1890. He had also moved to New York City to be closer to his family, who had settled there in 1887.[9] It is thus unlikely that Moses and Levy became acquaintances until much later, although certainly they long knew of one another. Given the fact that both were members of the CCAR, knew and had been greatly influenced by Adolph Moses, and shared a mutual interest in applied psychology and Jewish Science, their paths may well have crossed before August 1925, when Moses gave several talks, including a major address on the ideals of Jewish Science, at a week-long conference organized by Levy under the auspices of Temple Beth El in Rockaway Park, Long Island.[10]

In the summer of 1890, soon after moving to New York, Clifton Harby Levy briefly served as superintendent and organizer of a school for immigrant children sponsored by the Baron de Hirsch Fund. By September of that year, he had become rabbi of the Reform congregation Gates of Hope at 15 East 86th Street, a position he held for a little over a year. According to Levy, he left Gates of Hope after "failing to secure support for [his] idea of expansion."[11] Tellingly, he later left Tremont Temple in the Bronx for the same reason. In 1891, Levy married Sarah Lang, and in 1903, after Lang's death, he married Cora Bacharach, to whom he remained married for almost sixty years. From 1892 to 1894, Levy served as rabbi of Congregation Shaarai Shomayim in

Lancaster, Pennsylvania, and from 1894 to 1896 as rabbi of the Eden Street Temple in Baltimore. During his years in Baltimore, Levy also did postgraduate work in Semitics at Johns Hopkins University, helped found and edited the *Jewish Comment*, and worked to create the first United Jewish Charities in the United States.

By 1896, apparently "disgusted with the methods then in vogue in congregational life," Levy returned to New York City to devote himself to writing. In recollecting his years in Lancaster and Baltimore, Levy never elaborated on those congregational methods that he found to be so distasteful. Yet what he revealed about his earlier reasons for leaving Gates of Hope and what I have discovered about his reasons for leaving Tremont Temple in 1919 suggest that Levy disliked the control exercised by the officers and the boards of trustees

FIGURE 5.1. Rabbi Clifton Harby Levy, November 29, 1892 (age 25).
Published by permission of the Jacob Rader Marcus Center of the American Jewish Archives, Cincinnati, Ohio.

over every aspect of congregational life. As previously discussed, it was for the same reason that, only a few years later, Morris Lichtenstein became so eager to leave his position in Athens, Georgia.

Once in New York City, Levy contributed to various periodicals, including the *Independent, Outlook,* and *Review of Reviews,* as well as "all the New York newspapers," primarily writing on archeological and scientific discoveries, especially those that shed greater light on the historical context and/or religious content of the Hebrew Bible. Yet, without forgoing his writing, it seems that by 1907 Levy once again assumed a leadership role in Jewish congregational life. In May of that year, the Board of Trustees of the Tremont Temple Society, an association formed by a small group of laypeople in April 1906 to build a synagogue in the Bronx, hired him to officiate at their Rosh Hashanah and Yom Kippur services in the fall. While Levy has since been identified as the founder of the Tremont Temple,[12] that identification is erroneous. The minutes of Tremont Temple Society meetings held between September 1906 and May 1907 make it clear that Levy's involvement with the society did not begin until almost a year and a half after it had been established. Another rabbi apparently led the society's first high holy day services, held in September 1906, and Levy was first formally introduced, and gave a short address, to members of the board at their May 1907 meeting.[13]

In appreciation for the fine job he had done in leading high holy day services, society members voted on September 19, 1907, to make Levy an honorary member of the society, and by 1908 he had begun to officiate at Sabbath morning services and was again hired to lead high holy day services in the fall. On November 19, 1908, society members unanimously voted to become a permanent Jewish congregation, to be known as "Tremont Temple, Congregation Shaarei Rachamim [Gates of Mercy]." They also voted to empower the Board of Trustees to "take action in regards to securing the permanent services of Dr. C. H. Levy." On February 4, 1909, he accepted their offer.[14]

While Levy later maintained that he had "aided the Tremont Temple Society in becoming the Tremont Temple," he never described himself as their rabbi.[15] The minutes of meetings held by both the Tremont Temple Society and the Board of Trustees make it clear, however, that in 1909 Levy was indeed hired to become the congregation's rabbi for an annual salary of $900. Although his salary was raised to $1,200 in 1910, Levy continued to receive no more than a one-year contract from 1909 until his resignation in 1919. In marked contrast to members of the temple's Board of Trustees, who were elected to serve three-year terms, Levy was duly nominated and elected to a one-year term as rabbi at the annual congregational meeting held each spring.[16] Minutes of board and congregational meetings held between 1909 and 1919 continually identified Levy "as rabbi of the congregation," and the temple's stationery listed in its left corner the name, address, and phone number of its rabbi, Clifton H. Levy.

Yet minutes of Board of Trustees meetings also reveal what at times was a strained and, from Levy's perspective, no doubt an increasingly frustrating relationship between the temple's lay leadership and its rabbi. Years later, Levy maintained that he had been instrumental in helping the congregation "build its first story." While he never made it clear how he had done so, undoubtedly Levy did contribute to the work of the building fund and, in fact, was invited to attend the Board of Trustees meeting in December 1913 to report the number of monetary pledges that the Building Committee had thus far secured. Certainly, during the earliest years of the temple's existence, Levy helped bring in new members. By serving as the congregation's rabbi, a position for which no one else seems to have applied during those years, perhaps because the salary was so low (board members admitted as much among themselves and subsequently offered his successor $3,500 a year), Levy helped the Tremont Society transform itself into a religious congregation. With Levy officiating, services were held on Friday nights, Saturday mornings, and the Jewish holidays. A cantor and choir, initially selected by Levy, were hired for special services, including those held on the high holy days, and Levy often spoke on behalf of the congregational Choir Committee at meetings of the Board of Trustees. Throughout his tenure at Tremont Temple, Levy maintained an active interest in the curriculum of the temple's Sunday school and in the building of the temple itself, on which construction had begun by the summer of 1909.

Levy's influence and actions, however, were severely curbed by a lay leadership that constantly exerted its power. His suggestions were often dismissed, and accountability was demanded for all of his actions. Thus, for example, on November 14, 1912, the Board of Trustees held a special meeting "for the purpose of considering matters in connection with the rabbi, Dr. C. H. Levy." Though board minutes do not elaborate on these matters, subsequent minutes suggest that the issue at hand was Levy's having allowed the Boys' Club (what Boys' Club is unclear) to meet at the temple. In early December, at the board's regular meeting, a motion was carried that on Levy's satisfactory explanation at the special meeting held in November and at the request of the Religious School Committee, the Boys' Club was to be granted temporary permission to meet at the temple on December 15 and 29, from 2:00 to 4:00 p.m.[17]

Less than two months later, the board reported that it had come to their attention that "Dr. Levy, the rabbi of the Temple, officiated at a marriage ceremony at the Temple on Sunday, February 2, 1913, the sanction of the Board not having been attained by him for the use of the Temple on that occasion." The secretary of the congregation, the board member Newman Joel, was "directed to inform the Rabbi that the Temple is not to be used for any purpose except as stipulated by the bylaws without such sanction first having been granted by the Board."[18] In April 1913, "under instruction from the Religious School Committee," Levy formally asked the board's permission to hold a children's seder at the temple, a request that was granted. However, when Levy went on to remind the board that they had not yet made necessary arrangements for Shavuot services, their response was that they would take the matter up at the next meeting; according to the minutes of their meetings, they apparently never did so.[19]

In June 1915, the board once again held a special meeting regarding Clifton Harby Levy. Its purpose was to discuss various criticisms of Levy's Shavuot sermon. It is not clear whether these criticisms were from congregants or solely from the board members, who subsequently informed Levy in no uncertain terms that they did not approve of his sermon. Levy apparently admitted "that the sermon may have been somewhat indiscreet" and assured the trustees who called on him that he was "ready at all times to act in accordance with the wishes of the Board as regards his sermons and other matters relative to the services."[20] From 1915 through the beginning of 1919, the board continued to monitor Levy's words and behavior closely, occasionally inviting him to trustees meetings to discuss "various matters regarding the progress and welfare of the congregation," at other times choosing to discuss "matters relating to his lectures and visiting of members" among themselves. One of their concerns was that Levy did not devote sufficient time to the affairs of the congregation. When it was suggested that for the rabbi to do so, it might be necessary to increase his salary, the discussion abruptly ended, and the matter apparently was dropped.[21]

One area in which Levy maintained ongoing interest and concern was in the building and physical expansion of Tremont Temple. At the October 8, 1918, trustees meeting, a letter was read that Levy had recently sent to the board. In it he wrote of the advisability of buying some land to the north of the temple in order to expand what at present was a relatively small building with little frontage. A special board meeting was convened that November. After a lengthy discussion, the trustees voted to inform Levy that they were not in favor of purchasing the additional land as he had suggested. Rather than obsequiously following the board's wishes, as he had done in the past, Clifton Harby Levy decided to appeal to the temple's Sisterhood, whose fund-raising efforts had been indispensable to the congregation from its inception, and whose members included several of the temple's founders and wives of members of the Board of Trustees. The Sisterhood agreed to purchase the land suggested by Levy and apparently informed the board of their intention.

On February 11, 1919, the trustees unanimously passed a strongly worded resolution saying that the board was "very much opposed to the Tremont Sisterhood purchasing any property at this time and should the Sisterhood insist on purchasing such property, the Board of Trustees, believing that such action would be a detriment to the interests of the congregation, would be compelled to refuse its acceptance."[22] Given the fact that the board accepted the Sisterhood's gift shortly after Levy's departure, it may well be that the "action" to which the trustees referred in their resolution was not the purchasing of ad ditional property per se but rather the purchasing of property at the suggestion of the rabbi, who, after his proposal had been rejected, openly and defiantly challenged the board's power. It should be noted, however, that at the November 1918 meeting when the trustees first voted on Levy's suggestion, there was a separate, brief discussion, followed by a vote, to withdraw $1,000 from the congregation's account toward paying off the $10,000 balance due on the temple's mortgage. Thus, financial considerations may also have played a role in the board's rejection of Levy's proposal. Apparently, however, no such reasons were given either to Levy or to members of the Sisterhood.

In any case, Clifton Harby Levy had had enough. On February 14, 1919, he typed a formal resignation letter to the Board of Trustees and members of the Tremont Temple. Perhaps consciously or unconsciously, to underscore his anger and sense of alienation toward, if not abandonment by, the temple's male leadership, the letter was not written on the temple stationery bearing his name but rather on the stationery of the New York Board of Jewish Ministers, on which he was listed as secretary of its executive committee. Levy opened the letter by saying that he felt a crisis had arisen "in the affairs of the Tremont Temple." Now is the time to decide, he continued,

> whether it is to be a really effective, large and representative Jewish
> Centre, or a small, languishing and unprogressive congregation. So
> that the Temple might be erected on a proper scale, befitting its lo-
> cation on the Grand Concourse, I advocated the purchase of an ad-
> ditional lot north of our building of 69 feet. This would give us 94
> feet, a proper front for a real Temple, and for the expansion of the
> Religious School, as required by this growing neighborhood.

After expressing his appreciation to members of the Sisterhood for accepting and acting on his idea, he singled out the board, who, "in its wisdom, decided that it would not accept the lot and so notified the Sisterhood, through its president, thus checking the negotiations." Levy then made his intentions clear:

> In view of this decided and radical difference of opinion as to the
> future progress of the Tremont Temple, I deem it wise to offer my
> resignation, to take effect not later than February 28th, unless the
> Board and members of the congregation can agree to the larger plan
> of development for this Temple.[23]

In light of the firm hand exercised by the board in governing the congregation, it is not surprising that Levy's letter, sounding very much like an ultimatum, gave the trustees little choice but to accept his resignation.

After his departure, Levy apparently had little contact with Tremont Temple or most of its members. While a handful of members left the congregation, including at least one man nominated for membership by Levy himself, mem-

FIGURE 5.2. Clifton Harby Levy. Courtesy of Ruth Herman.

bership continued to rise even before a new rabbi was hired. Until then, worship services were led either by laypeople or guest rabbis, such as Morris Lichtenstein, who, in early June 1919, wrote to the Board of Trustees offering his
services to the congregation "whenever called on." Their response was to ask
whether he could officiate at services the following Friday evening and Saturday
morning. Whether or not Lichtenstein was interested in securing a full-time
position at Tremont Temple is unclear. There are no further references to him
in the board minutes, and at the trustees meeting in August 1919, when several
names were placed in nomination for rabbi, Lichtenstein's was not among
them.[24]

On only one occasion after his departure was Clifton Harby Levy formally
invited to return to Tremont Temple. In August 1920, the Board of Trustees
voted to invite him to take part in the dedication service of the newly expanded
building, to be held in early September. As there seems to be no extant program
of the service, it is unclear what part he played, although minutes from the
trustees meeting held two days before suggest that only the officers and trustees would take part in the opening processional. Even then, it seems, Levy,
and presumably the newly hired rabbi, Dr. David Klein, had to take a back seat
to the lay leadership of the congregation.[25]

In 1921, members of a Jewish New Thought group in New York City—the same group that eventually approached Morris Lichtenstein—approached Levy about becoming their leader. While he seems to have considered their invitation seriously, he made it clear that he could not serve them "unless they were ready to cooperate with the physician openly and fully."[26] Apparently they were not willing to accept his conditions. Subsequently, Levy continued to devote himself to writing, while at the same time participating in various communal and professional activities. By December 1924, several members of the New Thought group that had first approached him in 1921 called on him again.[27] According to Clifton Harby Levy, "after working under another leader for some time they . . . [had become] dissatisfied with his methods, and withdrew from his organization."[28] There appears to be no extant record of the names of those who approached him. Yet it is fairly certain that among them was Bertha Strauss, identified by Levy as "one of the pioneers of the Jewish Science movement." (In tribute to her, the center's handbook, *The Helpful Manual*, was published by the "Bertha Strauss Memorial Publication Fund," established by the center after her death in early 1927 to propagate the teachings of Jewish Science throughout the world.)

Levy never identified the leader with whom the group in question had been dissatisfied. Yet there can be little doubt that it was Morris Lichtenstein. Since it was at Bertha Strauss's invitation that Lichtenstein became leader of the society that she and Lucia Nola Levy had founded, and since there are no extant records of their having created another Jewish New Thought group prior to 1924, we can safely assume that it was to Lichtenstein that Levy was referring. Surprisingly, however, Bertha Strauss's name does not appear on the Society of Jewish Science's certificate of incorporation dated August 1922. Nor does her name appear in any of the Society of Jewish Science's early publications, including the *Jewish Science Interpreter*. Lichtenstein never referred to her by name; she apparently was not one of the society's practitioners and never wrote a testimonial to the *Interpreter*, as did several members. Thus, there is no evidence that Strauss ever joined Lichtenstein's Society of Jewish Science. Extant records contain no reference to internal dissension. Apparently, however, less than two and a half years after Morris Lichtenstein formally had assumed sole leadership of what had once been the Society of Jewish New Thought, a few of the group's early members were ready to create an organization of their own. That they asked Clifton Harby Levy to lead them indicates both their willingness to make greater use of physicians and Levy's willingness to place greater emphasis than he had previously on inner, divine healing.

Two other women who may well have approached Levy in 1921 and 1924 were a Mrs. Jacobs and Lucia Nola Levy.[29] In the January 1928 issue of *Jewish Life*, Levy announced that henceforth, February 26th should be celebrated by the Centre of Jewish Science as Founder's Day, in honor of the woman who helped develop Jewish Science as a movement, Bertha Strauss. He chose the date to mark the anniversary of Strauss's death, exactly one year earlier. Yet in discussing the establishment of Founder's Day, Levy also mentioned the work of Mrs. Jacobs and Lucia N. Levy, both deceased, who, together with Bertha Strauss, paved the way for the creation of Jewish Science as a movement. While Levy did not explicitly identify Strauss, Jacobs, and L. N. Levy as the group that had approached him, his insistence that the center acknowledge the pioneering work of all three women does imply that the "sacrifices which they made in the interest of the type of Judaism in which they believed"[30] included instigating the creation of the Centre of Jewish Science.

In the fourth issue of *Jewish Life*, published in June 1925, Levy credited Alfred Geiger Moses with having introduced the name and basic concepts of Jewish Science. His was the first attempt, he wrote, to help Jews understand that Judaism possesses all one needs to find help and healing from God "and that no Jew or Jewess need go to any other faith for spiritual sustenance." Comparing Jewish Science to the early nineteenth-century Wissenschaft des Judenthums—an intellectual movement that sought to bring the tools of modern scholarship to bear in objectively studying the origins and development of Judaism and, as such, helped give shape and legitimation to Reform Judaism— Levy maintained that his "little movement" was a "very modest attempt to go several steps further than either the scholars of Germany or Rabbi Moses in developing in full detail a system usable in any Synagogue, no matter what its doctrinal position, by which all of its adherents might secure as complete a spiritual apprehension of their faith as possible."[31]

As the foregoing quotation reveals, Levy identified Jewish Science as a Jewish religious movement. At the same time, however, he insisted that his movement was neither a "cult" nor an attempt to create a new branch of Judaism that would further divide the American Jewish community. Perhaps for that reason, he did not identify himself as leader of Jewish Science but rather as "Rabbi Clifton Harby Levy, Lecturer and Teacher." He maintained that his intent was to form a "spiritual bond of union, which would aid in the spiritual uniting of all Jews." To do so, he initiated a number of specific measures.

First, he developed a thirty-week course in spiritual culture to be used by individuals, lay-led groups, and rabbis within their congregations. Initially created for the Centre of Jewish Science in New York, the class lessons were mailed out five at a time, so that they could be studied without interruption, no matter how far away from New York City interested individuals or "centers of instruction" might be. Topics included "Love of and for God"; "The Conquest of Fear and Worry"; "Controlling the Body by the Spirit"; "Driving out Hatred, Anger, and Destructive Thought"; "The Process and Power of Spiritual Prayer"; "How Best to Utilize Silence and Meditation"; and "[Re]vitalizing Religion." Levy hoped that rabbis in particular would make use of his course in spiritual culture, for he believed that it was preferable to have the material taught by a "learned reader" who could add his own interpretations. He assured the American rabbinate that "scholars of various shades of [religious] opinion" who had read the material acknowledged that each of the lessons closely adhered to Jewish tradition. In fact, several rabbis outside of New York had already begun to form spiritual culture study circles of their own. Nonetheless, he realized that there were congregations in which the rabbi did not yet realize the pressing need for spiritual reeducation. In such cases, he advised that lay groups be formed, for if the results achieved at the center in New York were any indication, studying these lessons would have enormous, practical value.[32] As Levy wrote in the October 1925 issue of *Jewish Life,*

> these lessons point the way to the appreciation of Judaism as a vital
> force able to direct all life if we will but understand its infinite
> power. Written in simple language, so that all may understand, they
> carry conviction with them, and will add greatly to the Spiritual
> power of those who master them. As a first course in proving the
> need of utilizing the best results of modern thought for the solution
> of our religious problems, they should prove most interesting and
> valuable.[33]

By April 1926, he reported that several synagogues had begun to offer his lessons in spiritual culture. Singled out for special mention was Reform Temple Beth Emeth in Flatbush, Brooklyn, under the leadership of Rabbi Samuel J. Levinson, whom Levy described as "the earnest leader of that thriving congregation." Apparently, Rabbi Levinson's class grew to over 150 men and women. According to Levy, those enrolled had already begun to discover ways in which Jewish teachings could be applied to the realities and problems of everyday life. He also mentioned that a lay group led by the wife of a rabbi outside of the New York area was making "fine progress with these lessons," thus meeting a real spiritual need within their religious community. Finally, in a brief paragraph toward the end of the April issue, under the headline "Jewish Science Is Advancing," Levy listed a number of other congregations in New York and New Jersey that had recently begun to introduce a course in spiritual culture.[34]

By January 1928, Jewish Science study circles had been created at two other synagogues in New York, and a lay group had been organized in Greenwood, Mississippi.[35] A year later, *Jewish Life* listed the names of Jewish Science circles that either were in existence or in formation. It also provided the names and addresses of the synagogues where already existing circles met; the specific times of meeting; and the name of the rabbi, who presumably facilitated study of Levy's lessons in spiritual culture. All of the congregations mentioned were affiliated with Reform Judaism, although Levy failed to mention this, perhaps to imply that Jewish Science was broader in appeal than, at that point, it apparently was. Rabbis and congregations included Rabbi Samuel Levinson at Beth Emeth, whose study circle had been in existence for almost three years;

Rabbi Louis Gross at Union Temple in the Park Slope area of Brooklyn, a group that had already been meeting for two years[36] (although it disbanded several months later, after Gross and his co-rabbi were abruptly forced to resign from their positions[37]); Rabbi Samuel Peiper at Temple Ahavath Sholom in Brooklyn; Rabbis Simon and Rosenbaum at Washington Hebrew Congregation in Washington, D.C.; and Rabbi Maurice J. Bloom at Temple Beth Jacob in Newburgh, New York. Coincidentally, Bloom later served as rabbi of Tremont Temple. However, his real connection to Clifton Harby Levy, and in all probability the reason he agreed to write the memorial address about him for the 1962 *CCAR Yearbook*, was his own early interest in Levy's concept of Jewish Science.[38]

As a second strategy toward creating a spiritual bond among Jews, Levy advocated studying his lessons together with material presented in *Jewish Life*, since it too dealt with the great problem of guiding Jews toward God and the life of the spirit. Originally about thirty pages in length, later shortened to fifteen, then to eight, each issue included discourses initially delivered by Levy to members of the Centre for Jewish Science. It also included several short pieces Levy specifically wrote for it; letters to the editor; descriptions of activities held at the New York center; and, in some of the early, lengthy volumes, liturgies Levy developed for use in New York that already had proven effective in cultivating greater spiritual awareness. Early issues of *Jewish Life* also included prayers to be recited by children and adults at certain times of the day and brief passages, including biblical verses and quotations by such thinkers as Aristotle, Shakespeare, and Emerson, that readers might find of great practical and spiritual value. Subscriptions to *Jewish Life* initially cost $2.00 a year. One could also purchase a single issue for twenty-five cents. By 1927, with the size of the magazine cut in half, yearly subscriptions were reduced to $1.50 and single issues fifteen cents, while a year later, with the magazine again substantially shortened, the subscription rate became $1.00 for a year, and a single issue cost a dime. Coincidentally or not, Morris Lichtenstein's the *Jewish Science Interpreter* was also eight pages and had been so from its inception in February 1923, and cost $1.00 for a yearly subscription and ten cents for a single issue.

Levy encouraged his readers to tell their friends about *Jewish Life* and maintained that if they sent him their names and addresses he would gladly mail them a few sample copies. He also encouraged readers to keep their copies for reference and ongoing guidance. He made available leatherette binders, imprinted with the name of the magazine, at a reasonable cost. In 1925 he also published twenty-five of his addresses, reprinted from the first six issues of *Jewish Life*, in a hardbound volume entitled *Discourses on Judaism Applied to Living*. A special price of $3.00 was offered to those interested in purchasing both the *Discourses on Judaism* and a year's subscription to *Jewish Life*, normally $2.00 each.

Finally, Levy sought and publicized received rabbinic approval of his magazine. He wrote in the third issue of *Jewish Life:* "The letters which are coming to us daily from Rabbis all over the country are most encouraging, especially as many contain very fine offers of assistance in spreading *Jewish Life*, endorsing the purposes for which we stand." One rabbi wrote of the great need for a Jewish journal devoted to expressing the religious ideals of Judaism. Today's "so-called Jewish Journals, magazines and newspapers," he continued, "tell us what Jews are doing—not what Judaism is accomplishing. They are of course necessary too, but the more power to you for the attempt to give us a spiritually stimulating journal. May the *Jewish Life* magazine prosper!" In addition to sending initial copies of *Jewish Life* to rabbis all over the country, Levy brought the magazine to the attention of the New York Board of Jewish Ministers, of whose executive committee he had once been a member. The board, made up of Orthodox, Conservative, and Reform rabbis, offered Levy what he took to be personal expressions of interest and approval. An official letter sent to Levy from the board's secretary informed him that on March 25, the Executive Committee had noted the creation of Levy's new Jewish Science movement and looked on the movement and his magazine, *Jewish Life*, intended to foster its growth, with great interest. As Levy commented to his readers, "Who could ask more?"[39]

Third, in attempting to help unite American Jews spiritually, Levy advocated the creation of "soul clinics" in synagogues (and churches) throughout the United States. Reiterating his belief that Jewish Science needed to work within the synagogue, not outside it, he envisioned a specific organization or place within the synagogue that would offer treatment for those suffering from afflictions of the soul. While he admitted that theoretically, all houses of worship already offered such aid, in reality, he believed, most were not as direct as they needed to be in offering the kind of practical help that most human beings need at one time or another. He applauded the Roman Catholic Church for providing such daily help through the confessional and sadly noted that, in contrast, most Jewish religious institutions were "diffident about our inner troubles." While he did not propose introducing confessionals into Jewish houses of worship, he nonetheless believed that if Jews knew that they could "go for Soul-aid as they go to a medical clinic for physical treatment, the religious institutions would be serving their people far more effectively than is now possible."[40]

He entreated rabbis to minister to their congregants, encouraging them to discuss with congregants the problems that mentally ailed them, whether worry, fear, anger, lack of self-confidence, nervous exhaustion, or any number of other diseases of the soul. He emphasized the importance of offering concrete advice that drew on the teachings of Judaism in a way that was direct, frank, and helpful. Just as "every physician is more or less a confessor to his patients," so every rabbi needed to help his congregants "by receiving their confidences and suggesting to them the ways by which they may strengthen the power of their Souls." In short, he suggested that congregational rabbis

FIGURE 5.3. Clifton Harby Levy (on left) conducting services at United
Home for Aged and Infirm Hebrews, New York City. Published by
permission of the Jacob Rader Marcus Center of the American Jewish
Archives, Cincinnati, Ohio.

assume as one of their many roles that of pastoral counselor—a suggestion
that was soon taken seriously by leaders of Reform Judaism and, by the late
1940s, by leaders of Reconstructionist and Conservative Judaism as well.

Levy hoped to establish the first soul clinic at the Centre of Jewish Science's
first permanent headquarters, described in *Jewish Life* in January 1926 as oc-
cupying a single floor at 222 West 72nd Street. He envisioned its housing a
small chapel for Sabbath services and quiet, personal reflection; a religious
school; a reading room; and a soul clinic, staffed by "spiritual helpers" who
would be trained by him. Already, he claimed, "our Helpers are volunteering
to take full charge, day by day, so that every afternoon and evening the place
will be open, and some one in authority will be in attendance."[41] In addition,
he hoped that a medical faculty, presumably consisting of medical consultants,
would soon work with the center's spiritual helpers as part of a body clinic, to
be housed in the center's headquarters as well.

For whatever reason, the establishment of a headquarters at West 72nd
Street was short-lived. By the end of 1926, Sunday morning worship services

and Wednesday evening lessons in spiritual culture were once again being held by Levy at the Hotel Ansonia on Broadway between 73rd and 74th Street. For many years, they continued to be held in New York City, either at the Ansonia or at the Hotel Whitehall on Broadway at 100th Street. From its inception, the center held services on Sundays, in all probability to make it clear that what was being offered was a spiritual supplement rather than an alternative to synagogue services on the Sabbath. Levy did not explicitly say whether he envisioned the center as offering both Sunday and Sabbath services at the newly established headquarters, or Sabbath services alone. Yet he did say in *Jewish Life* that there would be Sabbath services, perhaps arousing the kind of rabbinic opposition he very much wanted to avoid. In any case, he soon made it clear that the aim of the Centre of Jewish Science was not to become a synagogue but to create a Jewish Science center in every synagogue that could be persuaded to do so.

Perhaps, he admitted, we may initially have tried to do too much. He thus abandoned plans for a reading room and, as of 1927, the establishment of a religious school and Sabbath worship services. He abandoned the idea of creating a body clinic, pointing instead to the hospitals that had begun to recognize the importance of chaplaincy work and to the efforts of such noted surgeons as Charles Mayo in Rochester, Minnesota, who vigorously supported such efforts. "Perhaps," Levy wrote, "the world will listen when [Dr. Mayo] speaks, for it doubts the suggestion of the religionist who is supposed to be speaking in his own cause [presumably Levy himself], but may believe the ultra-scientist who is still so broad of view that he welcomes and asks for the help of religion."[42] With rabbinic assistance, Levy also planned public gatherings at which physicians and rabbis discussed the importance of cooperation between medical and spiritual science. Perhaps the most successful was a gathering of over five hundred men and women at Union Temple in Brooklyn on May 7, 1928. The majority of those in attendance were members of Levy's Centre for Jewish Science and of the Jewish Science circles of Union Temple and Temple Beth Emeth. Short presentations were given by Rabbis Levy, Gross, and Levenson and by lay representatives of each of the Jewish Science groups, and there were lengthier addresses by two physicians, Dr. Roth and Dr. Sands, who, according to Levy, pleaded "for the cooperation of religion in their work." When "physicians tell us, as they did on that evening," he later wrote, "that the patients who come to them with many ailments are suffering chiefly from lack of a real, deep-seated faith," it helps those previously disinterested in Jewish Science to appreciate all that "the religionist can do to help the scientist in his labor for the betterment of human life." Such gatherings, he believed, served two important purposes: first, they helped legitimate Jewish Science as a Jewish movement that possessed "great vitalizing power for the rank and file" of American Jewry, and second, by underscoring the extent to which Jewish Science was capable of breathing new life into Judaism as currently understood, further stimulated "those who have begun to see the light to make still more strenuous efforts for the expansion of the [Jewish Science] movement."[43]

Similarly, Levy apparently abandoned the idea of creating self-designated soul clinics. Instead, he held conferences and spoke at synagogues throughout the United States about the importance of congregations opening a Jewish Science center or study circles of their own. He assured his listeners that doing so would not interfere in any way with their customs and rituals but would deepen the spiritual power of both congregants and rabbis. How many people came to hear him is unclear. However, in the October 1928 issue of *Jewish Life*, Levy announced that a "remarkable meeting" had taken place in Washington on October 1 at which "a thousand men and women gathered to learn of Jewish Science and listened for two hours!"[44] Presumably, Levy spoke at Washington Hebrew Congregation, where rabbinic support and congregational interest soon led to the formation of a Jewish Science study circle. Given the fact that no presenters' names were mentioned, one can conclude that the meeting was run by Levy himself.

To those who were apprehensive about the term *Jewish Science*, Levy admitted that he frequently had been asked: "[If Jewish Science is nothing more than] a movement within our religion . . . why not simply use the word Judaism since you are teaching only that which comes out of the Faith?"[45] His answer was that "Judaism" in and of itself did not sufficiently convey the particular emphasis of Jewish Science, which was the cooperation of Judaism with science and the importance of faith, or spiritual culture, as capable of developing the best and highest attainable by human beings. By November 1926, Levy spoke of the Centre of Jewish Science as having formed its own, ideal congregation called the Temple of Jewish Faith. Levy identified the congregation as a faithful band of men, women, and children "willing and eager to attain the most complete possible knowledge of the [Jewish] Faith," ready to do all that they believed to be right, and working "heartily and fearlessly" as a harmonious whole for the common good and greater advancement of humanity.

Its Sunday morning service drew on a brief liturgy comprised of traditional prayers and those presumably written by Levy himself. Printed in pamphlet form by the Temple of Jewish Faith, its cover identified the liturgy simply as "Jewish Science Service," with Clifton Harby Levy as rabbi. The service included an opening meditation; two affirmative prayers to be read in unison that focused on God as source of love, truth, wisdom, and health; and a silent petitionary prayer asking for help in filling the worshipers' souls with the consciousness of divinity. It also included the recitation of the Sh'ma, the central prayer of communal, Jewish worship (in Hebrew transliteration and English translation); a weekly lesson and discourse by Clifton Harby Levy; several musical solos; a closing prayer, similar in content and length to the "Adoration" of the Reform movement's *Union Prayer Book;* and a transliterated Kaddish, the mourners' prayer. On the back cover were three hymns taken from Reform Judaism's *Union Hymnal*, to be sung by a soloist or the congregation.

Like *The Helpful Manual*, the textbook of the Centre of Jewish Science published in 1927, the "Jewish Science Service" provides great insight into the ways in which Clifton Harby Levy, as Jewish Science lecturer, teacher, and rabbi, rearticulated, but did not substantially change, the substance of his earlier theological visions. Unlike Morris Lichtenstein, whose understanding of God as a divine mind was of a power or process within human beings, Levy more frequently drew on traditional images of divinity. Through prayers of petition and affirmation, his service described God as possessing great love, truth, righteousness, and eternal wisdom. God was envisioned as a great helper, capable of providing the necessary aid to face life's trials and struggles, and the source of all blessing, to whom "we lift our souls above all earthly things, that we may find our better selves in contemplation of Thy mercy, love, and goodness." The service also placed special focus on God as healer, emphasizing in its prayers of affirmation that the remedy for the world's needs lie within each of us, for as we grow up in godliness, we ourselves become righteousness, truth, and love. Yet, as *The Helpful Manual* also asserted, Levy believed that it was not by tapping into the divine mind within us that we become godly. Rather, it was by asking God to have pity on those who suffer and by receiving God's aid and everlasting mercy that one could "think and work with God, to help all who are in need."

Like Levy's "Jewish Science Service," *The Helpful Manual* (initially published in English and soon afterward in Yiddish translation) similarly emphasizes the role of God as healer. Here, too, in short prayers included throughout the manual, God is petitioned as an almighty savior who gives us courage and heals our pain. Prayer is described as "talking with God" so as to find the "fine reverence for Him and for His Universe," of which we are but a tiny particle. It is feeling near to God, rather than feeling one's own natural power, that drives out doubt and fear. Like Morris Lichtenstein's *Jewish Science and Health*, *The Helpful Manual* emphasizes the importance of God-consciousness. Yet, unlike Lichtenstein, who understood God-consciousness to be the recognition of divinity within us, Levy equated God-consciousness with a growing awareness of God's presence both within us and in the world. By placing ourselves in greater harmony with God and God's laws, we can feel "the inpouring [*sic*] of His power," rather than discover, as Morris Lichtenstein claimed, that divine power is something we, as human beings, naturally possess. *The Helpful Manual*, like Levy's lessons in spiritual culture, emphasizes the importance of contemplating, concentrating on, and consecrating ourselves to God. In contrast, Lichtenstein's *Jewish Science and Health*, like his other works, emphasizes discovering our very essence, namely, the divine mind within us that is the "spring which yields [us] life and vitality" and directs our everyday growth.[46]

The theological differences between Clifton Harby Levy and Morris Lichtenstein are readily apparent in examining a concept central to both: that of
divine love. To Levy and Lichtenstein, love was a divine attribute out of which
all existence was created. Healing the sick, strengthening the weak, cheering
the depressed, and giving hope to the despondent were all expressions of
God's love, although Levy's and Lichtenstein's understandings of the nature
of this love and the way it was made manifest considerably differed. To Lichtenstein, love was a divine gift that inherently resided within each of us. A
power akin to human power, it enabled us to enhance our happiness and to
better cultivate feelings of joy, tenderness, and sympathy for others. While he
believed that we must consciously call this divine gift into action, he insisted
that love is not a virtue one must struggle to acquire, for if all of God's powers
and attributes are inherent within us, divine love resides in the "depths of the
human heart," "knitted" or "intertwined with the very roots of . . . [our] being."
Consequently, Lichtenstein wrote, human beings were born to love one another, "for love wells from the Divine Mind, and the Mind knows no discrim-
ination, and has no favorites. . . . What is true of the Divine Mind is also true
of the attributes . . . [that God] expresses through [us]." What began as a chapter
on divine love thus ended as a chapter on the importance of human love, and
in particular, the human love of humanity. To Lichtenstein, such love was an
"all-embracing and transcendent expression" of our divinity, for "it knows no
barriers among races, creeds or social classes and gives to others, seeking
nothing in return." It is only through such love, he concluded, "that the salvation of mankind will be attained . . . [for] it is only when [human beings] . . .
learn to give full expression to the divine power of love within them, that
bloodshed will cease and war will be no more."[47]

To Clifton Harby Levy, loving others was an expression of our godliness,
our ability, in other words, to be like God. Unlike Lichtenstein, who saw this
expression as an inherent divine gift that needed to be cultivated, Levy understood it to be a learned, and often difficult, human achievement. For Levy, its
impetus lay not in the realization that divine and human power were akin to
one another but rather in the acknowledgment that the love of God, and consequently the love of others, was an obligation incumbent on each and every
Jew. Perhaps the theological differences here seem minor. After all, both Levy
and Lichtenstein understood divine love to be an attribute of God that can, and
should, be cultivated and expressed by human beings. Yet, as both undoubtedly
would have agreed, responding to a divine voice, even if it is heard as an inner
voice, is not the same as discovering the divine power that one innately possesses. For Levy, loving God was a precondition for becoming godly, while for
Lichtenstein, one didn't become godly but rather recognized the essential unity
of what is human and what is divine. Moreover, Levy equated the human love
for God with a higher ethical awareness, echoing classical Reform Judaism's
notion of the "God idea." On the other hand, Levy believed that God was more

than an ethical ideal. He wrote of trusting in God and feeling certain of the aid of "Almighty God, ever loving to those who seek Him in spirit and in truth."[48]

As in his addresses and articles, Levy reiterated in *The Helpful Manual* his belief in the importance of medical science. Indeed, the aim of the manual, as asserted on its first page, was to show those in need how "higher scientific living, applied to Judaism," could secure the well-being of mind, body, and spirit, "bringing health, happiness and lasting success to every one who [used] it diligently."[49] At the same time, however, the manual made it clear that physicians were helpers of God, for God was the only true healer. For that reason, Levy refused to identify those who completed his lessons in spiritual culture as practitioners or healers. Instead he identified them as spiritual helpers, a term not explicitly used but suggested in *The Helpful Manual* in the section entitled "Bringing Health to the Home." In answer to the question "How can one help when someone close to us lies in bed, filled with pain?" Levy answered:

> If we are cheerful, hopeful, confident, and spread the atmosphere of trust and courage around us we are working in accord with the law of God and helping the sufferer back to health and happiness. . . . We can help by aiding the sufferer in ceasing to think too much about the pain from which he or she shrinks. Cheerful conversation about impersonal matters [and] directing the interest to affairs of [the] moment . . . help to bring the patient back to a normal, happy state of mind, which must aid in restoring the calm and self-control which they need. . . . Flowers, music, all things cheerful and delightful, help, if the patient can be led to manifest interest, and even subconsciously the effect of music is felt.

Following these suggestions was a petitionary prayer, apparently written by Levy, to be recited by those seeking to help restore others to health. Addressed to God, it began: "Thou Healer of men, Who giveth strength to all, help Thou our loved one, who lingers in pain. Let Thine assurance of help and healing be fulfilled, giving courage, strength and peace to all who suffer." Asking God to bless "us all Thy children," it expressed the hope that God "teach us how best to help one another."[50]

While most of the prayers contained in *The Helpful Manual* were those of petition, Levy ended the manual with a lengthy prayer identified as "Our Affirmation." Primarily written in the first person singular, this prayer includes no mention of the benefits of medical science and only mentions in passing one's moral obligations to others. Rather, like the two shorter affirmations that lay at the heart of Morris Lichtenstein's Society of Jewish Science, its primary focus is on the personal attainment of happiness and health. Again, like Lichtenstein's affirmations, it assumes, but does not explicitly maintain, that both can be found, and indeed, for the individual reciting the affirmation, have already been found, within the context of the Jewish religion. "We affirm," it says,

> That God is Love, Truth and Wisdom supreme, and that I am made in His image.
> The more I know of God, the more I consider His Love and Mercy, the better may I conform my soul to His Truth and Wisdom, and the more fully may I live the Righteous life, through my completer [sic] Consciousness of God. . . .
> In me lies the remedy for the world's need; for I am Love, Truth, and Righteousness as I grow up in Godliness.
> I put away all fear, all anxious thoughts, all lack of soul or body, for God is my Aid and Helper and I need none else.
> With will attuned to the Will of God, I hearken to His Voice daily and hourly, and find truth, leading to higher thought and truer confidence. I think and work with God to help all who are in need, in weakness of body or soul. . . .
> Through Thine aid are we guarded from error of thought and deed, and by Thy mercy wilt Thou accept our words and each endeavor for the better understanding and the nobler life. Thou art our Hope, our Strength, Healer of all our woes, Savior from all sorrow.[51]

As rabbi of the Temple of Jewish Faith and titular head of the Centre of Jewish Science, Clifton Harby Levy saw as his primary goal the reawakening of Jewish religious consciousness through what he called spiritual reeducation. While his theological ideas may have been less consistent and at times less coherent than those of Morris Lichtenstein,[52] his understanding of Jewish Science ultimately had greater influence on the Reform movement, if not on American Jewry as a whole. By seeking the approval of other rabbis and working in cooperation with them, Levy helped promote the role of rabbi as pastoral counselor and the synagogue as a center of individual and communal spiritual revitalization. As a popularizer of Jewish Science, he succeeded in creating educational programs that other rabbis adapted for their synagogues; spoke to Reform congregations throughout the country on Jewish Science teachings; and held conferences at which physicians and rabbis gave major addresses advocating the collaboration of religion and medical science. He also raised greater rabbinic awareness, especially among Reform rabbis, of ways in which the insights of modern psychology could be beneficial in determining the goals and nature of contemporary Jewish religious practice.

In October 1925, at the annual meeting of the CCAR, Levy urged his Reform colleagues to take seriously modern scientific insights concerning the relationship between physical and spiritual disorders. "When the physicians come to us and tell us," he said, "that many of our ills are the result of mental causes, that if we teach our people to think right they will be right, is it not our duty to teach them?"[53] A year later, in an essay on Jewish Science in the *Jewish Institute Quarterly*, a journal published by rabbinical students at Stephen Wise's Jewish Institute of Religion, Levy similarly maintained that

> the greatest broad minded physicians freely admit that ninety per cent of the "cures" which they bring about are due to confidence in them and their medicines. . . . The Rabbi can help the patient to become an active coadjutor of the physicians, not simply a passive, unresponsive subject for experimentation. Psychologists state unhesitatingly that the patient who works with the physician, who . . . is filled with courage, and not depressed by endless fears, is already on the high road to recovery.[54]

By 1925, in order to see whether Reform synagogues might "devise a more adequate program and technique for coping with mental and physical infirmities" in keeping with its understanding of Judaism, the CCAR adopted a resolution empowering its executive board to appoint a committee that would look into the matter. Rabbis Louis Witt of St. Louis, Missouri, and Samuel Koch of Seattle, Washington, the authors of the resolution, explicitly said that their motivation in bringing forth this request was to discover whether "certain movements initiated within the synagogue," that is, Jewish Science, were compatible with the synagogue's "spirit and traditions."

The report of the nine-person Committee on the Relationship of the Synagogue to Mental and Physical Healing was presented by Louis Witt, chair of the committee, at the CCAR meeting held in June 1927 in Cape May, New Jersey. While he said that he found the term *Jewish Science* regrettable, as it was not indigenous to Judaism and suggested a "separatistic [sic] tendency," Witt asked conference members to approach the mind cure movement with a "positive and receptive, albeit critical and cautious approach." Following a personal presentation of the issues discussed by the committee, he offered its three recommendations for debate and endorsement. The first was that the conference recognize that

> Spiritual Healing, defined as the utilization of indwelling divine energies for the healing of the ailments of the body and mind, practiced by a technique that . . . [draws on faith and prayer and autosuggestion to set these] energies into action, and limited by the fullest cooperation with medical science as well as by the necessity of the conscious cooperation of the beneficiaries—is in keeping with the principles and traditions of Judaism.

Second, the committee recommended that the conference instruct its executive board to encourage and if possible help facilitate the publication of booklets on prayer and consolation to be used in Reform congregations. Third, the committee asked the CCAR to "respectfully petition" the authorities of HUC to consider creating a course in spiritual healing, "with a view to furnishing its graduates with a more adequate background and technique for their ministry of service."[55] The report was signed by five committee members, with the other four dissenting. Among the dissenters was Louis I. Newman, then the rabbi of Temple Emanu-El in San Francisco,[56] who published a scathing critique of Jewish Science several months later. In it he described the writings of Alfred Geiger Moses, Morris Lichtenstein, and Clifton Harby Levy as "inconsequential and absurd" and emphatically asserted that "the synagogue should strictly avoid any embroilment in the quackeries of religiotherapy."[57]

Critics of Jewish Science who discussed the recommendations at the Cape May meeting were far more tactful. While the recommendations were overwhelmingly rejected by a vote of 46 to 13, they were recommitted for further study. Alfred Geiger Moses apparently was not present at the meeting, but Morris Lichtenstein was and, during the lively discussion that ensued, spoke out at length about the success and importance of his work and, more generally, about the efficacy of affirmative prayer. Also featured at the conference was a special symposium on spiritual healing in which three major papers were presented. Dr. Bernard Glueck, in a presentation entitled "The Clinical Significance of Religion," provided evidence that one's religious outlook can greatly influence one's health. The rabbi and scholar Hyman G. Enelow, of Temple Emanu-El in New York City, a member of the aforementioned committee, one of the five in favor of its recommendations, and president of the CCAR from 1927 to 1929, delivered a paper entitled "A Note on Spiritual Healing in Jewish Tradition." Levy later reprinted these papers in *Jewish Life*. The third speaker was Levy himself, who gave a presentation entitled "Jewish Science—A System and a Method."

Clifton Harby Levy later cited this address as one of his life's most significant achievements. Published in both the 1927 *CCAR Yearbook* and in pamphlet form, it subsequently reached a wider audience, and for many years after it kept alive within the Reform rabbinate issues concerning medical/religious cooperation. In his address, Levy argued that the mind affects the body, just as the body affects the mind. Thus, rabbis and doctors needed to work with one another. As spiritual helpers trained to help those who suffered "in the most tactful and efficacious way," rabbis needed to lead them "to re-establish self-control, and the correct attitude toward life, with all of its difficulties." Our task, he said, "is to aid the sufferer to harmonize himself within, so that he may come into harmony with God." He believed that the advantages of doing so were many. According to Levy, rabbis identified with Jewish Science would discover congregants seeking their guidance as never before, would find themselves to be better tempered, and would start delivering sermons that were purposeful and concrete rather than abstract and academic. Finally, he predicted, new life would be breathed into a congregation once it awakened to the idea "that Judaism can be and should be applied every day and all day long to the fine art of living."[58]

At the 1928 CCAR meeting, the Committee on the Relation of the Synagogue to Mental and Physical Healing submitted its revised and final report. Its endorsement of spiritual healing was far more circumscribed. Indeed, the report contained few, if any, statements with which conference members would disagree. While saying that the synagogue could help cure spiritual ailments and, indirectly, physical ailments as well, the report also asserted Judaism opposed "every cult or creed that . . . maintains that there is no healing agency except the direct and unmediated action of the divine, on the human mind." Medical science, in other words, was an "efficacious way of healing the ailments of both the body and the spirit and is interpreted as itself an instrumentality of the divine will." The call for encouraging the publication of booklets on prayer and consolation was replaced with the more general hope that "a richer consolatory literature" be created, and the specific request for a course on spiritual healing was deleted in favor of the hope that rabbis receive "a more adequate training in the potency of the religious attitude, and function in a way that will make God real and close" to every Jew.[59]

Although the committee's revised report offered no recommendations on which conference members were to vote, members of the CCAR continued to discuss and debate issues that it raised throughout the late 1920s and 1930s. The discussion was kept alive by rabbis sympathetic to the work of Morris Lichtenstein and Clifton Harby Levy, including Louis Witt, who, soon after the 1928 CCAR convention, published his own book of consolatory literature under the auspices of the Reform movement's Union of American Hebrew Congregations. In addition, in 1936 the prominent rabbi S. Felix Mendelsohn of Chicago published a collection of his sermons that viewed spiritual healing within the contexts of Judaism and modern science under the title *Mental Healing in Judaism: Its Relationship to Christian Science and Psychoanalysis.* This discussion was also kept alive by Clifton Harby Levy, who remained an active member of the CCAR until his death in 1962. In 1937, in no small measure due to the efforts of Levy and others, HUC offered its first elective course on pastoral psychology as part of the rabbinical school curriculum. It was not taught by a rabbi but by the psychiatrist Abraham Franzblau, who evinced a strong interest in Judaism.[60] Since then, HUC, which in 1950 merged with Stephen Wise's Jewish Institute of Religion (becoming HUC-JIR), has required a course in pastoral counseling as part of its cluster of courses in professional development within the rabbinic program on its campuses in New York City, Los Angeles, and Cincinnati. More recently, other rabbinic institutions have introduced similar courses of study.

FIGURE 5.4. Portrait of Clifton Harby Levy at age 94 (c. 1961). Published by permission of the Jacob Rader Marcus Center of the American Jewish Archives, Cincinnati, Ohio.

In 1990, HUC-JIR established a rigorous postgraduate program leading to a doctor of ministry (D. Min.) degree in pastoral counseling. Open to ordained rabbis, priests, and ministers, it is cosponsored with the Postgraduate Center for Mental Health in New York City. Levy undoubtedly would have been enthusiastic about such a program, as it provides religious leaders with the kind of spiritual training he believed was so desperately needed. He also would have applauded the creation of the recently endowed Blaustein Center for Pastoral Counseling at HUC-JIR's New York City campus, established in partnership with the CCAR and in cooperation with the faculty of the Postgraduate Center for Mental Health. Under the auspices of the center, rabbinical students at HUC-JIR in New York are now able to establish a solid academic grounding in psychodynamics and pastoral counseling and are required to complete a number of supervised clinical experiences, including pastoral counseling internships and one year of congregational work as prerequisites for ordination. Under the leadership of the Reform rabbi Dr. Nancy Wiener, field work coordinator and instructor of pastoral care and counseling at HUC-JIR, the center is also working to create approaches toward teaching counseling skills that ground field experience reflections in Jewish texts, while providing the opportunity for clinical supervisors, most of whom are rabbis with certification in chaplaincy or counseling, to meet regularly for supervision as a means of enhancing their own professional development.

Though based in New York, the Blaustein Center has already begun to assist in the future development of counseling and chaplaincy programs at HUC-JIR's other U.S. campuses. Currently, rabbinical students on the Cincinnati campus enroll in the experientially based Clinical Pastoral Education (CPE) program, a national educational system that teaches pastoral care in a health-care setting. Students in Los Angeles, in addition to required fieldwork and related courses, are now able to take advantage of the programs and conferences sponsored by the recently endowed Kalsman Institute on Judaism and Health. Under the direction of Dr. William Cutter, professor of education and Hebrew language and literature and instructor in chaplaincy, who has described the Kalsman Institute as "founded on the principle that health and healing are a fundamental part of the Jewish religious experience," it aims to become the "intellectual center of the healing movement," by facilitating serious theological and philosophical discussion on Judaism and health; sponsoring national conferences on medical ethics; involving itself in advocacy around issues concerning health care provisions and ethics; training future religious and professional leaders to competently deal with these issues; and, at the same time, working to "develop new models of training for the broader field of health care in the United States."[61]

All of these efforts address needs that Clifton Harby Levy first identified and brought before the leadership of the CCAR in the mid-1920s. To him, they reflected the ideas and concerns of Jewish Science, including its insistence on the cooperation of religion and science, the role of rabbi as pastoral counselor, and the transformation of the synagogue into a spiritual center dedicated to the spiritual reeducation of American Jews. Yet Levy—unlike Morris Lichtenstein, who devoted almost all of his adult life to Jewish Science—maintained other interests. He continually wrote on a variety of subjects, and by the 1930s, developed a particularly strong interest in Jewish art. He published two books on the subject, including *The Bible in Art* (1936), and served as art editor of the Universal Jewish Encyclopedia. He also served on the boards of the Boy Scouts of America and the Society for the Prevention of Cruelty to Children. A member of B'nai Brith, he helped to establish the New York Association of Reform Rabbis, served as president of the New York Board of Rabbis, and was a founding member of the anti-Zionist American Council for Judaism.[62] While Levy formally listed the one-page *Ten Constructive Commandments* (1934) as his last published work on Jewish Science, Levy continued to serve as the Centre of Jewish Science's "teacher and lecturer" for the remainder of his life. Although he insisted that he was not the center's leader, it apparently ceased to exist after Levy's death.

6

Tehilla Lichtenstein and the Society of Jewish Science

In 1938, when Tehilla Lichtenstein succeeded her husband, Morris Lichtenstein, as leader of the Society of Jewish Science, she never dreamed that she would continue to serve as the society's spiritual leader for almost thirty-five years. Nor did she dream that in so doing she would become the first American Jewish woman to serve as leader of an ongoing Jewish congregation. Yet from 1938 until shortly before her death in 1973, in more than five hundred sermons and in scores of essays, lectures, and radio broadcasts, Tehilla Lichtenstein articulated and shared with thousands of men, women, and children her own understanding of Jewish Science.

From the society's inception, Tehilla worked closely with her husband to help ensure the society's success. Leadership firmly remained in Morris Lichtenstein's hands until his death in November 1938. Yet during the early years of the society's existence, Tehilla Lichtenstein served as principal of the religious school and editor of the *Jewish Science Interpreter*. In addition to the sermons by Morris Lichtenstein that appeared in the *Interpreter,* Lichtenstein edited and typed her husband's other writings, including his books, making whatever grammatical and literary changes she felt were necessary. The limited yet important role she initially assumed is not surprising in light of the fact that in 1922, the same year that her husband transformed and incorporated Bertha Strauss and Lucia Nola Levy's Society of Jewish New Thought into the Society of Jewish Science, Tehilla Lichtenstein gave birth to their first son, Immanuel, and in 1927 to their second son, Michael.

Despite her active interest in the society, Tehilla Lichtenstein was not listed as one of its seventeen original members. This number was comprised of nine men, including Morris Lichtenstein, and seven women, at least two of whom, Mathilda Jacobs and Rosa Morgenstern, were married and joined with their respective husbands, Hyman and Sidney.[1] Tehilla Lichtenstein, then, could have become a founding member had she chosen to do so. Instead, it seems that from 1922 to 1938, Tehilla Lichtenstein was busy raising her children, keeping a Jewish home, for example, preparing for the Sabbath and holidays and following the laws of *kashrut* (dietary laws), albeit in a modified form[2]; and helping her husband with what she considered to be his work. She also spent considerable time with other family members, including her parents, who died only a few years before Morris Lichtenstein; her sister, Esther Taubenhaus (1884–?), who lived in Texas but spent summers with Tehilla; and the sister to whom she was closest emotionally and geographically, Tamar de Sola Pool (1890–1981), the wife of David de Sola Pool (1885–1970), the rabbi of the Spanish and Portuguese synagogue, Shearith Israel, in New York City.[3]

Tehilla Lichtenstein was born in Jerusalem on May 16, 1893, to Chava (Eva) Cohen (1862–1931) and the Orthodox Rabbi Chaim Hirschensohn (1856–1935), an educator, community leader, and prolific scholar.[4] Chava's father was the prominent rabbi Sha'ul Benjamin ha-Cohen; Chaim's was the widely respected rabbi Jacob Mordecai (c.1806–1888). Both of Tehilla's grandfathers were renowned scholars and Roshei Yeshivah (heads of a school of higher Jewish learning). Jacob Mordecai established yeshivot in Pinsk, Safed, and Jerusalem, while Sha'ul Benjamin, who, like the Hirschensohns, had come from Russia to Palestine via Germany, established a yeshivah named *Etz Chaim* (Tree of Life) in Jerusalem, shortly after his arrival in 1858. On his mother's side, Chaim Hirschensohn was closely related to the Gaon of Vilna and Rabbi Isaac Elchanan Spector and apparently, on his father's side, to some of the great Hasidic rabbis.[5] Tehilla later claimed that she was a "direct descendent of a line of rabbis unbroken for five hundred years."[6]

Jacob Mordecai initially was reluctant to ask his wife, Sara Bayla (1816–1905), to leave her hometown of Pinsk, where she was active in numerous charities and managed the affairs of her father, a Talmudic scholar and philanthropist. Yet he apparently was haunted by a recurrent dream that he establish a yeshivah in Palestine. On what became a one-year journey, they spent time in several countries, including Germany and Austria, where they met with such rabbinic and Jewish communal leaders as Samson Raphael Hirsch, the founder of modern Orthodoxy, and the Rothschilds of Frankfurt. They also were given an audience with Chancellor Otto von Bismarck, from whom they received German citizenship, as well as the surname Hirschensohn.[7] While his parents were from Russia and he was born in Palestine, Chaim Hirschensohn consequently was known among Jews in Jerusalem as the "German rabbi."[8]

In 1848, Jacob Mordecai and Sara Bayla settled in Safed, at that time a nearly deserted town in need of religious revival. With funding provided by a number of German Jewish leaders, as well as by Sara Bayla, who apparently was wealthy in her own right, they built a yeshivah. They also built a non-Hasidic synagogue, the first in Safed, for although Jacob Mordecai came from a prominent Hasidic family, Sara Bayla's family were ardent *mitnaggdim* (Hasidic opponents). Unable to secure a minyan (prayer quorum of ten adult Jewish males),

> Sara Bayla went from village to village to search for Jews, offering them free dwellings and whatever food could be obtained from the outside. She ground the wheat which the Arabs brought from afar, baked the bread in an outdoor oven, raised some chickens, kept some goats, planted a vegetable garden on hard mountain soil—all this so that scholars might go on learning. . . . [Sara Bayla] gathered blankets from everywhere, and continually traveled on burros to Arab settlements to obtain food.[9]

She learned to speak Arabic and established good relations with their Arab neighbors. According to Tehilla's eldest sister, Nima Adlerblum (1883–1974), unlike others who, "profiting from the Turkish homestead law, had come to [Safed to] claim the deserted ruins as their own," her legendary grandmother "refused to take possession of any land until, after prolonged search, she had located the Arab owner and paid him for it."[10]

Fifteen years later, at the urging of the German rabbi Eliahu Guttmacher, the Hirschensohns moved to Jerusalem with their young sons, Yitzhak and Chaim, in order to establish a yeshivah that would heal the breach within the Ashkenazi community and help settle some of the grave disputes among Ashkenazim and Sephardim. Theirs became the first yeshivah in Jerusalem that were open to Ashkenazic and Sephardic Jews. Among the Ashkenazim, both Hasidim and Mitnaggim were welcomed as students and encouraged to study together. Under Sara Bayla's supervision, cottages were built for visiting scholars. Also built were a large dining room; a deep cistern for water; a courtyard, which became a reception area for greeting visitors as well as a place for debate and discussion; and several terraces situated on a large hill, facing the Mosque of Omar, near the Western Wall. According to Tehilla's sister, Nima, who was raised in Jerusalem, her grandparents' aim was to revitalize Jerusalem as a "religious center from which sufficient strength would radiate to combat the dangers abroad." Consequently, European rabbis as well as local people "from among Hassidim, Mitnaggdim, Sephardim, Yemenites, outstanding scholars as well as humble people," joined in discussions and debates at what became known as "Sara Bayla's courtyard."[11]

The marriage of Chaim Hirschensohn to Chava Cohen was arranged by their parents, who knew one another even before the Hirschensohns moved to Jerusalem. On the day of their wedding, Chava apparently was twelve and Chaim eighteen. Chaim Hirschensohn, who became a rabbi, like his father and his older brother, Yitzhak, assumed leadership of the yeshivah after his father's death. He continued to write on such subjects as biblical and rabbinic interpretation; kabbalah (Jewish mysticism); medieval Jewish philosophy (according to Nima, he was regarded as the foremost authority in Jerusalem on Maimonides' *Guide for the Perplexed* and other medieval classics); ethics; Jewish education; and *halakhah* (Jewish law) and the modern world. Describing the Torah as "my life, my way of living, and the source of life of our whole people,"[12] he believed that there was no essential conflict between halakhah and modernity. He thus attempted to transform the yeshivah his parents had created into a modern seminary focusing on the study of rabbinic texts as well as on ways halakhic laws and regulations could be applied to changing conditions. Nima later wrote:

> Finding a new interpretation, deducing legitimate corollaries from some Talmudic point, gave him immeasurable joy. Even the younger children of our household, Tamar and Tehilla, coming back from school and noticing his beaming face, would guess the cause and exultingly exclaim, "Avi ['my father,' the name that Chaim Hirschensohn's children, and later their spouses, always called him], *hidashta hiddush hayom* (You have discovered something new today)." With twinkling eyes, and an expression of delight to which no pleasure could compare, he said in his usual, gentle voice, "*ken, barukh ha-Shem, hidashti eizeh hiddush* (Yes, thank God, I have added something new)."[13]

Chaim and Chava Hirschensohn raised five children: Nima (Nechama); Esther, who was a year younger than Nima; Benjamin, Tamar, and Rachel Tehilla, who later identified herself simply as Tehilla. They also had a daughter, Hinde Raisl, who died when she was five years old, sometime before Nima was born, and a son named after Chaim's father, Jacob Mordecai, who was born before Benjamin and died at the age of three months.[14] Both Chaim and Chava (affectionately called Immi, "my mother," by her children and later, their spouses) enthusiastically worked with Eliezer Ben Yehuda to revive Hebrew as a modern language. Although, unlike Ben Yehuda, they did not wish to transform Hebrew into a purely secular language, they remained close associates and friends, believing, as Ben Yehuda did, in the importance of spreading Hebrew as a spoken language. Like him, they insisted on speaking Hebrew to their children. It seems that the Hirschensohns continued to do so even after they settled in the United States.[15]

This association with Ben Yehuda, and Chaim Hirschensohn's subsequent attempt to transform the German-funded Laemel Schule in Jerusalem into a model Hebrew-speaking school, was one of many reasons why Hirschensohn eventually was put in *cherem* (excommunicated) by a Bet Din (rabbinic court of three), an action that was apparently instigated by the Brisker Rov, a leading

Hasidic rabbi. It also led the German sponsors of the school, who were un-willing to substitute Hebrew for German in secular subjects, to withdraw their support.[16] While Chaim Hirschensohn was not excommunicated until the early 1890s, the Laemel Schule, founded by Hirschensohn in 1887 as a modern Orthodox institution that offered classes in both religious and secular subjects, aroused opposition from its inception.[17] Indeed, it created such antagonism within the Orthodox community that Hirschensohn endured numerous con-frontations with traditionally religious rabbis opposed to the introduction of secular study. On at least one occasion, stones were hurled through the school's windows.

No longer able to earn a living, unwilling to accept charity from abroad, and feeling spiritually exiled within his own community, Chaim Hirschensohn felt that he and his family had no choice but to leave. It was not, then, as some scholars erroneously have claimed, that Hirschensohn left Palestine at the in-sistence of the Turkish government, in apparent opposition to his Zionist ac-tivities.[18] Rather, it was opposition within the Jewish community itself that caused his departure. The family settled in Constantinople (now Istanbul), which, like Palestine, was part of the Ottoman Empire. Hirschensohn contin-ued the educational work he had begun in Jerusalem, establishing a modern Orthodox day school that flourished even after he left for the United States. He also took advantage of the educational opportunities available to his chil-dren through the Alliance Française. Believing that a secular, European edu-cation was an important precondition of full acceptance in the modern world, Hirschensohn immediately enrolled Nima, Esther, and Benjamin at the Alli-ance Française, and eventually Tamar and Tehilla as well. By 1901, Nima and Esther were studying at the Alliance in Paris, Benjamin in Jerusalem; during the next twelve years, up through Tamar's year at the University of Paris fol-lowing her college graduation, the five siblings, including Tehilla, frequently wrote to one another in French.

Financial insecurity continued to plague the Hirschensohns during their years in Turkey, and by 1903, Chaim, Chava, Tamar, and Tehilla left for Frank-furt, Germany, en route to the United States. Nima and Esther left the Alliance to join them there, while Benjamin and Esther's future husband, Jacob Tau-benhaus (1884–1937), at Chaim Hirschensohn's urging, had gone to America a year earlier to complete their studies and find jobs (Benjamin as an engineer, Jacob as an agronomist) not available to Jews in Europe. Before the Hirschen-sohns left Frankfurt, however, Chaim received a letter from Constantinople informing him that he had been chosen as a delegate for the sixth Zionist congress in Basel, Switzerland. A guest card was enclosed for Chava, enabling her to accompany him. Tehilla and Tamar, at least, went with him as well. It was at this meeting that Theodor Herzl proposed accepting the British offer of Uganda as the location of a future Jewish state. In protest, the eastern Eu-ropean delegates stormed out of the meeting. According to family legend, it was at that moment that Chaim Hirschensohn encouraged ten-year-old Tehilla and thirteen-year-old Tamar to move to the front of the room and sing the Zionist anthem, "Hatikvah." Apparently their singing was so beautiful and so moving that the delegates, who were on their way out the door, turned, walked back, and took their seats. While there are no historical records to document this event, the legend still persists within the family that it was Tehilla and Tamar who saved the Zionist movement![19]

After accepting Baron William Rothschild's invitation to study Talmud with him for several months in London, which presumably offered much-needed financial remuneration, Chaim Hirschensohn sailed for New York. His wife and daughters soon followed. Not long after, he became rabbi and *nasi* (head of the Orthodox community) of Hoboken, New Jersey, a position he held for over thirty years. He served as spiritual leader of several small Orthodox congregations in the Hoboken area and spent a great deal of time on his scholarly writings, most of which eventually were published with the financial support of his congregations.

Like her sisters, Tehilla Lichtenstein received an adequate Jewish education. Clearly, she could read and write Hebrew, had familiarity with Jewish liturgy, and studied the Bible and later rabbinic texts, presumably including those written by her father. She also was well versed in the daily practice of halakhah, especially in regard to those obligations incumbent on women. Given the fact that her mother married at twelve, the type of religious education Chava Hirschensohn received, before and after her wedding, is instructive. According to Tehilla Lichtenstein's sister, Nima Adlerblum, as soon as their mother got married,

> Avi engaged an instructor to enlarge her Hebrew knowledge. She studied the weekly *parashah* (portion of the Torah) assiduously, which gave her occasion to exchange *divre Torah* (matters of learning) at Sabbath meals. She had been taught by her father that talks on the Sabbath are to be devoted to holy matters only. On Fridays, [her mother-in-law] Sara Bayla would wake her early to complete the *parashah* and receive instructions on the *kugel* [noodle pudding].[20]

With variations, the religious education of Tehilla and her sisters was undoubtedly much the same.

In addition, an ardent Zionism, that indelibly shaped their understanding of Jewishness and Judaism, was central to their formal and informal religious education. Ivria Sackton, Nima Adlerblum's daughter, was told by her mother that one important consequence of Chaim Hirschensohn leaving Jerusalem was that in securing a Western education for his children, and especially in deciding to send his oldest children, Nima and Esther, to Paris, "he substituted Zionism for the observance of *halakhah*. Because his children were going to the secular schools of the Alliance Française, he did not expect them to keep the Sabbath. He believed in freedom of choice (a nineteenth-century idea). He took away their freedom to accept or rebel."[21] As his children got older, it seems that Chaim Hirschensohn gave each of them great freedom in terms of religious observance and equated Jewish loyalty with speaking Hebrew and with Zionism. According to his son-in-law, Rabbi David de Sola Pool, he "used the Balfour Declaration as the base line for his calendar, dating the years from the time it was signed."[22] Yet while he consciously permitted his children to cease being Orthodox, he encouraged them, both by words and by example, to regard Jewish learning as a lifelong pursuit. Its aim, he insisted, was not to make the present a "static copy of the past" but rather to let the past and present creatively function together as a means of finding the proper meaning of the Torah and of life itself.

While Tehilla Lichtenstein may have received a better Jewish education than many Orthodox women of her generation, it paled in comparison to the secular education she and her sisters received. As a young girl in Constantinople, in addition to studying such basic subjects as arithmetic and reading, she studied drawing and drama, both of which she showed a particular talent for and apparently enjoyed immensely. She continued with her study of modern Hebrew and became quite adept in German, and especially French, which she continued to study through college. A letter she wrote in 1913, two years before her graduation from Hunter College, indicates that she also studied Greek and Latin, American literature, English literature, history of education, and art history. She received a bachelor of arts degree in 1915, with a major in classics and a minor in English. With the wholehearted encouragement of her parents, she subsequently enrolled in graduate school, receiving a master's degree from Columbia University in English literature. She continued to study at Columbia, working toward her doctorate in English literature until 1920, when she married Morris Lichtenstein, whom she apparently had met at the university the previous year.

Supportive of her husband's work, and especially his great dedication to Jewish Science, she did all she could to help him. Yet it was never her intention to succeed him as the society's leader. In fact, both Tehilla and Morris Lichtenstein hoped that one of their sons would some day do so. Yet in November 1938, when Morris Lichtenstein died, Immanuel was only sixteen years old and Michael eleven. Neither had any intention of becoming a rabbi, as their mother undoubtedly realized. Thus, Tehilla Lichtenstein's assumption of religious leader came about by circumstance rather than design. Wanting to maintain control over the beliefs and future direction of the society, Morris Lichtenstein specified in his will that should neither of his sons be willing to succeed him, it was his wish that his wife, Tehilla, take his place. With assurances of cooperation and support from society members, she reluctantly agreed to do so.[23] A copy of Tehilla Lichtenstein's 1939 tax return shows the seriousness with which she approached her new position. Listed as her principal occupation was "spiritual leader."

On Wednesday, November 15, 1938, just over a week after Morris Lichtenstein died, the Board of Directors of the Society of Jewish Science held a special meeting at which Tehilla Lichtenstein formally agreed to fulfill her husband's wishes by becoming its leader. As she wrote in an open letter to members of the society, she saw the great outpouring of love she and her sons had received as both a tribute "to our beloved founder" and "a sign that we are to go forward together in the work which he created, which has enriched and will continue to enrich our people."[24] That she was able to do so took both personal resolve and courage. An ad paying tribute to Morris Lichtenstein in the 1939 *Society of Jewish Science Year Book* reveals the extent to which Tehilla Lichtenstein neither saw herself as cofounder of Jewish Science nor aspired to a leadership position. Amid numerous ads of thanksgiving appears one placed by "R.T.L." Since few, if any, outside of Tehilla's family knew that her full name was Rachel Tehilla, most readers of the *Year Book* had no idea that this lengthy, anonymously placed ad was in all likelihood written by Tehilla Lichtenstein herself. Written in italics, it began by expressing deep gratitude to God for the many blessings showered on the author and the author's friends. It then continued: "One of the greatest of these blessings was my having been guided to Jewish Science, led by so great a teacher as our dearly beloved Rabbi, Dr. Morris Lichtenstein, who will ever be with us in Spirit." It concluded by identifying the author as a "a grateful and ardent Jewish Scientist."[25]

According to the *New York Times*, on Sunday morning, December 4, 1938, over five hundred people came to hear Tehilla Lichtenstein, the society's new spiritual director, help conduct services and deliver her first lecture.[26] While many of those in attendance simply might have come out of curiosity, she continued to attract a loyal following. Among them were the hundreds of men and women who were members of the society under "the rabbi's" tenure, none of whom seemed to have left when Tehilla succeeded him as leader, as well as new members gained through an aggressive membership campaign conducted over the next few decades. Though the total number of members never significantly grew, by the early 1950s those on the society's mailing list, presumably meaning those who subscribed to the *Jewish Science Interpreter*, totaled close to two thousand. Tehilla Lichtenstein's following also included members and nonmembers who went to the 11:00 a.m. service on Sunday mornings while their children attended the Society's Sunday school, open to any Jewish child from the age of six on, who was not affiliated with any other Sunday school, free of charge. Finally, it included what she described as "thousands on thousands" of men and women who, beginning in early September 1943, listened to her radio broadcasts on station WMCA at 9:45 a.m. on Sunday mornings.[27] The broadcasts undoubtedly attracted some in the New York area to the society, and indeed, Tehilla made a point of telling her listeners that the society would be very happy to welcome all who wished to attend their services. The broadcasts prompted many listeners to subscribe to the *Jewish Science Interpreter* and possibly join the society itself.

Her understanding of the historical significance of the role she had undertaken is clear. The entry on Jewish Science that appeared in *The Universal Jewish Encyclopedia*, published in 1942, was signed by Tehilla Lichtenstein. Referring to herself in the third person, she wrote that "Mrs. Lichtenstein [currently] occupies the pulpit which her husband established, being the only woman in the United States holding a rabbinical post."[28] While she never claimed to be a rabbi, and in fact, regularly invited rabbis to officiate at high holy day services, the initial intention of the society's board and of Tehilla herself to find a "member of the rabbinate, as yet unselected," to work with her never came to fruition.[29] Indeed, it was an idea that was never seriously pursued. Undoubtedly, the support that she received, inside and outside of the society, made a difference.

Within the society, members like Rebecca Dreyfuss, to whom Tehilla Lichtenstein continually referred as "Dr. Lichtenstein's foremost disciple," provided great moral and financial assistance.[30] Also offering her unwavering support was Ruth Fauer, an ardent Jewish Scientist who wrote and published in 1935 a pamphlet called *The Influence of Jewish Science in Healing*, which discussed the teachings of Jewish Science and the benefits of joining the society. Trained as a practitioner by Morris Lichtenstein, Ruth Fauer continued to serve as a practitioner and member of the Women's League during and after the thirty-five years in which Tehilla Lichtenstein served as the society's leader. In so doing, she helped practitioners and Women's League members, among others, feel a greater sense of continuity with the past and connection to one another.

Rebecca Dreyfuss remained a member of the society's Board of Directors, honorary chair of the Women's League, and organizer of the annual donor luncheon of the Women's League until her death in November 1942. Briefly succeeding Rebecca Dreyfuss as chair was the practitioner and longtime member Jennie Bloom. Ruth Fauer also assumed this role for a short time, preceded and followed by the indefatigable Anna Moser, who was also a practitioner and longtime member of the society. She, as well as her husband, Samuel Moser, whom Tehilla trained to be a practitioner and who, under her leadership, served for several decades as an officer and member of the board, were deeply devoted both to Morris and Tehilla Lichtenstein and to Jewish Science.

Over the course of the next several decades there were others involved in the Women's League, many of whom also were practitioners and/or members of the Board of Directors, who gave Tehilla Lichtenstein their wholehearted encouragement and support. Most notable was the deeply spiritual, warm, and tireless Sarah Fellerman (1896–1981), who served as president of the Women's League for more than twenty-five years. Until her death, she, like her husband,

Martin, who was also a life member of the Society and a member of its Board of Directors, devoted herself to Jewish Science. At the same time, she actively supported more than twenty other Jewish organizations in the United States and Israel.

Seriously injured in 1943, Sarah Fellerman was in constant pain and on crutches until the late 1970s, when an operation improved her ability to walk, even on occasion without crutches. Yet she never bemoaned or complained about her condition. "Self-pity," she said, "is not my career. I pray to live and to be useful and to be given the courage and strength to carry on for those less fortunate [than me]."[31] In April 1958, the annual donor luncheon was held in her honor. In recognition of this occasion, Tehilla Lichtenstein dedicated the April 1958 issue of the *Jewish Science Interpreter* to Sarah Fellerman, the only individual so honored either before or since.

In the tribute she delivered at the luncheon, Tehilla called her "another Rebecca Dreyfuss in our midst," thanking her for giving Jewish Science "her devotion and service in greater measure than any other of her beloved causes" and for being "closer to us than to all others . . . [and considering us] her dearest friends."[32]

Other longtime Women's League members included Ruby Melker, who formed a small Jewish Science group in Brooklyn; Anne Jacobs, whose husband, Morris, was a member of the society's Board of Directors and a devoted

FIGURE 6.1. Tehilla Lichtenstein and David Snyder, financial secretary, at the home of Sarah Fellerman in Jersey City, New Jersey (early 1960s). Courtesy of Doris Friedman.

friend to both Morris and Tehilla Lichtenstein; and Helen Miller, who for many years chaired the entertainment committee for the Women's League donor luncheon. Gifted with a beautiful singing voice, Miller opened the league's fortieth anniversary luncheon in 1962, held in Tehilla Lichtenstein's honor, by singing the "Star-Spangled Banner" and "Hatikvah." After she was widowed (her husband, Harry Miller, was also a member of the society), she married Julius Harwood (d. 1983), a board member and dedicated Jewish Scientist. Until her death in January 1998 at close to 101 years old, Helen rarely missed a Sunday service. In later years she usually attended with two other longtime members, her sister, Marion Ellis (d. 1996), and their sister-in-law, Sarah Rosenfeld (d. 1987), whose husband, Ben (d. 1982), had also been an active member. As Helen told me in 1983, more than forty-five years after she had joined the society, she "wouldn't miss [Sunday services] for the world," for it set her "thinking right" for the whole week, "and when you think right you do right."[33]

Also providing Tehilla Lichtenstein with emotional support and, as an attorney, with important legal advice, was Harry Hartman, a Jewish Science practitioner, member of the board, and chairman of the society for several years after Tehilla became its leader. He and his wife, Jennie, who was an active member of the Women's League, were devoted to Tehilla Lichtenstein and the

FIGURE 6.2. Left to right, sisters Helen Miller Harwood and Marion Ellis, at Jewish Science services in 1987. Courtesy of the Society of Jewish Science.

work of the society until they died. After he stepped down as chairman of the
society in 1943, Hartman remained on the board as honorary chairman for
almost twenty more years. Succeeding him was Abraham Goldstein (1907–
1998), who first joined the Board of Directors in 1939, immediately after Tehilla
Lichtenstein had become the society's leader.

As a board member and soon after as chairman, he provided Lichtenstein
with invaluable, and very much appreciated, personal and financial support.
His wife, Mildred (1912–), was also an active society member and remains so
today. Among the early activities she was involved in were those sponsored by
the Women's League, including its Rebecca Dreyfuss sewing circle that made
and distributed layettes for infants in need. To a large extent, the Goldsteins
helped the society remain financially solvent both before and since Tehilla
Lichtenstein's death. Initially drawn to Jewish Science because of Morris Lichtenstein, they were greatly devoted to, and continually inspired by, Tehilla Lichtenstein. As the society's chairman, Abe Goldstein was in charge of overseeing
its affairs, looking to secure a permanent space for meeting and worship, and
constantly searching for new ways of propagating the teachings of Jewish Science. In addition, he assisted Lichtenstein during services on Sunday morn-

FIGURE 6.3. Mildred and Abraham Goldstein. Courtesy of Mildred Goldstein.

ings, leading the congregation in prayer while she delivered the lecture around which the service focused. He later succeeded her as leader and remained chairman until his death.

During the years Tehilla Lichtenstein served as leader of the society, other members assisted at worship services. Among those serving as ushers were Fred Schaefer, who for many years was a teacher in the Society's Sunday school, and the orchestra conductor Harry Salter (d. 1984), best known as creator and musical director of the hit radio and television show *Stop the Music*. His wife, Roberta, was the daughter of the popular evangelist Aimee Semple McPherson. During the summer months, which Tehilla Lichtenstein usually spent at Fire Island with her family, Abe Goldstein continued to assist at services. Sam Moser conducted the service while Goldstein read one of her, or the rabbi's, lectures. For a few summers in the early 1950s, Sam Moser conducted services by himself, and on at least one occasion he delivered his own lecture entitled "The Malady of Our Age—Inner-Excitement," while there were some summers when services were conducted by different members, with no preannounced leader. By the late 1950s, Friday night services at the society's newly built synagogue in Old Bethpage, Long Island, were led by Abe Goldstein, often with the assistance of Sam Moser and other Jewish Science members.

From the time she assumed leadership of the Society, Tehilla Lichtenstein encouraged the creation of new groups, especially those that might attract younger members, and got members of the society to chair them. Thus, for example, in March 1939, Marguerite Flegenheimer, who succeeded Tehilla as principal of the society's Sunday school in 1938 and whose husband, Monroe, was a Jewish Science practitioner and longtime member of its Board of Directors, agreed to direct a parents' group that would meet twice a month "to discuss matters of particular interest to parents and children." Also in March 1939, Adele Hartman (Harry and Jennie Hartman's daughter), together with Harry Cohen, agreed to lead the newly organized Teen Age Group of Jewish Science that promised boys and girls "whose age ends with a 'teen" fun and comradeship two Sunday afternoons a month at the True Sisters Building.[34] By October of that year, plans were made to establish a Young Folks' League "for the study of Jewish Science teachings and for the promotion of sociability among the young people of our organization."[35] By the mid-1940s, the aims of these short-lived groups were assumed by the Junior League of Jewish Science, which, with the active support of Tehilla Lichtenstein, met twice a month either at the Jewish Science office in the True Sisters Building or at the home of one of its members. During the years in which this small yet active group existed, its mostly female membership held parties, luncheons, and holiday celebrations; studied Jewish Science together; helped with the Oneg Shabbat (reception) following Friday night services; and helped teach in the Sunday school.

In the early 1940s, after returning to New York from a brief move to

Chicago, where they launched a small Jewish Science group, Anna and Sam Moser helped establish two new groups aimed at promoting greater involvement and sociability among Jewish Science members. Both groups were undoubtedly instigated and certainly encouraged by Tehilla Lichtenstein. Anna Moser created and for many years served as chair of the Women's Business and Professional Group of Jewish Science. By the early 1950s, still under her leadership, this group was renamed the Business and Professional Group of Jewish Science, indicating that membership was also open to men, although it is unclear whether any became members. In early 1944, Sam Moser organized a men's club. Unfortunately, it was as short-lived as the men's club established in 1930 under the leadership of the practitioner and devoted society member Meyer Pesin. By 1950, a new group, the Men's League of Jewish Science, chaired by the board member Harry Lee Goldby, came into being. Like the Women's League and the Business and Professional Group, it identified itself as an auxiliary of the society. Yet despite its claiming to have met with "immediate success, both in the size of its membership, and in the enthusiastic activity with which its programs and projects are being planned," it merged four years later with the Business and Professional Group. With a combined board of directors and officers representing both groups, the renamed Men and Women's Business and Professional Group of Jewish Science met for several years, until the death of Anna Moser.

In 1936, the practitioner and ardent member Tillie Siegel began to hold a brief Jewish Science service, followed by tea and coffee, in her apartment on East 96th Street on Wednesday evenings. With Tehilla Lichtenstein's encouragement, the group, which grew to about twenty in number, continued to meet for over a decade, with younger members like Mildred Goldstein affectionately referring to their hostess and prayer facilitator as "Aunt Tillie."[36] The April 1939 *Interpreter* announced the creation of a Jewish Science reading room in the True Sisters Building, open to the public every Wednesday evening from 8:00 to 10:00 p.m. Henrietta Diamond (1891–1980), a practitioner and ardent member of the society, was in charge and "glad to welcome" anyone interested in the teachings and publications of the Society of Jewish Science.

Within months of her husband's death, Tehilla Lichtenstein began to offer a Jewish Science practitioners' course, which she continued to do throughout her tenure as the society's leader. For many years, she also offered adult education classes, which focused on the Bible, Jewish Science, and Hebrew study. While under her leadership, membership in the society never grew beyond what it had been in the 1930s, through her considerable efforts, the number of practitioners rose dramatically. In the late 1930s and early 1940s, Tehilla Lichtenstein offered weekday afternoon Jewish Science healing sessions at the True Sisters Building, as her husband had done. Yet as early as 1942, a Jewish Science clinic was opened at the True Sisters Building during the weekdays from 10:00 a.m. until noon, with practitioners providing their services. By the end of the 1940s, with almost thirty active practitioners in and outside of the New York area, most of them trained by Tehilla Lichtenstein, those in need of healing or with personal problems for which they sought assistance were encouraged to call the society's office for referral to the authorized practitioner who lived nearest their residence.

During the many years she served as leader of the Society of the Jewish Science, Tehilla Lichtenstein maintained a relatively small yet extremely loyal lay following. Out of a membership that each year numbered approximately five hundred men and women, some, like Rebecca Dreyfuss, Ruth Fauer, Henrietta Diamond, the Hartmans, the Goldsteins, the Fellermans, and the Mosers, were initially drawn to the Society because of Morris Lichtenstein yet quickly came to recognize Tehilla Lichtenstein's own extraordinary gifts as an individual and as a religious leader. Others, who joined in the 1940s or early 1950s and became devoted, lifetime members—like Jack Botwin; Doris Friedman; Fred Schaefer; Harry Leventhal, who served for many years as vice-chairman; Sam Sobel, who became the society's treasurer; and David Snyder, its longtime financial secretary—were attracted both to the teachings of Jewish Science and to the model of leadership displayed by Tehilla Lichtenstein itself.

By all accounts, Tehilla Lichtenstein was warm, sincere, generous, and approachable. She was also extremely bright, dedicated to Jewish Science, charismatic (some described her as angelic), and inspiring. As Jack Botwin (1920–) put it, when she spoke from the pulpit, "you could hear a pin drop. She always spoke, loud and clear (every word a pearl), and you felt as if she were speaking the Word of God to you directly." But off the pulpit, she was someone you could talk to and laugh with. "She was," he continued, "[regular] Tehilla."[37]

For over thirty years, Tehilla Lichtenstein was driven to and from Sunday morning services, first at the True Sisters Building and by the 1950s, at Steinway Hall, by Jack Botwin. She often was driven to other services and meetings by Doris Friedman (birth date unknown–1998), who helped lead services for several decades after Tehilla Lichtenstein's death and edited a collection of Lichtenstein's essays, published in 1989 as a book entitled *Applied Judaism*.

Like Botwin, Friedman was trained by Tehilla Lichtenstein as a practitioner and became a member of the society's Board of Directors. She also became a teacher in the society's Sunday school and, by 1955, its principal. Like Botwin, she continued to view Tehilla Lichtenstein as a spiritual mentor even after her death, drawing on small anecdotes and personal memories that continued to keep the powerful message of Jewish Science alive for her, as they still do for Jack Botwin.

Once, in the early stages of researching this book, I was driving into New York City on a Sunday morning with Doris Friedman to attend Jewish Science services at the Barbizon Plaza Hotel. At that time (the mid-1980s), services were led by the board member Harry Hauptman, with Doris leading the congregation in the visualization and affirmations and reading a sermon by Morris

FIGURE 6.4. Jack Botwin at age 22 (1943). Courtesy of the Society of Jewish Science.

or Tehilla Lichtenstein. There happened to be a good deal of traffic that morning, and as we got closer to Central Park South, where the Barbizon was located, it seemed as if finding a parking space was going to be difficult, if not impossible. I remember turning to Doris, who was driving, and nervously asking, "Do you think we'll find a space?" and in the soft, clear, measured tones with which I remember her always speaking, she said, "Don't worry. We'll find one." "Once," she continued,

> I was driving in New York [City] with Mrs. Lichtenstein. We couldn't find a parking space anywhere [near where we needed to be]. She told me that she was going to visualize an available parking space,

FIGURE 6.5. Doris Friedman, c. 1990. Courtesy of the Society of Jewish Science.

[which she did], and within minutes we had found one. [Since then, whenever] I drive into New York, I visualize an available space, and one is always there.

And, of course, one soon was. What Doris Friedman was describing to me wasn't a miracle. Rather, it was the power of positive thinking, or, as she would have said, the power of positive prayer.

In addition to the support Tehilla Lichtenstein received from members of the Society of Jewish Science, she received considerable encouragement from her family. Tehilla and her eldest sister, Nima, were not particularly close, perhaps because of their ten-year age difference, differences in temperament, frequent geographical separation, and Nima's lack of involvement in Jewish congregational life. Yet their great commitment to Zionism, strong sense of Jewish self-identity, and bonds of family loyalty led to a relationship that was mutually supportive. On the other hand, from the time she was a young child, Tehilla felt extremely close to her sister, Esther, despite the nine-year age gap and later geographical distance between them. She was also close to Esther's husband, the plant pathologist and university professor Jacob Taubenhaus, who became engaged to Esther when Tehilla was only six years old. As early as 1924, Taubenhaus began writing to the *Jewish Science Interpreter*, simply identifying himself as "J. J. Taubenhaus, Professor, Texas State University," describing his interest in Jewish Science and wishing the society the best of success.[38] When Esther was studying in Paris (1901–1903), she and Tehilla frequently wrote to one another. After Esther got married and moved to Delaware (1910–1916), Tehilla enjoyed lengthy summer visits with her and Jacob. Even after Taubenhaus became chief of the division of plant pathology and physiology at the Agricultural and Mechanical College in College Station (later renamed Texas A&M University), the sisters continually kept in touch, sometimes writing long, affectionate letters to one another. In one such letter, written after Jacob's death, Esther thanked Tehilla for the help and moral support that Tehilla had given to her and her daughter, Ruthie.[39] Sharing Tehilla's interest in the religious education and communal involvement of younger generations of Jews, Esther Taubenhaus played a major role in the founding of the Hillel Jewish student association in 1921 at what today is Texas A&M University. During the years in which Tehilla was leader of the society, Esther frequently visited her in New York and for many summers stayed with her at Fire Island, an island off the coast of Long Island, New York.

Only three years apart in age and for the most part raised together, Tehilla and her sister Tamar enjoyed a special friendship that lasted for almost eighty years. Perhaps more than anyone else, it was Tamar de Sola Pool who gave Tehilla the confidence and the courage to take Morris Lichtenstein's place as leader of Jewish Science. By the time Tehilla Lichtenstein assumed this role, Pool had already taken on positions of communal leadership, including, from 1930 to 1935, that of president of the New York chapter of Hadassah, the large and enormously successful women's Zionist Organization of America. From 1936 to 1946, Pool was editor of *Hadassah* magazine and from 1939 to 1943 Hadassah's national president. In addition, as early as 1934, she joined the struggle to help save Jewish children from Nazi persecution. As a member of the governing board of Hadassah's Youth Aliyah and organizer of its speakers' bureau, she worked to rescue and resettle European Jewish children in Palestine. After World War II, she organized training centers that provided children in detention camps in Cyprus with both teachers and textbooks. Tamar de Sola Pool was long active in a number of other Jewish organizations and institutions, including the World Zionist Council; the American Jewish Committee (becoming the first woman member of its executive board); the Sisterhood of Congregation Shearith Israel in New York City, where her husband served as rabbi; and the National Council of Jewish Women, for which she served as director. She was a member of the Board of Governors of Hebrew University in Jerusalem, an honorary chair of the Jewish National Fund, and, in 1948, founder and chair of the Hebrew University Hadassah Medical School building fund. Like her younger sister, Tehilla, Tamar was a woman of deep religious faith who "never lost sight of the meaning of Jewish tradition." Her belief in God, passion for preserving the Jewish past, involvement in synagogue life, and great commitment to Judaism and the Jewish people motivated her to coauthor three books with her husband: *The Haggadah of Passover* (1955); *An Old Faith in the New World* (1955); and *Is There an Answer?* (1966). Marjorie Lehman wrote: "A visionary, an inspirer, as well as an activist . . . when Tamar de Sola Pool passed away on June 1, 1981, the world Jewish community lost one of its most altruistic supporters."[40]

In light of all this, it is perhaps not surprising that during the thirty-five years in which Tehilla Lichtenstein led the Society of Jewish Science, Pool provided her sister with constant emotional and physical support. Letters, photographs, and the reminiscences of those who knew them all testify to the great extent to which Tamar stood by Tehilla's side. Abe Goldstein later credited Pool with having played a crucial role in Tehilla's agreeing to become the Society's leader. While Tehilla Lichtenstein, he said,

> initially did not believe that she should undertake a responsibility that heretofore had never been given to a woman in modern America, Mrs. Pool had quite the opposite view. She insisted that her sister do this, and prayed with her to receive Divine guidance. After several days, when our Board of Directors offered the formal leadership to Tehilla Lichtenstein, she then knew that she must accept it.[41]

During Lichtenstein's first year as leader of the society, Pool attended its Sunday service every week. She continued to do so on a regular basis until Lichtenstein's death. In addition, she unfailingly attended the annual donor luncheon given by the Women's League, as did her husband, Rabbi David de Sola Pool. Invited as honored guests of the society, they both sat on the dais with Tehilla. At the 1962 luncheon, it was Tamar who delivered the formal tribute to her sister. Throughout Lichtenstein's tenure as leader, Tamar spoke at a number of other Jewish Science functions and continued to do so after Tehilla died. Even after they were married, Tamar and Tehilla usually spent summers together, either traveling or, as was more frequently the case, relaxing at Fire

Island. Tehilla regularly rented a place at the Fire Island community of Ocean Beach, where Tamar and David de Sola Pool had long owned a home. In fact, the Pools helped found Fire Island's first Jewish community; its first formal (Orthodox) Sabbath service was led by David de Sola Pool in 1945 in the Pools' living room.⁴²

Married to Tamar in 1917, David de Sola Pool provided his sister-in-law, Tehilla, with the same steadfast support he had long given to his wife. His presence at Jewish Science functions and his public endorsement of the society helped legitimate both Jewish Science as a Jewish movement and Tehilla Lichtenstein as a religious leader. A renowned scholar, author, editor, and translator of seven books of Sephardic Jewish liturgy, the British-born Pool came from a distinguished rabbinic family. After earning his doctorate summa cum laude from the University of Heidelberg in 1907, shortly after his twenty-second birthday,⁴³ he moved to New York City to become rabbi of the Spanish and Portuguese (Orthodox) congregation, Shearith Israel, a position he held for forty-nine years. In 1928 he began what became a more than forty-year tenure as president of the Union of Sephardic Congregations. He also assumed leadership roles in several Zionist organizations, Jewish educational associations, and such Jewish communal organizations as the Jewish Welfare Board (JWB), for many years serving as its national vice president. Deeply committed to meeting the many needs of those serving in the American armed forces, as his work for the JWB clearly revealed, he served as chair of the Chaplains' Committee of the JWB in 1940 and headed the U.S. Committee on Army and Navy Religious Activities from 1940 to 1947.

Both of Tehilla's parents, Chaim and Chava Hirschensohn, died before 1938; had they been alive, they may well have encouraged and supported their daughter's assuming the role of Jewish congregational leader. With the exception of Lily Montagu, the founder and later leader of the Liberal Jewish movement in England and from 1928 to 1963 the lay rabbi of the West Central Liberal Jewish Congregation, a woman assuming such a role was unprecedented. Within the context of Orthodoxy, even modern Orthodoxy, it was, and remains, halakhically questionable, if not prohibited. However, given Chaim Hirschensohn's views concerning religion and modernity, his consequent desire to provide his children with a first-rate secular education, even if that meant their compromising their own religious observance, and his genuine respect for Morris Lichtenstein and, it seems, the society he created, there is no reason to believe that Chaim Hirschensohn would have stood in the way of Tehilla's carrying out her husband's request that she succeed him as the society's leader.

On December 6, 1938, exactly one month after Morris Lichtenstein died and two days after Tehilla Lichtenstein preached her first sermon as society leader, a memorial was held in the auditorium of the True Sisters Building in tribute to Morris Lichtenstein. Among the speakers was David de Sola Pool, who, as the *Jewish Interpreter* noted, "spoke on Rabbi Lichtenstein's personality, revealing with a vibrant emotion which he communicated to his listeners, the many-sidedness and depth and warmth of our Founder's character."[44] This much-valued public support for Tehilla and Morris Lichtenstein continued for over thirty years. David de Sola Pool officiated at the formal unveiling of Morris Lichtenstein's gravestone in 1940, and in all probability at his funeral as well. Like his wife, Tamar, he delivered a formal address at several Women's League luncheons, including those held in the early 1940s, just after Tehilla had assumed leadership of the society, and he gave a formal tribute to Morris Lichtenstein at the 1962 donor luncheon given in Tehilla's honor. On April 22, 1952, Harry Leventhal formally presented Pool with the Jewish Science Humanities Award, annually given by the Men's League of Jewish Science.

David de Sola Pool wasn't the only rabbi who paid tribute to Morris Lichtenstein at the December 1938 service held in his memory. William Rosenblum of Temple Israel and Louis I. Newman of Rodeph Sholom, the spiritual leaders of two of the largest and most prestigious Reform congregations in New York

FIGURE 6.6. Harry Leventhal (standing) about to present Rabbi David de Sola Pool with the 1952 Jewish Science Humanities Award. At dais, left to right: Harry Hartman, unknown, George Weisblum, Harry Leventhal, David de Sola Pool, Tehilla Lichtenstein, Abraham Goldstein, Tamar de Sola Pool, Anna Moser, Samuel Moser, Sarah Fellerman. Courtesy of the Society of Jewish Science.

City, did so as well. William Rosenblum, who apparently often had expressed "interest in and admiration for Jewish Science," spoke about Morris Lichtenstein's contribution to Jewish thought, while Louis Newman, who a decade earlier had been an outspoken critic of Jewish Science, discussed the significance of Morris Lichtenstein's writings. Clearly, the legitimation such tributes afforded Jewish Science encouraged Tehilla Lichtenstein to carry on her husband's work. The invitations she soon received to speak at a number of major Reform and Conservative synagogues in the New York area encouraged her as well.

Throughout her thirty-five years as leader of the Society of Jewish Science, Lichtenstein continued to receive public accolades that spurred her on, as she continued working toward revivifying among American Jews what she considered to be the first requirement of Judaism, namely, "a whole-souled awareness of God's presence and God's goodness" within each person.[45] Among the most notable and personally meaningful tributes she received were those from Eleanor Roosevelt and Golda Meir, then foreign minister of Israel. They were sent on the occasion of the 1962 luncheon given in Tehilla's honor. The letter she received from Eleanor Roosevelt, typed on personal stationery and signed by her, wished "Mrs. Lichtenstein" congratulations and good wishes. "You are performing," she wrote, "an outstanding spiritual service to your fellow man [sic] and I want to commend you for the work you have done and hope that you may be given the strength to carry on for many years to come."[46] On May 10, Golda Meir sent a lengthy telegram addressed to David de Sola Pool, which may well have been read by him at the May 1962 luncheon. It said:

> Pleased to join Tehilla Lichtenstein's many admirers in wishing her well on the occasion of the luncheon in her honor. Her magnificent service for forty years with the Society of Jewish Science should be a beacon to all of us, and especially to Jewish women everywhere, to whom the love of Israel and its spiritual heritage is [the] guiding maxim of their life's labor. I wish Tehilla Lichtenstein many more years of fruitful activity and happy achievement.[47]

Tehilla Lichtenstein's vision of Jewish Science as something that "reveals to the Jew the great treasures that are contained within Judaism"[48] owed a great deal to the writings of Morris Lichtenstein. Indeed, she maintained that her own spiritual vision was both inspired by his writings and in strict accordance with his entire philosophy of life and religion. Identifying herself as his disciple and clearly revering him, she denied that she ever consciously modified his teachings. Yet a comparison of their sermons reveals that the spiritual visions of Morris and Tehilla Lichtenstein were not identical. While most of his sermons focused on what the human mind could know, hers explored the feelings that led to such knowledge. Morris Lichtenstein emphasized the principles or "fundamentals" of Judaism, while Tehilla emphasized the daily experiences through which these fundamentals might be revealed.

Given Jewish Science's claim to be nothing more than applied Judaism, Morris Lichtenstein constantly attempted to show how Jewish teachings might be applied to the realities of life. Yet he primarily spoke in generalities. He spoke about sickness and suffering, "man" and his character, and nature and its observable changes. Tehilla Lichtenstein, on the other hand, used concrete examples, drawn from her experiences or her imagination. Having spent much of her life as a wife and mother, most of her personal examples related to motherhood, marriage, and the home.[49] Thus she described human progress as going forward "like vacuum machines, picking up the bad with the good," and, in discussing human regret, spoke of a young boy's wishing he could relive his party so as to choose strawberry over vanilla ice cream and to sit nearer to the cookies. In giving advice "About Ruling Others and Yielding to Others," she reminded her congregants that just as "there is not much joy in . . . anxious and intense motherhood,"[50] so it is important to know when to leave one's friends alone.

On the joys of motherhood, she maintained that one could learn a great deal from children about the promise of life, the reality of truth, and the beauty of nature. The child "is still unworldly, untainted, uncontaminated by worldly standards and worldly desires and worldly ambitions" and thus "in nearness to God and his distance from worldliness [is wrapped] in the mantle of holiness." It is this quality in the child," she continued, "Which most charms us, which most captivates us, which leaves us breathless, [and] which makes the whole world fall prostrate and worship."[51] She further enjoined her adult audience to actively draw on their own childhood memories. Thus, for example, she asked them to remember:

When we were children, we delighted in the fairy tale of Aladdin and his wonderful lamp, which when he rubbed it, instantly made the all-powerful genie arise at his side. We loved to hear Ali Baba say the words, "open, sesame," which swung wide the gates of the cave and admitted him to a world of untold riches. We have the formula too, which will open up all the riches of life, of living, of power in living. Our formula lies in the realization of the potency that is part of every human soul . . . of the endless tools we each have for making life a good and wonderful thing, of the tremendous bounce and adaptability which is part of the human spirit. . . . If you think yourself weak, incapable, beaten in the face of life, life can easily smash you; but if you think yourself strong, nothing can touch you; for you are strong. . . . The word *strength* can be your open sesame, your Aladdin's lamp, to the power which you must have to meet life as the master, the conqueror, which you were meant to be.[52]

In discussing the importance of self-control, Morris Lichtenstein emphasized self-direction, self-assertion, and self-expression. Tehilla Lichtenstein also preached on this subject, but her sermon, entitled "Controlling the Tongue and the Temper," consciously sought to ask listeners to think of the importance of self-control in terms of their own experience. "If," she asked,

> you had a sharp-bladed instrument in your hands that could cut and slash and wound and mar and even kill, would you hurl it violently at those that you loved? Would you throw it at your children, at your life-companion, at your dearest friends? Your answer to this question is, of course, a horrified "No!" You may even think the question is absurd. But the fact remains that you have such an instrument in your possession, and that [in impatiently or angrily reproaching others] you are hitting out with it every day, hurting and destroying with it those whom you love best in all the world.[53]

In "Cures for Minds in Distress," Tehilla Lichtenstein described the causes of stress. Morris Lichtenstein previously had described its causes as "rapidly multiplying needs [that] have intensified man's struggle for existence to an unlimited degree, and in consequence . . . [have] drained his nervous strength . . . to the point of exhaustion."[54] In contrast, using specific examples and thus creating a more personal, even intimate tone, Tehilla said:

> We are all subject to disappointments and sorrows; they are part of the woof and warp, part of the indicated pattern of life. Who has not known the loss of a loved one? Who has not suffered setbacks in his business? Who has not been shocked by the disloyalty of friends or the suffering of dear ones or a thousand and one ill fortunes that are part of the heritage and destiny of [humankind]?[55]

Tehilla's focus on daily experience led her to emphasize relationships between human beings far more than had her husband. Among those that she explored were relationships between husband and wife; parent and child; siblings; friends; Jews and non-Jews; individuals of different generations, ethnic, or national backgrounds; and relationships among nations. She believed that their significance was twofold. First, such relationships underscored the conviction that as God's children we have a responsibility toward one another, and second, they awakened feelings of love that served as a model of the relationship between the individual and God.

Morris and Tehilla Lichtenstein most frequently spoke of God as the divine mind within and responsible for all of creation. On occasion, they also described God as a benevolent, loving, and accessible father, recognizing that anthropomorphic images of God were often an effective, though not necessary, means of visualizing what one believes to be the qualities of the divine. Thus, for example, because the biblical Psalmist believed in God's "unshaken and unshakable might," he visualized God as a fortress or rock, just as believing in God's ever-abiding care led the Psalmist to see God as a shepherd. In Tehilla's words, "[The Psalmist's] belief in God's Divine attributes enabled him to transmute those abstract attributes into concrete images; he believed and therefore he saw God's goodness, strength and love. . . . believing is seeing and . . . visualizing will bring about that which you [see]."[56] Drawing on her own experiences sometimes led Tehilla Lichtenstein to visualize divine attributes through less traditional, anthropomorphic images. On at least several occasions, for example, she, unlike her husband, envisioned God as a loving and protective mother. Without specifically referring to God as "she," she saw an analogy between running to one's mother and entering into the divine presence. We run to God, she maintained, as we do our mothers, saying, "I need you and want your strength" and as our mothers are there for us so too is "He [sic]." "God," she insisted,

> has given each one of us, whether blessed by the stimulus of poverty
> or blessed by the ease of affluence, the same equalizing gift—our
> mother's love, which is, on this earth, the nearest thing, the closest
> thing, to the love that God bears for [humanity]. Mother's love is of
> the same substance, it is of the same divine fabric, and expresses
> itself in the same boundless way.[57]

In describing God not only as a parent but also as a brother, Tehilla Lichtenstein emphasized the nonhierarchical nature of the human-divine relationship. Using the model of friendship, she enjoined her congregants to help God. Once you do so, she concluded, you will "count with God as much as God counts with you."[58]

Given Tehilla's educational background, it is perhaps not surprising that the Jewish sources on which she drew were limited. She relied most heavily on the words and insights of the Hebrew Bible. Like her husband, she most frequently quoted from the Psalms, especially those that emphasized God's goodness, greatness, compassion, creative power, and direct response to all who turn to God in prayer. Among her favorites was Psalm 139. She never tired of quoting the following "wondrous lines," which she believed were the most beautiful ever written.

> Whither shall I go from Thy spirit?
> Or whither shall I flee from Thy presence?
> If I ascend up into heaven, Thou art there;
> If I make my bed in the netherworld, behold Thou art there.
> If I take the wings of the morning,

> And dwell in the uttermost parts of the sea;
> Even there would Thy hand lead me,
> And thy right hand would hold me.

To her, this psalm reflected "the loftiest, purest, most rational and most intellectual conception of God that . . . [Judaism had] reached in its evolution from almost primitive anthropomorphism to the deepest understanding of God as immanent and omnipresent Divine Mind." As such, it served to remind us:

> Words are not necessary when we are addressing the Divine Mind
> within us . . . [nor are they] necessary when we are invoking the Divine forces within us into action; we need only to declare to God . . .
> that which we wish to have brought about; and this we do with our
> mind . . . [and] imagination. . . . God is in us as He is with us and
> about us, everywhere.[59]

On occasion, Tehilla quoted brief lines or sayings from the Talmud and, in at least one sermon, appreciatively mentioned Maimonides' nonanthropomorphic understanding of God. More frequently, she quoted from the sermons, essays, and books of Morris Lichtenstein, whom she continually referred to as "our founder." Describing him as a "great lover of Judaism" who sought "to revive the religious consciousness of the Jew and to counteract the inroads of Christian Science in our midst,"[60] she dedicated herself to carrying out his work. In November 1939, exactly one year after his death, she and members of the society's Board of Directors declared that the first Sunday of November would henceforth be known as "Founder's Day," to be observed each year in Morris Lichtenstein's memory. Certainly, Tehilla's understanding of God as divine mind came from him, as did her understanding of the divine attributes, the importance of visualization, and the efficacy of affirmative prayer. So too did her recognizing that as important as it was to do well, being well was also a necessity.

Surprisingly, she never mentioned any of Chaim Hirschensohn's writings, including those on the modern revitalization of Judaism, a concern they shared.[61] Yet, like Lily Montagu, who also was raised in an Orthodox home and received a secular education that far surpassed her religious one, Tehilla Lichtenstein often drew on her considerable knowledge of British and American literature. As a former classics major, she drew on the teachings and history of the ancient Greeks and Romans as well.

The British authors whose works she cited included William Shakespeare, William Thackeray, William Wordsworth, William Blake, Percy Bysshe Shelley, Robert Louis Stevenson, Rudyard Kipling, Matthew Arnold, and Robert Browning. Not surprisingly, the American author she referred to most often was Ralph Waldo Emerson. She found particular inspiration in poetry and wrote a number of sermons whose titles and themes were based on poems she had read, including "The Captains and the Kings Depart" (1939), drawing on a line from Kipling's "Recessional," "A Perfect Day" (1941), based on Browning's "Pippa Passes," and "Into the Heart of Things" (1943), whose title paraphrases a line by William Wordsworth, perhaps her favorite poet.

In numerous sermons, Tehilla Lichtenstein contrasted Jewish teachings with those of the ancient Greeks and Romans. Thus, for example, she began a sermon on Jewish education by discussing the very different course of study Plato recommended for the Greek child and what Cato believed every young Roman male ought to know. She contrasted Plato's understanding of the world with that of Judaism and emphasized the markedly different attitudes of Hedonism, Stoicism, and Judaism toward pain and despair. Other sermons looked at ancient Greek philosophy more appreciatively. For example, "Know Thyself," published in the *Jewish Science Interpreter* in July 1939, drew on an idea first articulated by Socrates, whom Tehilla Lichtenstein praised as "the most beloved of men and among the greatest thinkers of all time." Yet even here, Tehilla sought to go beyond Greek thought, insisting that knowledge should not be an end in and of itself but rather an "instrument for better living."[62]

Both Morris and Tehilla Lichtenstein envisioned Judaism as a communal religion. However, while he placed greatest emphasis on revitalizing the religious consciousness of Jews, Tehilla Lichtenstein placed equal emphasis on the revitalization of Judaism. For her, discovering the joys of spirituality and applying Jewish teachings to daily life were essential but not sufficient. She saw the chief aim of Jewish Science as making contemporary Jews better Jews, leading them to love and understand Judaism, making its practice a part of their lives, and finding in Judaism the solution to their problems not only as individuals but also as a people. "Jewish Science," she wrote, "has been accused of being a personal religion, and that is exactly what Jewish Science is." Yet that does not mean that its primary focus is on one's own needs or desires. Rather, it means that Jewish Science personally "identifies itself with every phase of Judaism, with the ritual, with the ethics, with the philosophy, with the national aspirations of Judaism. Nothing that touches the Jew or Jewish life at any point is foreign to the interests of Jewish Science."[63] While it is a purpose of Jewish Science to bring the blessings of Judaism to contemporary Jewry, "it is equally our purpose," she insisted, "to strengthen Judaism, to save it, to preserve it, and transmit it to the generations to come."[64]

To Tehilla Lichtenstein, Jews were more than a religious group. Far more than her husband, she insisted that they were also a people and a nation, inextricably linked by ties of land, language, and history, with memories of a common past and a shared sense of responsibility for the future. Just as our ancestors lived in and for Judaism, so must we, she maintained, find the same beauty and strength in Judaism that they did. Yet our obligation is not only to ensure the future existence of Judaism. It is also to ensure the continuity of the Jewish people. In the summer of 1940, responding to the threat of Nazi Germany, she wrote:

> [For almost four thousand years], the Jews have accepted Judaism as the reason and the condition for their existence. The Jewish people exist for Judaism, and they exist because of Judaism, it is that which assures their eternal existence, and they need have no fear of destruction. God is still with us, His sheltering wings are still about us; He will save us from the wrath of our foes.[65]

In a small pamphlet entitled *What to Tell Your Friend about Jewish Science*, published in 1951, Tehilla Lichtenstein made her belief in the centrality of Jewish peoplehood clear. While Jewish Science is motivated by both love of Judaism and love of the Jewish people, these emotions, she said, are not quite identical to one another. Our love of Judaism is a love "for a great host of human ideals, springing from . . . the truth of the presence and the nature of God," while our love of the Jewish people means that

> we love every man and woman who bears the Jewish name as our own kin, our closest brethren, who have shared with us our blessings and our travail, our glorious spiritual heritage and our heavy burden of suffering, our dangers, and our hopes, our struggles for life, and our service to [both God and] humanity.[66]

While Morris Lichtenstein minimized the concept of divine election, Tehilla stressed the importance of Jews' viewing themselves as members of a chosen people. She insisted that despite what others might believe, "there is no arrogance involved in that claim; only a sense of destiny . . . [and] great responsibility."[67] In sermon after sermon, she made these responsibilities clear. The Jewish holidays afforded her a particularly good opportunity to link the notions of responsibility and peoplehood together. All of the holidays, she maintained, have as their intent and focal interest a consciousness of God and "a recognition of the God of Israel." Their function is "to remind us that God is, that God is good, that the Jewish people are the recipients of His goodness."[68] Rightly recognizing that only the high holy days lack historical connotation—a clear reminder that the other holidays have such connotation—the sermons delivered on other Jewish holidays combined history lessons with spiritual exhortation.

Succoth, the festival of the fall harvest, inspired sermons that stressed the double purpose of the holiday, identified by Tehilla Lichtenstein as "the duty to our people and the duty to God." In building a *sukkah* (hut), as did our ancestors over three thousand years ago, we are reminded, she said, of both a period in Jewish history which we should not forget and "our dependence on

God's goodness, without which we could not exist."[69] In the late 1930s and early 1940s, she spoke about Chanukah as a time of thanking God for having stood beside the Maccabees as they fought against heathenism and iniquity and for continuing to be with the Jewish people in the fight against Nazi terror. Just as God gave our ancestors the confidence to triumph over their Hellenistic oppressors, so, she insisted, God fills us with the hope that Hitler will soon be defeated. Similarly, she maintained that Purim invokes memories of the biblical Haman who unsuccessfully attempted to murder the Jews of Persia, while reinforcing and celebrating Jewish self-identity, even in the face of such modern-day Hamans as Adolph Hitler.

According to Tehilla Lichtenstein, Jews who observe Passover with the attention and earnestness it demands not only fulfill a religious obligation but also are given three gifts. First is an increased awareness of and joy surrounding one's family. In preparing for Passover, those who live under the same roof feel a great sense of "unity in joyful anticipation" of the seder while they are reminded of those relatives not with them, though they wish they could be, on the seder night. The second gift is an intensification of love, loyalty, and sense of oneness with the Jewish people. At the seder,

> we are carrying the heavy loads of brick on our bent and weary
> backs, we are groaning under the burning Egyptian sun, we are
> wincing with pain at the merciless whiplash of the Egyptian over-
> seer. And we, not just our ancestors, now see coming toward us the
> redeemer which God has sent us, we see the radiant figure of Moses
> . . . [we] have been saved, rescued, liberated, from the tyrannous
> Pharaoh, from that cruel bond-master, by the mighty hand of God.

Finally, she said, reinvoking the concept of chosenness, Passover "commemorates the world's emancipation, through the instrumentality of the children of Israel, from idolatry, from spiritual ignorance, from moral and ethical baseness and unawareness."[70]

The dual significance of Shavuot was emphasized in numerous sermons by Tehilla Lichtenstein. Its celebration of the barley harvest was placed in historical and geographical context, recalling an entire people offering "the first and the finest of the fruits of their toil" to God, gratefully declaring in the Jerusalem Temple the many gifts that they had received, both as individuals and as a people. At the same time, the traditional belief that it was on Shavuot that the Torah was given to Moses and, through him, to the Israelites as a whole, also established Shavuot as the celebration of the spiritual birth of the Jewish people. Tehilla reminded her listeners that it was on that day that "God said unto us, through Moses, 'If you will do as I command you, you shall be a peculiar treasure unto me, my chosen people.' And we answered, 'Whatever Thou commandest, that we shall hear and obey.' " Each year, she continued, the festival of Shavuot once again seals in our hearts the pact that we as a people made with God, reminding us that it is the upholding of God's law to which one can attribute the miracle of Jewish survival.[71]

Perhaps one can explain the different levels of importance Tehilla and Morris Lichtenstein attached to the concept of peoplehood as a product of the different decades in which they lectured and wrote. Like most Reform rabbis trained at HUC during the first decades of the twentieth century, Morris Lichtenstein deemphasized the concept of Jewish peoplehood and wrote little about Jews as a past, present, or future nation. On the other hand, by the time Tehilla Lichtenstein became the society's leader, the Reform rabbinate had already begun to place new emphasis on Jews as a people, rethinking its earlier position of anti-Zionism. Indeed, in 1937, four years after Hitler's rise to power, the CCAR formally adopted a new set of guiding principles at its annual meeting in Columbus, Ohio. Subsequently known as the Columbus Platform, it identified Judaism as the "historical religious experience of the Jewish people" and Palestine as a land hallowed by Jewish memories and hopes that held "the promise of renewed life for many of our brethren." We therefore affirm, it continued, that it is the obligation of all Jews "to aid in upbuilding . . . [the land of Israel] as a Jewish homeland by endeavoring to make it not only a haven of refuge for the oppressed but also a center of Jewish culture and spiritual life."[72]

Most likely, however, Tehilla's emphasis on Jewish peoplehood and her ardent Zionism had little if anything to do with changing attitudes within the Reform rabbinate. Nor, in all likelihood, was she significantly influenced by Reform rabbis like Judah Magnes, Abba Hillel Silver, and Stephen Wise, who had been ardent Zionists long before Hitler came to power. Her love of the Jewish people and strong emotional attachment to the land of Israel began in her childhood and continued throughout her life. She, like her parents, siblings, and other members of her family, were born in Palestine and were committed Zionists and strong supporters of the state of Israel. As previously noted, her parents had been close associates of Eliezer Ben Yehuda, and her sister, Tamar de Sola Pool, was the national president of Hadassah, was actively involved in numerous organizations and institutions in Israel, and spent a great deal of time there with her husband. Tehilla's sister, Nima Adlerblum, was a Zionist activist who considered the land of Israel to be the "starting point as well as the final goal of Jewish destiny."[73] Adlerblum shared a warm friendship with Hadassah founder Henrietta Szold, with whom she corresponded about the role of Zionism and Hadassah in contemporary Jewish life. She enjoyed many extended visits to Israel and moved there in 1971 with her husband. She died in Jerusalem in 1974. Tehilla Lichtenstein once wrote that if anyone could prove that there was a single Zionist who loved America less than a non-Zionist she "would be ready to cede the entire Zionist aspiration." However, she doubted that such an individual existed, for she believed that

the heart is infinite in its capacity, and it grows in stature and depth
and beauty and tenderness when it makes room for more love, more
loyalty, [and] more friendship. . . . To say that we can truly love only
one land, or only one group, is like saying that a mother can truly
love only one child. But that is not the way of love. We love . . .
[America] all the more because we love [the land of Israel].[74]

There is no way of knowing whether Morris Lichtenstein would have lectured on contemporary issues, including the plight of European Jewry, had he
lived longer. Given the fact that few members of his family survived the ho-
locaust, he might have broadened his focus beyond the individual to include
communal, national, and international concerns. Yet none of the sermons written by Morris Lichtenstein between 1933, when Hitler became chancellor of
Germany, and early November 1938—three years after the Nuremberg Laws
had stripped German Jews of citizenship and over six months after the annex-
ation of Austria—addressed political or social issues. Instead, the sermons'
focus continued to be the spiritual needs and capabilities of the individual.
They could have been delivered at any time and in any place.

In sharp contrast, Tehilla Lichtenstein often delivered lectures that simultaneously addressed spiritual and political concerns, for she firmly believed
that one's individual life is "interwoven with and . . . interdependent with the
destiny of the world."[75] Even before the outbreak of World War II, she spoke
out against the "maniac[al] voice of Germany's ruler" and the totalitarian governments that supported him, leaving the small countries of Europe "trembling
and cowering" and our "Jewish brethren" both hopeless and helpless.[76] She
discussed at length the rise of anti-Semitism, not only in Europe and South
America but also in the United States, claiming that "eight hundred separate
organizations in this country . . . [were] being subsidized by Germany to spread
the doctrine of anti-democracy and anti-Semitism."[77] In January 1939, hoping
that war might be averted but fearing it soon would become a reality, she made
it clear that the war was not one for Jews to fight alone. Rather, it needed to be
fought by "all who love everything that is good and pure in human striving."
Yet, as she also made clear, the war against fascism needed to be more than a
physical combat. Like all wars, it also needed to be a spiritual combat, using
all of one's strength to obtain a "victory for God." In order to do so, she maintained,

we must fight propaganda with propaganda, we must spread the
truth with the same zeal with which they spread lies, we must be as
fanatic in our support of democracy as they are in their support of
fascism. We must spread the doctrine of love, justice, equality, [and]
righteousness, with the same burning fire that they use to spread
the doctrine of hate, autocracy, power, [and] ruthlessness.[78]

Tehilla Lichtenstein flatly repudiated the belief held by some devout Jews that the persecution of European Jewry was both a divine punishment for contemporary Jewry's lack of religious observance and a divine lesson that might drive nonreligious Jews "back into the fold." God, she insisted, is not punishing the Jewish people or "whipping us back to our faith." Rather, anti-Semitism and Jewish persecution are the result of the human "inability, as yet, to express fully the divine essence which God has instilled within [us]." Once this ability is realized, "anti-Semitism, which is hate, will be supplanted by love, understanding, [and] brotherhood." In the meantime, she continued, Jews need to turn adversities into blessings, as did their ancestors before them. Just as Jews, as a nation, have long had an "inner consciousness of power and destiny" that helped them overcome adversity and "wring beauty from calamity," so can individuals, despite everything, retain their sense of dignity and find within themselves new talents, abilities, and unsuspected strength. Through adversity, one often gains the wisdom to distinguish between true and false values, discovering the importance of "friendship, real love, true simplicity, [and] joyous contact with nature and God."[79]

Sermons written after the war painted a less rosy picture of adversity. While Tehilla Lichtenstein continued to emphasize the ever-present possibility of finding happiness, health, and courage within oneself, she acknowledged that one

> cannot know complete happiness, even through the expression of all his [or her] inner Divine attributes, until another condition is met . . . not by him [or her] alone, but by . . . all humanity. . . . We are as much part of one another as we are part of God . . . and our individual happiness is dependent on the happiness of all humanity. . . . The terrible thing about our enemy . . . which makes him the anti-God, the Satan incarnate, is that he would deny the earth's bounty to some of humanity, and reserve it only for others. That is the greatest crime in the eyes of God; that is the greatest thwarting of God's plan for mankind. That is why we solemnly believe that it must be defeated.[80]

In the meantime, Tehilla cautioned against the temptation to succumb either to fear or despair. Reflecting her deep-seated belief in the power of the mind, she maintained that such defeatism would actually bring about what we most fear, namely, the triumph of fascism and the end of democracy, humaneness, and human dignity. Yet at the same time she insisted that one not ignore or become indifferent to the very real danger with which the entire world was threatened. "Denying things," she said,

> will not make them disappear. . . . The more we refuse to look at reality, and acknowledge it, the more we render ourselves impotent for

the time when we shall be forced to face it, and the more we increase our chances of defeat. . . . [Many people today] would go on
blithely, fiddling while Rome is burning, somehow inwardly convinced that they themselves are immune to the travail that has
seized mankind. They are due, unfortunately, for a rude awakening.
Individual immunity is a condition no longer existent in this world.
. . . If there is one thing that we have learned, or should have
learned, from this stupendous calamity . . . it is that humanity is
one. . . . The experiences of every individual affects the life and fate
and nature of the whole of humanity and humanity affects the life
and fate and nature of each individual within it.[81]

Believing in the power of visualization, she suggested that one way to
respond to world events was by imagining the world as one wished it to be. If,
for example, one wished, as she did, for a world in which the oneness of
humanity was recognized and human relationships consequently were based
on justice, love, and equality, one needed to clearly visualize such a world and
then "go ahead and make it." "We must see success before us," she maintained,
"just as Hitler sees success before him." Yet we need to see success more vividly
and assuredly than he. We may know that the forces of good, which history
repeatedly has shown to be invincible, are on our side. Yet for goodness to
triumph, we must see success and do our share toward achieving it.

Fascism, however, wasn't the only evil against which Tehilla Lichtenstein
preached during the late 1930s and 1940s. In numerous sermons, she forcefully criticized the economic, political, and social injustices that continued to
exist in American society. Contrasting the image of America as a land of liberty,
equality, and justice for all with the harsh realities of American life, she urged
her congregants and readers of the *Jewish Science Interpreter* to do all that they
could to make America the country they ideally visualized it to be. She pointed
out that "corruption, self-seeking, over zealousness for profits, abuses of un-
derlings, and miscarriages of justice, have always been part of the American
scene, not because, but in spite of, democracy" and insisted that it was the duty
of every American to do all he or she could to correct such abuses.[82]

During the depression, she drew a vivid picture of Americans engaged in
what she called "the struggle for sustenance," offering advice on how best to
engage in what admittedly was an uphill battle. To those who were presently
unemployed, she made it clear that bemoaning one's fate, "studying the statistics of unemployment, and figuring that with so many seeking the same job,
you have no possible chance of securing it,"[83] deciding that one's former work
was the only kind of work one was fit for and that certain types of available
jobs were beneath one's dignity, and resigning oneself to relying on the generosity of sympathetic friends and relatives were not the best ways to face
unemployment. Instead, she argued, one first needed to find the courage to

believe and affirm that one was meant to receive, and if sought after *would* receive, some of the Earth's superabundance of bounty. Tehilla then suggested several affirmations that might be recited to help gain such courage. Underlying each was an assertion of faith—in oneself, in others, and in the powers implanted within each of us by God.

Beginning in the 1950s, she publicly advocated greater equality for women within American society generally and, more specifically, within Jewish religious life. In January 1951, a reporter from the *New York Post* asked what she thought of the recent decision by the Reform Temple Beth Israel in Meridian, Mississippi, to have Paula Ackerman succeed her husband, Rabbi William Ackerman, as the congregation's spiritual leader. Her reply was that she saw the decision as indicative of a new and wholesome trend. "For too long," she said, "American women have shared the privileges of the synagogue without sharing in the responsibilities as much as is right. Yet the strength of a synagogue often rests on the women and they should have more leadership."[84] That same year, in a speech delivered at the Conservative Park Avenue Synagogue in New York City, thirty-two years before faculty members of the Jewish Theological Seminary agreed to ordain women as Conservative rabbis, Tehilla Lichtenstein expressed ideas that may be commonplace now but certainly were not then. Arguing that women's subordination was not intrinsic to Judaism but rather developed as a result of "the general low esteem in which women were held in the Middle Ages," she forthrightly declared:

> In answer to the question[s], "Shall women receive religious equality
> in Judaism?" "Shall they be called to the Torah . . . counted in a quo-
> rum . . . ordained if qualified and called to the pulpit?" I naturally
> answer a simple "yes." And I cannot conceive of any valid objection
> to giving women, if they wish it, the same rights and privileges and
> opportunities that are granted to men in this field. It is a long time
> now that the world admits that women are human beings, that they
> have a soul, and some will even grant . . . a mind. If God has be-
> stowed on her equality of spiritual and intellectual endowments,
> how can we take it on ourselves to forbid [a woman] equal standing
> before God?[85]

Like Morris Lichtenstein, Tehilla Lichtenstein gave numerous sermons on how to develop one's own inner powers. Yet by the time she became leader of the Society of Jewish Science, Christian Science was no longer perceived to be a threat to the American Jewish community. Indeed, by the late 1930s, Christian Science's popularity, in general, had long peaked. Thus, the vast majority of Jews who were attracted to Jewish Science during the years in which Tehilla Lichtenstein served as the society's leader were not those who had been previously or were potentially attracted to the teachings of Mary Baker Eddy. Consequently, Tehilla did not need to present the society as a Jewish countermovement to Christian Science, as had both Morris Lichtenstein and Clifton Harby Levy. She continued to be influenced by her husband's teachings and continued to cite his works. Yet by the late 1940s, many of Tehilla Lichtenstein's lectures took a different direction, sharing much in common with those of such inspirational religious leaders as Norman Vincent Peale.

The son of a Methodist preacher, Norman Vincent Peale (1898–1993) was one of the most popular preachers of the twentieth century and one of its most influential religious figures. The pastor of Marble Collegiate Church in New York City from 1932 until 1984, he was the author of forty-six inspirational books, including the bestselling book *The Power of Positive Thinking*, which, since its publication in 1952, has sold almost twenty million copies in forty-one languages. In 1935, Peale launched a weekly radio broadcast on NBC, *The Art of Living*, which remained on the air for a record-breaking fifty-four years. His sermons apparently were mailed to more than 750,000 people a month. In addition, in 1945, he and his wife, Ruth, helped found the enormously popular *Guideposts* magazine as a nondenominational forum for the sharing of inspirational stories. Still in print, with a current circulation of over four million, it now also has an interactive Web site for those who wish to become part of the "*Guideposts* magazine community."

Tehilla Lichtenstein and Norman Vincent Peale were great admirers of one another. According to several members of the Society of Jewish Science, when Jews came to Peale for help, he regularly referred them to her. While some religiously conservative Christians denounced, and still denounce, his teachings as not authentically Christian, he claimed to be teaching "applied Christianity," just as Tehilla and Morris Lichtenstein identified Jewish Science with "applied Judaism." Peale's Christian faith expressed itself in numerous theological statements that continued to differentiate his message from that of Jewish Science. For an example, one need look no further than the daily affirmations each suggested that one recite. Of the two formulated by Morris Lichtenstein, and later expounded on at length by Tehilla, the first affirmation spoke of trusting in God, the English equivalent of the Hebrew concept of emunah (faith), while the second proclaimed one's inner "God consciousness," a phrase initially meant to echo Mary Baker Eddy's notion of "Christ consciousness" but also echoing the biblical, prophetic identification of God as the "still, small voice" within.

In contrast, *The Power of Positive Thinking* begins with the story of a man filled with self-doubt who came to Peale for help and includes the affirmation Peale suggested he recite several times daily in order to overcome his feelings of inferiority. Taken from the New Testament, Philippians 4:13, it says: "I can do all things through Christ which strengthens me." While other religious affirmations appear throughout *The Power of Positive Thinking*, this quote from Philippians appears more often than any other. Indeed, the chapter entitled "I Don't Believe in Defeat" uses this affirmation as its focus. Perhaps tellingly,

FIGURE 6.7. Dr. Norman Vincent Peale. Copyright: *Guideposts*, 66 East
Main St., Pawling, NY 12564.

neither the book nor chapter titles of any of Peale's works reveal the deeply
Christian nature of his work. Yet implicitly if not explicitly, his intended audience was Christian. He advised his readers as follows.

> Every day of your life conceive of yourself as living in partnership
> and companionship with Jesus Christ. If He actually walked by your
> side, would you be worried or afraid? Well, then, say to yourself,
> "He is with me." Affirm aloud, "I am with you always." Then
> change it to say, "He is with me now." Repeat that affirmation three
> times every day.[86]

Yet despite the Christian theological basis of Peale's teaching, reflected in
the specific quotations and texts from the New Testament on which he frequently drew, many of his "how to" sermons and book chapters contained little
theology. Instead, like most of Tehilla Lichtenstein's "how to" addresses, they
primarily offered sound, practical advice. Among that offered in *The Power of
Positive Thinking* was advice on how to relax, cure heartache, get people to like

you, and "expect the best and get it." Other books included chapters on how to become more efficient, successful, happy, calm, and more happily married. These and other topics were similarly addressed by Tehilla Lichtenstein. Among the dozens of "how to" lectures and essays she wrote were those on "How to Achieve Inner Poise"; "How to Achieve Happy Relationships"; "How to Overcome Worry"; "How to Give and How to Take Criticism"; "How to Throw Away Happiness"; "How to Build Up Your Personality"; "How to Become Unpopular"; and "How to Influence Your Enemies and Make Them Your Friends." One of her lengthiest, and most compelling, essays offered advice on how to achieve what Tehilla Lichtenstein understood to be "successful living."

Asserting that the three essential components for a successful life were achievement, joy, and love, she differentiated each from one another. While she believed that "achievement must be impregnated and surrounded by joy, and pursued against a background of love," she maintained that she was not speaking here about the joy derived from achievement or the love for humanity that frequently motivated one's work. Rather, she insisted, "I mean the joy of life, joy in living, apart from one's work, and I mean love for those intimately locked into our own close circle." She therefore admonished her readers:

> Work, strive, achieve something in life; make the utmost of your abilities, of your powers, of your talent; but never lose the power of joy because of a too intense pursuit of your labors; never lose the power to experience joy or to give joy, for that is too great a loss; if necessary, separate yourself from your work for a while . . . let go of it at frequent intervals, so that you can see a world outside your own intense interests. . . . By successful living I mean a life worth living, a life that is really worthwhile.[87]

These words easily could have been written by Morris Lichtenstein. Certainly, they express sentiments he very much shared. Yet Tehilla Lichtenstein didn't just write these words. She actually lived them. Unlike her husband, whose life *became* Jewish Science, Tehilla regularly spent time with her children, family, and friends, not just during the summer, when leadership was assumed by others, but throughout the year. Despite, or perhaps because of, her role as leader of the Society of Jewish Science, Tehilla Lichtenstein practiced what she preached. As her son, Michael, once told me, "everyone who knew her, knew that she enjoyed life." She enjoying traveling, spending time at the beach, eating out, and relaxing with family and friends. When she was in her fifties, she tried skiing because her son, Immanuel, had taken a great interest in it (although apparently she only stood on her skis and watched Immanuel), and in her seventies she taught Michael's then six-year-old daughter how to roll down a hill.[88] "As long as you have concepts of what is good," she once wrote,

you have the time to pursue that good; so long as you have visions
. . . of what you would like to attain, you have time to make those
visions . . . [a] reality; so long as you have attachments, love . . . [and]
admiration for people, you have time to express this love. . . . You
have time; you have all the time in the world.[89]

Taking these words to heart, Tehilla Lichtenstein attained a life of remarkable
balance.

7

Spiritual Healing, Divine Assistance, and Peace of Mind

By her own admission, Tehilla Lichtenstein believed that what all human beings wished for most was peace of mind. In a sermon delivered in 1940, she argued that "when we say we want wealth or security or position or love or countless things, what we really want is . . . surcease from the pain and mental restlessness which the lack of these things is inducing in us." Identifying this desired state as peace of mind, she described it as "a state of inner harmony with life, with outward circumstances, with other human souls about us, with ourselves and with God."[1] In an interview with the writer John Appel, Lichtenstein apparently differentiated between spiritual healing, the focus of her husband's work, and her own focus on God's help in times of trouble.[2] Yet a careful examination of her sermons reveals that for her, spiritual healing and divine assistance were very much related to, indeed inseparable from, one another. Thus, she rhetorically asked:

> If you have faith in God's presence and God's goodness, will you let illness or the thought of illness invade your mind and rob you of peace? Or will you realize that God's goodness has planted in you recuperative powers which will come to the fore and battle your illness and pain and discomfort and restore you to vigor and health? . . . Will you let the fear of want darken your mental horizon and render you helpless in the struggle for sustenance? Or will you know that God's goodness has expressed itself in the abundance with which He has filled the world, and in the capacities and faculties He has given you for reaching out

and obtaining your share of this abundance. . . . We have but to reinstate in our consciousness the Presence of God . . . [sensing] that He
is ever at our side . . . [expressing] Himself through us . . . and we
shall achieve . . . [that which is most] desired.[3]

Within the Jewish community, Tehilla Lichtenstein was not alone in ex-
tolling the virtues of peace of mind. Alfred Geiger Moses, Morris Lichtenstein,
and Clifton Harby Levy had all emphasized its importance, and indeed, Lichtenstein entitled one of his books *Peace of Mind*. Yet by the late 1940s, the
Jewish leader most closely associated with this phrase was the Reform rabbi,
author, and spiritual leader (of Temple Israel in Boston) Joshua Loth Liebman
(1907–1948). His bestselling *Peace of Mind*, published in 1946, made him a
nationally renowned and frequently quoted figure.[4] The book's purpose, as
Liebman made clear, was to draw on and correlate psychological and medical
insights concerning human nature, and the individual's infinite capacity to
change, with enduring religious ideas. In so doing, he placed greatest emphasis
not on the healing power of God but rather the "healing power of psychology."[5]

FIGURE 7.1. Rabbi Joshua Loth Liebman. Published with permission of
the Jacob Rader Marcus Center of the American Jewish Archives,
Cincinnati, Ohio.

Citing the work of Sigmund Freud, Karen Horney, Paul Schilder, Erich Lindemann, and other pioneers in the fields of psychiatry and psychotherapy, Liebman credited the "psychiatric mirror" with revealing those "inward flaws and spiritual crevasses" inherent within every human being.[6] Unlike Tehilla Lichtenstein and other proponents of Jewish Science, he did not believe that one could achieve peace of mind by affirming that one was calm and cheerful, free of envy, hate, and worry. Rather, he wrote, human beings are by their very nature "split souls," and such emotions as worry, fear, loneliness, guilt, and pain are part of human nature. To achieve peace of mind, one must learn how to control, not repress, such emotions. Indeed, he maintained, such emotions are sometimes desirable. Thus, for example:

> Our soldiers and sailors [in the recent World War] experienced fear when they went into combat; that very emotion intensified the flow of adrenalin, mobilized their physical and mental energy and ena- bled them to meet the objective menace with skill and success. A soldier who did not know how to be afraid was a danger to himself and a menace to his comrades.[7]

Similarly, in civilian life, when one experiences physical pain, fear of what it means usually sends one to a doctor, and thus, "the warning signal proves to be our friend rather than our foe." Today, he wrote, "the menace of the atomic bomb" and the fear that atomic energy "will become a weapon of universal destruction rather than a tool of planetary health is a realistic fear" that is indispensable in planning new strategies to master contemporary social and economic dangers. Thus, he concluded, "just as our endocrine glands, which regulate our physical health, require just the proper amount of secretion, so likewise in our mental life a certain degree of anxiety is normal and healthy."[8]

To Liebman, the value of modern psychology was its realistic, complex understanding of human nature, which, when fearlessly confronted and ver- balized, rather than denied or condemned, paved the way toward mature con- science and inner peace. At the same time, he believed that religion was also important in its ability to deepen the quality of life, teach human beings how to treasure one another, and "make life strong and brave and beautiful as our answer to the forces of death."[9] While his book was aimed at a general audi- ence, Liebman singled out the teachings of rabbinic Judaism as having had the wisdom to create almost every outlet for healthy-minded grief currently advocated by psychologists. In contrast, he faulted modern religious liberalism, Jewish as well as Christian, for discouraging emotion, and its rabbis and min- isters for arranging funerals that discouraged tears and "undignified scenes" at the grave and hid the coffin beneath a blanket of flowers and the earth under an artificial carpet of green.[10]

Refusing to sugarcoat reality, Liebman offered a vision that was unremit- tingly honest. Drawing on modern psychologist insights, he firmly believed that healthy-mindedness could only be achieved by unflinchingly examining one's life and one's emotions. Thus, for example, he wrote:

> For those who have lost loved ones during the tragic war, all of the rest of life will be but a half loaf of bread—yet a half loaf eaten in courage and accepted in truth is infinitely better than a moldy whole loaf, green with the decay of self-pity and selfish sorrow which really dishonors the memory of those who lived for our up building and happiness.[11]

Perhaps, he continued, it is "all a matter of compensation." Just as a man who loses use of one of his senses develops another sense organ more keenly, so those who suffer the loss of someone they loved may be forced to develop new interests and friendships. Such efforts won't bring our loved ones back, but we may receive comfort, even healing, knowing that "we never lose the power to weave new patterns of interpersonal relationships and to make ourselves richer, more creative, more interesting, and more interested characters."[12]

Published shortly after the war, Liebman's book responded to an emotional need felt by millions of Americans. As Rebecca Alpert has said, much of this need "was a reaction to the cumulative effects of the depression, World War II and the beginning of the atomic age. That reaction took the form of an increased interest in issues of mental health and individual well-being, and an upsurge of an interest in faith."[13] The theological questions Liebman raised in *Peace of Mind* were complex and timely and remain so today. Among the issues he explored were God's responsibility for evil, the personal or psychological factors underlying atheism, and the nature of and challenges to contemporary religious faith. His answers were straightforward and often biographical. He singled out Mordecai Kaplan's view of divinity as a transnatural power for recently having helped him discover a pathway to God that intellectually satisfied his own "wrestling spirit."[14]

Liebman's ideas gained greater acceptance among members of the Reform rabbinate than did the ideas of Jewish Science for a number of reasons. First, in the 1940s and 1950s, the basic premise of spiritual healing, namely, that the mind affects the body, had not yet gained widespread acceptance within the medical community. In contrast, as the Reform rabbi Jacob Weinstein, Liebman's friend and successor at Kehillath Anshe Maarav (KAM) Temple in Chicago, pointed out, *Peace of Mind* offered "some very concrete examples of the joint field of religion and psychotherapy," which, by 1946, was understood to be scientifically valid. Thus, Weinstein continued, "we need more material of this kind with definite suggestions as to how the Rabbi who may not be trained in psychology can make these findings available to the congregation."[15] Second, as Rebecca Alpert has observed, Liebman was the first rabbi to establish formal contacts with the already well-established Protestant pastoral counseling community. In so doing, he brought to the attention of the Reform rabbinate an adaptable model for the unification of religion and psychiatry.[16] Last, the Columbus Platform of 1937 advocated a return to many of the "emotional elements of religion" that American Reform Judaism previously had discarded. This subsequently led a growing number of Reform rabbis to recognize religion's important psychological function. Rabbi Samuel Cohon (1888–1959), architect of the Columbus Platform, said in *Judaism: A Way of Life*: "When religion functions properly, it helps to overcome the conflicts of personality, to remove inner tensions, to bind together the loose ends of character, and to re-center the unconscious mind on the ideas and ideals, the way and values that make life worthwhile."[17]

Peace of Mind was the first of what became a "whole flood of postwar religious bestsellers."[18] These included works by Norman Vincent Peale, whose first bestselling book was *A Guide to Confident Living*, published in 1948, and Bishop Fulton Sheen, whose *Peace of Soul* was first published in 1949. Among the Reform rabbis who attempted to duplicate Liebman's success were the Los Angeles rabbi Edgar Magnin, author of *How to Live a Richer and Fuller Life* (1951); Louis Binstock, of Temple Sholom in Chicago, author of three self-help books, the first of which was published in 1952[19]; and Hyam Schachtel, the rabbi of Temple Beth Israel in Houston, Texas, who wrote three such books, including *The Real Enjoyment of Living* (1952).[20] In 1958, Rabbi Israel Chodos of Los Angeles's Conservative Sinai Temple published *Count Your Blessings*, which presented facts in support of his thesis that ongoing progress in American society made self-improvement an ever-present possibility.[21] Liebman himself wrote a sequel to *Peace of Mind*, published in 1948; it was titled *Psychiatry and Religion*.

Yet, as much as these books shared in common, they were far from identical. As Fulton Sheen maintained, in an implicit critique of Liebman, "peace of mind" did not necessarily mean the attainment of that "peace of soul" that comes from a return to God and happiness.[22] Sheen attacked Freud and psychoanalysis, while Liebman emphasized the many important insights they provided. Norman Vincent Peale's power of positive thinking offered reassurance through religious faith. In contrast, Binstock's "faith in faith" did not refer to the power of God, the soul, or religion but rather, as Donald Meyer has written, "implied a kind of heroic psychological pulling-oneself-up-by-the-bootstraps operation that was far from mind cure, for in mind cure the belief that the power of faith was in fact the power of divine Supply was aimed precisely to dispute any notion of the adequacy of pure psychological heroics."[23]

On the surface, Tehilla Lichtenstein's message most resembled that of Peale. Yet, unlike Peale, whose faith was grounded in Christianity and whose intended audience, even when not explicitly stated, was clearly Christian, Lichtenstein preached as a Jew to other Jews. Moreover, although helping others overcome self-doubt and attain happiness, health, and other desirable conditions were goals that she and Peale very much shared, her aim went beyond the attainment of individual well-being. Of equal concern was the revitalization of Judaism and the Jewish people. Thus, while many of Lichtenstein's "how to" lectures offered more sound advice than theology and some drew on insights gleaned from modern psychology, she repeatedly returned to religious themes, emphasizing in particular the wisdom of Jewish teachings, the responsibilities of chosenness, and the importance of recognizing that the divine mind can be invoked, evoked, and put into action. She insisted that one's power could be increased, "not from without, but from within; it is not outside of you, it is all there within, an endless fount, and endless capacity, infinite and endless since it is part of God; you have only to recognize it as such and release its outward expression."[24]

At the same time, Tehilla Lichtenstein emphasized the importance of finding a balance between personal and communal religion. As essential as she believed it was to tap one's inner powers, she also felt that "complete spiritual expression" could not be achieved without sharing one's religious thoughts and actions with others. She maintained that

> the practices and ceremonies of communal religion, satisfy a deep
> human instinct . . . to be at one with . . . all others like ourselves, to
> feel part of a meaningful, integrated group in humanity. . . . Any
> holy day, observed with others, any ceremony practiced with the con-
> sciousness that it makes us one with our people, is a fine and elevat-
> ing and essential experience of the Jewish soul.[25]

Tehilla Lichtenstein understood personal religion to be the true goal of Judaism. Yet she believed that the renewal of inner spiritual strength depended on the inspiration, vision, and direction gained through the repeated experiences of communal worship and observance.

In 1953, a New Thought synagogue opened in Los Angeles. Its founder and leader was the businessman S. Pereira Mendes, son of the distinguished English-born rabbi Henry Pereira Mendes (1852–1937), who was one of the founders of the Union of Orthodox Jewish Congregations in America, the Jewish Theological Seminary, and the Federation of American Zionists, as well as the rabbi of Shearith Israel, the Spanish and Portuguese Synagogue in New York City. As the spiritual leader of Shearith Israel, Henry Pereira Mendes was assisted for many years by Rabbi David de Sola Pool, who later became his successor. It is noteworthy that the name S. Pereira Mendes chose for his New Thought synagogue was Shearith Israel as well. Shearith Israel in Los Angeles was established with the help of the Reform movement's Union of American Hebrew Congregations (UAHC) and special assistance from Rabbi Samuel Cohon. Yet, according to Mendes, a Reform rabbi recommended by the UAHC proved to be " 'unprepared and inadequate,' " and consequently he decided to lead the congregation himself.[26] On June 20, 1954, the New Thought Synagogue, as the congregation became known, formally joined the UAHC.[27] It retained membership through 1961. Throughout this period, the congregation remained small and continued to struggle financially. It did, however, employ a cantor and organist, receive occasional help from student rabbis, and establish a religious school.

Mendes and his wife, Reva, first become involved in New Thought through the Institute of Religious Science and Philosophy, founded by Ernest Holmes. Both later credited what they had learned at the institute as leading to Reva's complete recovery from a chronic illness from which she had suffered.[28] In a self-published booklet describing the nature and goals of his synagogue, Mendes maintained that the basic belief on which it rested was that "God can heal as well as hallow." This concept found greatest expression in the congregation's commitment to helping others find the solace of mind, body, and soul that Judaism, as a religious faith, was capable of providing. Reminding readers that the "synagogue should stress its power to help . . . and apply its healing efficacy to the uttermost," Mendes described the New Thought Synagogue as a place for "successful, well-adjusted men and women, happy in their acceptance of self and relation to their fellow beings and to God."[29]

During the nine years of its existence, worship services primarily were conducted from the Reform movement's *Union Prayer Book (UPB)* but added, in Mendes's words, "more Hebrew and more dignity,"[30] in keeping with the Sephardic tradition. In light of the fact that the *UPB* contained little Hebrew, the reference to Shearith Israel's additional use of Hebrew is clear. Less clear, however, is Mendes's claim that his services were more dignified, given the *UPB's* overriding emphasis on congregational decorum. It may be, as John Appel suggests, that Mendes equated dignified worship with the adoption of "more ceremonious ritual,"[31] presumably including the wearing of *kipot* (skullcaps) by male worshipers and possibly *tallitot* (prayer shawls) as well.

The sermons Mendes delivered were usually based on the weekly Torah portion, emphasizing the reality and power of God. Integral to the service was a guided meditation, using the formula prescribed by the New Thought teachers Ernest Holmes and Frederic Bailes, with whom the Mendeses had studied. Services apparently included no other special prayers or designated periods of silence.[32] At other times, however, congregants undoubtedly were encouraged to read Reva Mendes's *Words for Quiet Moments*. Published in 1956, this slim volume offered private meditations that, as Alpert points out, were not substantially different from the affirmations suggested by Jewish Science. The following is one rather lengthy example.

> As I turn to the inner world of consciousness, I know I am entering
> into the Secret Place of the Most High, where I dwell under the
> Shadow of the Almighty. The worries and fears that have seemed so
> real drop from me in the conscious awareness of the Divine Pres-
> ence indwelling [within] me and everywhere present. No longer can

phantoms of fear stake a claim in my thoughts. I am free of all anxiety in the light of the truth of God's Imminence [sic] and unfailing response. Strength and courage are established within me and I know myself equal to all demands made on me in my daily livingness [sic]. In confidence and joy I greet the day, with thanksgiving I accept my good and know that it is now being made manifest.[33]

The congregation was financially strapped from its inception, and its unsuccessful attempt to erect its own building led to its demise in 1962. Yet while it was in existence it regularly held Friday night services and sponsored lectures, study circles, young adult groups, and social organizations.[34]

Coincidentally, it was also in 1962 that the Centre of Jewish Science in New York City closed, following the death of its leader, Clifton Harby Levy. While interest in pastoral psychology and counseling grew among members of the Reform rabbinate,[35] and within the next few decades among increasing numbers of American Jews as a whole, by 1963 Tehilla Lichtenstein's Society of Jewish Science remained the only Jewish organization with particular focus on spiritual healing. Indeed, in 1956, again coincidentally, the same year Reva Mendes published her *Words for Quiet Moments*, the society realized a dream that neither the New Thought Synagogue in Los Angeles nor Levy's Centre of Jewish Science was able to achieve, namely, erecting a temple of its own.

The Society of Jewish Science's building fund was formally established in 1951 under the direction of the members Henry Perlmutter and Sam Sobel. The initial plan was to erect or substantially renovate a building on the east side of Manhattan between 57th Street and 90th Street, but available sites proved too costly. A more affordable property subsequently was found in Forest Hills, Queens, on 71st Avenue and 100th Street, near Continental Avenue.[36] At the annual membership meeting that November, Tehilla Lichtenstein presented a resolution, later voted on and passed, empowering the society's Board of Directors, through Abraham Goldstein as chairman, "to enter into a contract for the purchase of a temple site in Queens County, and to conduct for the time being, Friday evening services in a [vacant] building" presently on the property."[37] Sunday morning services would continue to be held in the True Sisters Building in Manhattan.

There seem to be no extant records concerning future negotiations or payments toward the purchase of the Forest Hills property. However, beginning in January 1955, for approximately two years, services were held in the Forest Hills area. Throughout 1955, except during the summer, Monday evening services and lectures were held at the Forest Hills Inn in Station Square at Continental Avenue—close, if not identical, to the site the society planned to purchase. The following year, these services were moved to Wednesday evenings in the Howard-Johnson building on Queens Boulevard and continued at least through the fall of 1956, and possibly the spring of 1957.[38] As late as October

1953, with plans to purchase the Forest Hills site having fallen through, several members continued to hope that the proposed temple would be built in New York City.[39] Yet while funds were still being raised, property in Manhattan had not been secured, and plans to proceed appeared to be at a stalemate. On October 21, a congregational meeting was held at the initiative of the society's chairman, Abraham Goldstein. He proposed building the synagogue on an acre of land he and his wife owned in Old Bethpage, Long Island, which they would give to the society.[40] Those present unanimously voted to accept the generous offer, although a few members later rescinded their pledges on the grounds that they were not in favor of supporting a synagogue outside of Manhattan.[41]

In November 1953, a groundbreaking ceremony was held on the Goldsteins' property at the northeast corner of Round Swamp Road and Smiths Road in Old Bethpage. Over a year later, in February 1955, Mildred Goldstein, the property's legal owner, granted the deed to the Society of Jewish Science as a contribution from her and her husband.[42] As Abe Goldstein explained to society members in a letter dated October 27, 1953, he and Mildred hoped that, given the area's expanding Jewish population, the erection of a synagogue in Old Bethpage would bring Jewish Science to many Jews previously unaware of its "great teachings." This synagogue, as they envisioned it, was to be "the first of a series to be built in various communities" throughout the United States, as a means of helping Jewish Science "realize its ideal of bringing the blessings of Judaism to all our Jewish people."[43]

The opening of the synagogue was marked with a lengthy service of dedication held on Wednesday, May 30 (Memorial Day), 1956. Perhaps the most significant moment in the society's then thirty-four-year history, the ceremony began at 2:00 p.m. With the congregation assembled in front of the synagogue entrance, a prayer and tribute to Morris Lichtenstein was read, and Immanuel and Michael Lichtenstein unveiled a plaque honoring his work and dedicating the synagogue to the furtherance of his teachings. After a formal procession into the sanctuary, the board members Morris Jacobs, Sam Sobel, Sam Moser, Harry Leventhal, and Oscar Weisblum shared the honor of placing the society's first Torah scroll into the newly built ark, followed by the congregation's reciting in unison, in Hebrew and English, what Reform Judaism often referred to as the watchword of the Jewish faith: "Sh'ma Yisrael, Adonai Eloheinu, Adonai Echad. Hear O Israel, the Lord is our God, the Lord is One." Additional prayers in English and Hebrew were led or recited by society leaders, including a prayer of invocation read by Abe Goldstein, recalling the building of Solomon's Temple in Jerusalem and the Jewish people's dedication to God, and another, read by Harry Leventhal in front of the already lit *ner tamid* (perpetual lamp), that vowed on behalf of the congregation to "keep the light of Israel's faith undimmed, that with ever increasing splendor it may cast its radiance into our lives and into the lives and hearts of all [humanity]."[44]

FIGURE 7.2. Jewish Science synagogue, Old Bethpage, Long Island. Courtesy of the Society of Jewish Science.

The service was highlighted with music, including the congregational sing-ing of hymns and several solos, possibly sung by Helen Miller, and featured a special dedication sermon by the society's leader, Tehilla Lichtenstein. In slow, clear, and measured tones, she maintained that the synagogue was not the society's first house of worship, as they had been worshiping together for many years, but its first "earthly possession," a "precious jewel house" to be theirs for many years to come, should they deserve it. Asking the congregation to rise, she asked God to help make their lives "glorious instruments for good" and, in the light of Jewish faith and the teachings of Morris Lichtenstein, to recognize that God's abode is not above the universe but within it. "All that God created," she insisted, "contains God. And above all, and beyond all, God is contained in the heart and spirit of [every human being]." God, she contin-ued, is contained within each of us in the form of goodness, love, nobility, mind, and power, along with "with the added grace of free will." Yet, if we bring God in with us, "the *Shekhinah*" (divine presence) can also be found in "our little synagogue, which we already love, because it speaks of the labor of so many hands and hearts over so many years." Embracing the religious role she had long ago assumed, she described the society as a "laymen's" congregation representing an important experiment in Jewish life. Within our fellowship, she said, each holds equal rank. Thus, in dedicating ourselves to doing the will of God by fulfilling our obligations to others, ourselves, and the world, each of us "can don the robes of priesthood" and become what God ordained the Jewish people to be.

Only toward the end of her sermon did Tehilla Lichtenstein speak of goals specifically associated with Jewish Science. She emphasized the importance of renewing one's spiritual strength, and becoming a healthy and happy human being, as well as a good Jew. Finally, ending on a personal note, she expressed great appreciation to those who had made it possible for her to serve as the society's leader. She confessed that, given the magnitude of the task, and her own inadequacies, she knew that alone she could do nothing. "But I was not alone," she added. "You were with me [and] together, we've served God and tried to reawaken the religious consciousness of Jews, keeping within Judaism those seeking strength elsewhere." For Tehilla Lichtenstein, spiritual healing was only one of the many aims of Jewish Science. As her dedication sermon made clear, such healing was a basic and essential aspect of Judaism. Yet believing that Judaism's understanding of religious obligation was both personal and communal, she viewed spiritual healing not as an end in itself but rather as a means of summoning such inner divine powers as strength, courage, and optimism to apply Jewish teachings to all of the realities and challenges of contemporary life.

For the next twenty years, the Jewish Science synagogue in Old Bethpage offered Friday night services, conducted by society members, and high holy day services, led by a Reform rabbi and featuring an organist and choir. Seeking to attract young families, a religious school was soon opened, along with classes in the teachings of Jewish Science and preparation for bar (and eventually bat) mitzvah. There were no application or membership dues, although separate fees were established for tickets to high holy day services, religious school attendance, b'nai mitzvah classes, hiring a rabbi to officiate at one's bar or bat mitzvah, and the use of the synagogue for b'nai mitzvah celebrations. The November 2, 1955, edition of the *Farmingdale Post* featured a lengthy article about the Society of Jewish Science and the consecration services to be held that Sunday at the site of its future synagogue on the corner of Round Swamp Road and Claremont Street.[45] It also included an architectural rendering of the outside of the completed one-story, white, wooden structure, with what appeared to be a bell tower atop the middle of the roof and a star of David above it.[46] Six months later, newspaper ads and radio announcements, placards displayed in store and restaurant windows, and prominently placed notices in the *Jewish Science Interpreter* publicized the Sabbath services and weekly lesson held at the synagogue of Jewish Science in Old Bethpage at 8:30 p.m. on Fridays. On the bottom of the placards, in small letters, was the phrase "Health and Happiness Through Judaism," easily read as both a goal and a promise.[47]

Extant records provide no indication as to how many individuals and families took advantage of all that the synagogue provided prior to the fall of 1976, when, according to a synagogue mailing list, adult membership totaled 128. Long before then, however, b'nai mitzvah celebrations, classes, and worship services conducted from the *UPB* began to be offered. For several years after Tehilla Lichtenstein's death in 1973, the society employed the Reform rabbi Edward Miskin to conduct services and hold classes in New York City and Long Island. In July 1976 he was replaced by Rabbi Michael Werthman, whose contract was abruptly terminated less than a year later.[48] According to David Goldstein, the termination had to do with the society's discovery that his claim to have received rabbinic ordination in Israel proved to be false. No extant records confirm or disconfirm either this statement or the belief that Werthman helped instigate a lawsuit filed against the society in 1977 by several Old Bethpage families, demanding greater financial and administrative control over the synagogue and its activities.[49] Settled two years later, apparently in favor of the society's New York office, identified as the "home center," the lawsuit soon led to the closure of the Old Bethpage synagogue and with it the hope that other Jewish Science synagogues would be built in the future.

As the lawsuit made clear, those who sent their children to the synagogue's religious school, paid for bar/bat mitzvah lessons, or financially contributed in other ways, were considered affiliates of the society but not members. To be a member, one needed to pay dues to the home center in Manhattan. Archival records from the late 1950s and 1960s indicate that out of an adult membership that, by then, totaled no more than two hundred, only a handful lived in Long Island. Whether or not they were part of the Long Island synagogue group is unclear. However, leadership firmly remained in the hands of Tehilla Lichtenstein, who preached at Sunday morning services in New York until shortly before her death, and the society's officers and Board of Directors, all of whom attended services in Manhattan and were members of the home center. On at least one occasion, however, Tehilla offered a rigorous thirty-session, two-hours-a-week course in Jewish Science healing at the Old Bethpage synagogue that was similar, if not identical, to the practitioners' course she continued to teach in Manhattan. Its purpose was to offer thorough insight into those principles of Jewish Science that "make it so effective an instrument for divine healing and effective living." She maintained that successful completion of the course, along with earnest application of the lessons, "should put into your possession the Jewish religious methods of healing and counseling which will make you a source of great strength to yourself, [to] those within your immediate circle, and to those whom you may wish to serve as practitioner, adviser, and friend."[50]

By 1957, Sunday morning services in Manhattan were no longer held in the True Sisters Building but in the air-conditioned auditorium at Steinway Hall on West 57th Street, where they remained for several decades. The small pamphlet used during worship included several prayers, including the Shema, in Hebrew and English; the 23rd Psalm, which was recited as an affirmation ("The Lord *is* my shepherd, I *shall* not want . . ."); the two affirmations of Jewish Science; and several hymns, taken from the Reform movement's *Union Hymnal*, including Eyn Keloheynu ("There is none like our God . . ."), with which the service undoubtedly closed. The pamphlet also informed worshipers that there was a "healing period at every service"; that is, a period of silence, guided meditation, or visualization, and the communal recitation of Jewish Science's affirmations, led by Tehilla Lichtenstein. While the Society of Jewish Science retained historical, liturgical, and, in terms of rabbinic assistance, institutional ties to the Reform movement, Lichtenstein herself, who was not a Reform rabbi and whose closest family members were Orthodox, saw value in the many spiritual paths Judaism offered. At one spiritual practitioners' meeting, held at her home in March 1960, she facilitated a discussion on the three major branches of Judaism. At her request, three practitioners, each of whom was identified, if not affiliated with, one of American Judaism's three major religious movements, described what he or she found most significant in Orthodoxy, Conservatism, or Reform. Summarizing the discussion and articulating her own belief, Tehilla Lichtenstein said that "each form of our Jewish religion is a vehicle for expressing our faith in God."[51]

Two or three years before she died, Tehilla Lichtenstein developed Parkinson's disease. According to her son, Michael, her illness was not severe and thus was successfully concealed from the congregation. One particularly strong tremor, however, while not affecting the clarity of her thinking, precipitated a physical decline that left her functioning but physically "never quite the same."[52] She stepped down from the pulpit in late 1972 but remained leader of the society until her death, from a stroke, on February 23, 1973. Buried next to her husband and parents in Riverside Cemetery in Saddle Brook, New Jersey, Tehilla Lichtenstein came to be formally recognized as the society's cofounder. That April, a memorial service was held in the Old Bethpage synagogue. It featured a formal tribute by Bernard Martin (1928–1982), a Reform rabbi, author, and professor of Jewish Studies at Case Western Reserve University in Cleveland. A longtime supporter of the society's work who conducted high holy day services at the home center for many years, he described Lichtenstein as a truly "liberated woman, long before that phrase gained its present popularity," contributing to the world as a wife, mother, and "creative and productive human being." "For the work of teaching, counseling and healing to which she felt herself called, and which brought blessing into the lives of so many people," he maintained,

> she was uniquely equipped both in qualities of mind and heart. . . .
> It was clearly her profound religious confidence and trust that made
> it possible for Tehilla Lichtenstein to live and work as she did. She

had the strongest and most unshakeable faith in God and her fellow
man [*sic*]. . . . The work that she and her dear husband began and
carried on so nobly for many years will go on. There are those
whom she and Rabbi Lichtenstein inspired deeply, and they and others as well will continue to advance the cause of Jewish Science and
thereby not only bring blessings to many, but also keep the memory
of its founders forever fresh and green.[53]

The Society of Jewish Science has since kept the memory and teachings of
Morris and Tehilla Lichtenstein very much alive. In large measure, this has
been due to the generous financial support of Abraham and Mildred Goldstein,
the dedication of a small yet enthusiastic and devoted membership that, as of
2003, numbered 120, and the many more who subscribe to the *Jewish Science
Interpreter*, which is published eight times a year and regularly includes one or
more of the Lichtensteins' sermons. The teachings of the Lichtensteins have
been kept alive due to the tireless efforts of such individuals as Abe Goldstein;
Doris Friedman; Jack Botwin; Harry Hauptman, who served as executive director for about eight years and helped conduct services in New York during
the late 1970s and early 1980s; and Helen Miller Harwood, longtime board
member and inspiration to many, who for more than sixty years rarely missed
a service, sang at high holy day services and other special events, and unfailingly procured entertainment for the society's annual luncheon. Indispensable for the past twenty years has been the lifelong member David Goldstein
(1949–), Abraham and Mildred's son, who is currently the society's executive
director and has long assumed responsibility for the society's daily affairs and
the preservation of its records.

The society continues to keep Morris Lichtenstein's books in print and has
published a collected volume of Tehilla Lichtenstein's sermons, as well as a
small pamphlet on her life and thought, written by Rebecca Alpert. Available
for purchase are several cassette tapes of Tehilla's radio broadcasts and sermons, the latter read by Doris Friedman. Worship services are still offered on
Sunday mornings at 11:00 a.m. in Manhattan. Since 1996, they, as well as
classes, board meetings, and special events, have been held at the society's new
headquarters, a beautifully renovated five-story brownstone at 109 East 39th
Street. Its small, tastefully decorated sanctuary features rich, burgundy carpet-
ing, upholstered chairs in a soothing pattern of burgundy and taupe, a large
desk from which the service is led and the Torah read on holidays, and the
walnut ark and ner tamid from the Old Bethpage synagogue, painstakingly
preserved in storage for twenty years. Inside the ark are several Torah scrolls,
including the scroll placed in the ark at the synagogue's dedication ceremony
in May 1956 and, in a metal case, an exquisite Oriental-Sephardic scroll, which
was a gift to the society from Martin and Sarah Fellerman shortly after their
purchase of it in 1960. Worship services are led by Rabbi Perry Berkowitz,

FIGURE 7.3. Abraham Goldstein at entrance of the Society of Jewish
Science's new headquarters in New York City (1996). Courtesy of Society of
Jewish Science.

who studied at both the Jewish Theological Seminary and HUC and was privately ordained within the Jewish Renewal movement.[54] Preceding the 11:00
a.m. service, his sister, Rabbi Leah Berkowitz, who also received private ordination, leads a weekly Torah study class, comprised of a bright and clearly
interested group of attendees.[55]

Before the class begins, there is much socializing and an informal breakfast, prepared by Mildred Goldstein and other class members in the kitchen
adjoining the spacious room in which Torah study is conducted. Finally—
largely through the efforts of Abe Goldstein, who for many years lived with
his wife, Mildred, in Israel; David Goldstein in New York; and Jack Botwin in

FIGURE 7.4. David Goldstein (center) with members Morison Gampel and Selma Foer at the Murray Hill Neighborhood Street Fair, June 2002. Courtesy of Society of Jewish Science.

Los Angeles—a number of Jewish Science groups have been and continue to be created. For more than fifteen years, a group met regularly in Netanya, Israel, and over the past several decades there have been, and in most cases still are, groups in the Bronx; Piscataway, New Jersey; Orlando, Florida; Albuquerque, New Mexico; and several groups in the greater Los Angeles area.

Both Tehilla and Morris Lichtenstein imbued their lives with an unshakable sense of optimism, including a belief in Jewish Science's success. In terms of numbers and influence within the American Jewish community, their optimism does not seem to have been well founded. At its peak the society attracted less than one thousand members, no more than half that number during Tehilla Lichtenstein's thirty-five-year tenure as leader, and it has just over a hundred today. One can only speculate as to the reasons for the society's numerical failure.

First, throughout the 1920s and early 1930s, despite those rabbis who gave their wholehearted support, there remained either opposition or indifference to Jewish Science both within the Reform movement and among Jewish communal leaders as a whole. Second, the Society of Jewish Science, like Clifton Harby Levy's Centre of Jewish Science, never developed a strong organizational base. Dependent on the efforts and financial contributions of an extremely small number of men and women, both were centered around devotion to a charismatic leader, who, because of his or her uniqueness, could never fully be replaced. Thus, Levy's Centre of Jewish Science closed after he died, just as the Society of Jewish Science lost a number of members after Morris Lichtenstein's death in 1938. Many of those who remained initially did so out of loyalty to Lichtenstein and the fact that his hand-picked successor was his wife, Tehilla, who continued to identify herself as his disciple. Shortly after assuming leadership of the society, Tehilla Lichtenstein attracted a loyal following of her own. Yet those who succeeded her, like Abe Goldstein, primarily functioned as organizational rather than spiritual leaders. Certainly Abe Goldstein, Doris Friedman, and Harry Hauptman, who led services after Tehilla Lichtenstein's death, were deeply spiritual human beings, as are David Goldstein and Perry Berkowitz today. Yet just as the spiritual leader of Christian Science remains Mary Baker Eddy, so the spiritual leaders of the Society of Jewish Science remain Morris and Tehilla Lichtenstein. Without their teachings and lived examples, there would be no Society of Jewish Science.

Third, without either rabbinic study or ordination, Tehilla Lichtenstein lacked the stamp of authentication shared by Morris Lichtenstein, Clifton Harby Levy, and the first formulator of Jewish Science, Alfred Geiger Moses. Moreover, according to many of those who knew her, her major interest was not in increasing society membership but rather in the spiritual reawakening of even one previously indifferent Jew.[56] Finally, Jewish Science's emphasis on God, prayer, and spiritual healing may have held great appeal in the early 1900s to those initially attracted to Christian Science. Yet by the late 1920s, as the general appeal of Christian Science declined, so, it seems, did the appeal of Jewish Science. Perhaps its spiritual understanding of Jewish self-identity simply didn't appeal to what had become an increasingly secular American Jewish community. During the late 1930s and 1940s in particular, American Jews as a whole were probably, and understandably, less interested in spiritual healing than in defeating fascism, rescuing the Jews of Europe, and ending the war. Moreover, throughout the 1970s, if not later, most leaders of Reform Judaism, the movement with the greatest historical ties to Jewish Science, placed less emphasis on personal religious growth than on the importance of social action. Yet I suspect that were Tehilla and Morris Lichtenstein alive today, they, like the society's current members, would remain optimistic about Jewish Science's future success, if not as a separate movement, at least as a means of helping Jews find health and happiness within the framework of their own religion.

Over eighty years after the creation of the Society of Jewish Science, a growing number of Americans, including American Jews, have evinced great interest in spiritual healing. While prayers and psalms recited on behalf of those who are ill, either in body or spirit, have long been part of the Jewish tradition, special healing services now exist in Jewish communities throughout the United States. An early inspiration and resource for their creation was the Jewish Healing Center (JHC), established in 1991 "to develop effective means of meeting the spiritual needs of Jews during times of illness," helping them to achieve spiritual wholeness through "Jewish texts and practices that can help one cope with [suffering], illness, [and] pain."[57] According to the Reform rabbi Nancy Flam, the JHC's first associate director, "we may not be able to make disease disappear, but we can profoundly affect how we cope with illness."[58] Emphasizing the connection between the mind and the body, she pointed to recent scientific studies suggesting that one's thoughts and words have great impact on one's health. She also singled out specific talmudic texts that describe human love, attention, compassion, presence, and bestowal of dignity as that which is capable of spiritually and physically healing others.

The Jewish Healing Center emerged out of an idea first conceived by Reform rabbi Rachel Cowan, as newly appointed director of Jewish life at the Nathan Cummings Foundation. In early 1991, at Cowan's instigation, she,

FIGURE 7.5. Rabbi Rachel Cowan. Courtesy of National Center for Jewish Healing, a program of JBFCS, New York, N.Y.

Rabbi Nancy Flam, Rabbi Susan Freeman, Ellen Hermanson, and Nessa Rapoport, all of whom were dealing with illness or loss, including Cowan,[59] met to discuss ways of coming to terms with their suffering. After studying and reflecting on the challenges of spiritual healing, they unanimously agreed that a Jewish Healing Center would be a unique and essential resource to the American Jewish community. Thanks to a generous three-year grant from the Cummings Foundation, they subsequently set out to create a center whose intent was not to replace but rather to complement normative medical care.

At a day-long inaugural conference in April 1991, thirty-five rabbis, scholars, medical professionals, patients, and former patients came together "to grapple with the question of what Jewish healing means, and to share their notions of what the Jewish Healing Center should be."[60] A distinguished group of panelists discussed such issues as the Jewish struggle with suffering; learning from other healing traditions; Jewish visions of wholeness and health; and Jewish healing in the future. Panel members included the writer and scholar of Jewish mysticism Rabbi Jonathan Omer-Man, who that same year founded Metivta, a center for contemplative Judaism in Los Angeles, and Rabbi Zalman Schachter-Shalomi, a writer, teacher, and founder of the P'nai Or Religious Fellowship in Philadelphia, widely recognized as a pioneer of Jewish spiritual renewal, who has since founded and serves as director of the interfaith Spiritual Eldering Institute. Other panelists included the Orthodox rabbi, author, teacher, and clinical and organizational psychologist Tsvi Blanchard, who currently serves as director of organizational development for the National Jewish Center for Learning and Leadership (CLAL) and has long maintained a deep interest in issues related to spirituality and health; the Jewish physician Herbert Benson, a pioneer in mind/body studies, bestselling author, and founding president of the Mind/Body Medical Institute at Harvard Medical School, and Dr. Samuel Klagsbrun, a psychiatrist and hospital executive medical director and the author of *Preventive Psychiatry* (1989), who currently is an adjunct professor of pastoral psychology at the Conservative movement's Jewish Theological Seminary.

By the fall of 1991, the Jewish Healing Center had opened offices in San Francisco and Brooklyn that soon sponsored a number of programs, publications, and special events. With the center itself located in San Francisco, Nancy Flam became West Coast director, while the Conservative Rabbi Simkha Weintraub, the center's program consultant, helped direct activities on the East Coast.

The center saw its work as divided into four major categories: (1) providing direct services to seriously ill Jews, their friends, and their families; (2) organizing training programs in pastoral care for rabbis and chaplains and workshops on ethical and spiritual issues for physicians; (3) sponsoring research, particularly on the connection between the mind and the body; and (4) creating

FIGURE 7.6. Rabbi Nancy Flam. Courtesy of National Center for Jewish
Healing, a program of JBFCS, New York, N.Y.

a library and resource center. Three years later, many of these goals had been
accomplished. Among the center's most significant achievements was the creation of Kol Haneshama, a Jewish hospice program founded and directed by
the Conservative rabbi Amy Eilberg, who became a staff member of the Healing Center in 1992.

Emphasizing the *mitzvah* (obligation) of *bikkur holim* (visiting the sick),
Eilberg maintained that even when there is little hope for cure, all Jews are
commanded to visit the sick, bringing them "a sense of context, meaning,
continuity, and hope." "Among professional pastoral caregivers," she continued,

> this quality of relationship is called the ministry of presence: the
> simple, sacred, healing act of standing with someone in pain. When

FIGURE 7.7. Rabbi Amy Eilberg. Courtesy of the National Center for Jewish Healing, a program of JBFCS, New York, N.Y.

we can meet a person in need fully, with no plans, no demands, no agenda, but to be there in all of our humanness, then moments of healing happen, and moments of awareness of God's presence as well.[61]

The early success and growing interest in the work of the Jewish Healing Center led to renewed funding from the Nathan Cummings Foundation, as well as local funding to create and support healing centers in Jewish communities throughout the United States. With the generous support of local Jewish federations, foundations, and individuals, the Jewish Healing Center in San Francisco became the Bay Area Jewish Healing Center, now a program of the Mount Zion Health Fund. Working in collaboration with a number of local

Jewish organizations, including the Bureau of Jewish Education, it offers rabbinic counseling, at home and in hospitals, hospices, and other care facilities, and provides spiritual support groups, healing, and memorial services; the largest Jewish library in the Bay Area on death and bereavement; and education and training for synagogues, health-care workers, and volunteers.[62] Having moved with her family to Massachusetts in 1996, and continuing since then to lecture and write on Judaism and healing, Nancy Flam currently serves as director of the Spirituality Institute, created in 1999 as a retreat-based learning program for Jewish leaders. Amy Eilberg, who, like Flam, continues to write and lecture on Jewish healing, is a pastoral counselor and spiritual director in private practice in Palo Alto, California. Like Rabbi Eric Weiss, the current executive director of the Bay Area Jewish Healing Center, she has undertaken extensive study at Mercy Center's Spiritual Directors' Institute, a Catholic spiritual direction program. Drawing on mystical and contemplative Jewish texts, her primary teaching goal is to find "an authentic Jewish language for spiritual direction."[63]

In 1994, the Cummings Foundation helped establish the National Center for Jewish Healing (NCJH), a resource center to help local Jewish communities meet the spiritual needs of Jews confronted with illness and loss. In 1996, Simkha Weintraub became (and still serves as) its rabbinic director. According to Weintraub, the NCJH was created to nurture the growth of the nascent Jewish healing movement and "to help Jews who are suffering receive support, guidance, and solace from the Jewish tradition and the Jewish community. [That is], to help them access Jewish spiritual resources."[64] Currently cocoordinated by Susan Rosenthal and Susie Kessler, who is also coordinator of Makom: The Center for Mindfulness, at the Manhattan Jewish Community Center, the NCJH has created Jewish spiritual support groups of all kinds and initiated projects for visiting the sick and public education programs on trauma response planning, Jewish end-of-life care, and other related issues. It has also established training programs for Jewish professionals working in areas of spiritual counseling and healing and, among its most important work, continues to publish a variety of materials that "strive to intertwine the rich spiritual resources of Jewish life and tradition with contemporary wisdom on health and healing."[65] Among them is the NCJH's newsletter, the *Outstretched Arm*, formerly the newsletter of the San Francisco–based Jewish Healing Center, and Simkha Weintraub's edited volume *Healing of Soul, Healing of Body: Spiritual Leaders Unfold the Strength and Solace in Psalms*, a project of the NCJH, published in 2000.[66]

As of 2000, there were more than twenty Jewish community-based healing centers throughout the United States and Canada, located in such cities as Framingham, Massachusetts; Ventnor, New Jersey; Pittsburgh, Pennsylvania; Baltimore, Maryland; Wilmington, Delaware; Washington, D.C.; Memphis, Tennessee; Jacksonville, Florida; St. Paul, Minnesota; St. Louis, Missouri; Phoe-

FIGURE 7.8. Rabbi Simkha Weintraub. Courtesy of National Center for Jewish Healing, a program of JBFCS, New York, N.Y.

nix, Arizona; Dallas, Texas; San Diego and San Francisco, California; New York City; and Toronto, Ontario.[67] By 2003, the number had grown to over thirty-five.[68] Most, however, are not independent centers but are healing networks or programs housed within local Jewish family services agencies. Among them is the New York Jewish Healing Center, a program of the Jewish Bureau for Family and Children's Services (JBFCS), which shares its offices with the National Center for Jewish Healing. Simkha Weintraub, who is an accredited social worker specializing in family therapy as well as a rabbi, serves as rabbinic director of the NCJH, the JBFCS, and the New York Healing Center. He also is an adjunct faculty member at the Jewish Theological Seminary, offering a course in pastoral counseling.[69] Jewish healing conferences, special programs, or retreats focusing on Jewish mysticism, meditation, and the search for spiritual wholeness currently are being offered not only by healing centers but also through the joint efforts of synagogues, Jewish community centers, local federations and social service agencies, hospices, hospitals, Jewish chaplains, local boards of rabbis, seminaries, and such summer camps as the Conservative movement's Camp Ramah.

Among the most well-known and successful Jewish retreat centers is Elat Chayyim, a transdenominational center for healing and renewal, founded in 1992 under the auspices of the Alliance for Jewish Renewal (ALEPH). Although its historical roots lie in the Jewish renewal rather than healing center movement, it offers special classes that include explorations of various Jewish paths toward healing, workshops on combining aspects of the Twelve Step program with Jewish spiritual practices, and a "full range of" healing services that includes private spiritual and pastoral counseling.[70] Its outstanding faculty have included Zalman Schachter-Shalomi; Nancy Flam; Amy Eilberg; Rabbi Michael Lerner, social activist and editor of the progressive *Tikkun* magazine; Rabbi Jeff Roth, cofounder and executive director of Elat Chayyim and a serious practitioner of meditation and experiential liturgy; and Rabbi Shefa Gold, who teaches about the healing potential of chanting, prayer, and contemplation and like Roth, is both a Reconstructionist and Renewal rabbi, with private ordination from Zalman Schachter-Shalomi. The poet Marge Piercy has taught several times on poetry as self-expression and midrash (interpretations of biblical texts); the Reconstructionist rabbi Sheila Weinberg has offered a workshop in meditation; and Rabbi Arthur Waskow, an author, social activist, and director of the Shalom Center (an affiliate member of ALEPH) continues to lead retreats, offer activist training sessions, and teach courses on personal and communal transformation.

Dozens of synagogues in such cities as Boston; Philadelphia; West Hartford, Connecticut; Washington, D.C.; Phoenix; Los Angeles; and Chicago presently offer liturgical services of healing. These congregations hold such services themselves or cosponsor them with several congregations in the area, usually alternating their designated location. In New York, for example, Congregations Kol Ami of White Plains and Westchester Reform Temple in Scarsdale have cosponsored monthly healing services led by the singer and songwriter Debbie Friedman since 2000. Other synagogues, such as the Conservative congregation Temple Beth El in Stamford, Connecticut, have intensified efforts to incorporate healing prayers into their Sabbath morning service, including the congregational singing of Debbie Friedman and Drorah Setel's Mi Shebeyrach, Judaism's traditional prayer recited on behalf of those who are ill or recovering from illness. According to Temple Beth El's rabbi, Joshua Hammerman, the recitation of such prayers is among "the most powerful points of the service." They aren't meant to "invoke some kind of magical cure." Rather, "through the act of prayer, and especially through communal prayer . . . [they] create a greater sense of connection [to God and one another]."[71]

Among those interested in Judaism, spirituality, and healing, including those instrumental in the founding of Elat Chayyim, are rabbis and laypeople associated with the Jewish Renewal movement. A small network of autonomous Jewish groups seeking to transform the contemporary Jewish community and infuse new life into Jewish religious practice, several are part of the loosely based ALEPH. Others, like Rabbi Michael Lerner, the activist, author, and editor of *Tikkun*, are less interested in Jewish renewal as a movement than as an individual and communal path toward healing and transformation. "Jewish renewal," he maintains,

> is an attempt to make us more fully alive to God's presence in the world, to build a life that is God-centered, and to provide us with a way of reclaiming the unique spirituality of Judaism, deeply embedded in political consciousness but not reducible to a particular political agenda or to a set of moral injunctions. Because Judaism is a way of life, Jewish renewal is an attempt to reclaim and rejuvenate that way of life for those who have abandoned it and for those who have transformed it into neatly demarcated ritual obligations and beliefs.[72]

While there are some, including Michael Lerner, who see a clear connection between healing and individual and communal transformation, not all of those who currently visit, or use the resources of, Jewish healing centers are necessarily interested in Jewish renewal.[73] Indeed, because most are under the auspices of Jewish Family Services agencies, whose programs are open to everyone, many have attracted non-Jews, of whom some are related to Jews and others have simply been attracted to the kinds of programs, such as bereavement support groups, these centers offer.[74]

Like the leaders of Jewish Science, those involved in creating new forms of Jewish spirituality, healing centers and support groups, meditation workshops, and retreat centers like Elat Chayyim see their work, at least in part, as one of outreach to nonaffiliated and affiliated Jews. In placing greatest emphasis on those coping with suffering and illness, Jewish healing centers have a narrower focus than Jewish Science, although some centers recently have expanded their work to include those who are physically healthy but "emotionally fatigued and spiritually needy."[75] While the leaders of Jewish Science viewed the concept of obligation as both personal and communal, the great commitment to political activism espoused by *Tikkun* magazine and renewal groups like the Shalom Center stands in marked contrast to Jewish Science's more inner-directed aims. Still, Jewish Science's major goals of applying Jewish teachings to everyday life and finding happiness and health within a Jewish context are goals these newer expressions of Jewish spirituality very much share. Long before most Americans, including most members of the medical community, either understood or acknowledged the connection between the mind and the body, Christian Science, Jewish Science, and New Thought espoused theologies that made this connection central to their understanding of God's goodness, compassion, and healing power. Today, most psychologists and neurologists agree that the mind and the body are not all that different and that "the well-being of one is intimately intertwined with that of the other."[76] It seems that most Americans, including most Jews, have come to believe this as well. An important, previously unwritten chapter in American Judaism, and especially, in the history of Reform Judaism in the United States, Jewish Science predated the current interest in Jewish spirituality by at least seventy years. As a movement, Jewish Science may remain little more than a footnote in American Jewish history. Yet its overriding message, that in order to *do* well one must *be* well, has become particularly meaningful to thousands, if not hundreds of thousands, of American Jews. It may well be Jewish Science's greatest legacy.

Notes

CHAPTER I

1. *American Hebrew* 88 (March 17, 1911) 20: 386.

2. Henry Frank, *Why Is Christian Science Luring the Jew Away from Judaism?* (San Francisco: Princess Press, 1919), 32–33.

3. For a fuller discussion, see Carroll Smith-Rosenberg, "The Hysterical Woman: Sex Roles and Role Conflict in Nineteenth Century America," in *Disorderly Conduct* (New York: Knopf, 1985), 197–208.

4. Dr. Maurice Fishberg, "Health Problems of the Jewish Poor," paper read at Jewish Chatauqua Assembly, July 27, 1903, reprinted in *American Hebrew* 73, 11 (July 31, 1903): 335–336.

5. Clara Lowenburg Moses, "My Memories," typed manuscript, American Jewish Archives, Cincinnati, Ohia (henceforth AJA). This memoir has recently been published as Clara Lowenburg Moses, *Memoir of a Southern Jewish Woman*, ed. Wendy Machlovitz (Jackson, Miss.: Museum of the Southern Jewish Experience, 2000).

6. Jacob S. Shield, "Christian Science and the Jewish People," *Christian Science Journal* 19 (February 1902): 690.

7. Jeanne L. Teller, letter to the author, April 20, 1984, Germantown, Tennessee.

8. Horace M. Kallen, "Judaism by Proxy," *American Hebrew* 99 (September 29, 1916): 682.

9. *American Hebrew* 92 (April 4, 1913) 23: 642–643.

10. Frank, *Why Is Christian Science Luring the Jew?* 20.

11. A later exception was a lead editorial titled "The Jewish Peril" that appeared in the *Christian Science Monitor* in June 1920. Howard M. Sachar, *A History of the Jews in America* (New York: Vintage Books, 1992), 315.

12. Samuel N. Deinard, *Jews and Christian Science* (Minneapolis: Deinard, 1919), 10.

13. Shield, "Christian Science and the Jewish People," 688.

14. Paul Cowan, *An Orphan in History* (Toronto: Bantam Books, 1982), 65.

15. Max Heller, "A Jewish Apologist for Christian Science," *American Israelite* 58, 44 (May 16, 1912): 4.

16. Evidence for this can be found in letters and testimonials by Jews published during the early decades of the twentieth century in the *Christian Science Journal*, the *Christian Science Sentinel*, and the *Jewish Science Interpreter* (henceforth *JSI*), articles in the *American Israelite* that appeared during the same period, and books such as Deinard, *Jews and Christian Science*, Frank, *Why Is Christian Science Luring the Jew*, and Paul Cowan, *An Orphan in History*.

17. Elizabeth Stern (pseud. Leah Morton), *I Am a Woman—And a Jew* (New York: Sears, 1926), 334.

18. Heller, "Jewish Apologist for Christian Science," 4.

19. Stephen S. Wise, "Why Jews Turn to Christian Science," *Free Synagogue Pulpit: Sermons and Addresses by Stephen S. Wise* (New York: Bloch, 1921), 6:147, 163.

20. Mordecai M. Kaplan, "A Program for the Reconstruction of Judaism." *Menorah Journal* 6, 4 (August 1920): 193.

21. Rabbi Horace J. Wolf, "Some New Types of Jewish Womanhood," *American Hebrew* 93, 19 (September 5, 1913): 483.

22. Etta Naftal, "A Personal Document," *JSI* 1, 1 (February 1923): 2.

23. *Peace of Mind*, one of several books written by Morris Lichtenstein, was first published in 1927. In 1946, long after the Jewish attraction to Christian Science had reached its peak, the Reform rabbi Joshua Loth Liebman (1907–1948) published a best-selling book of the same name. Unlike Lichtenstein, but like Rabbi Alfred Geiger Moses, another early proponent of Jewish Science, Liebman emphasized the importance of both psychology and religion as keys to inner peace. The phrase "peace of mind" was also used by those in the Protestant-based alliance New Thought, discussed at greater length in the next chapter.

24. (Mrs.) S. J., letter in *JSI* 11, 7 (August 1933): 5.

25. E.J.S., letter in *JSI* 2, 9 (October 1924): 3.

26. Jean A. McDonald, "Mary Baker Eddy and the Nineteenth-Century 'Public' Woman," *Journal of Feminist Studies in Religion* 2, 1 (spring 1986): 105.

27. Mary Baker Eddy, *Science and Health with Key to the Scriptures* (Boston: First Church of Christ Scientist, 1875), 192.

28. Eddy, *Science and Health*, 311.

29. Eddy, *Science and Health*, 161.

30. Eddy, *Science and Health*, 175.

31. Eddy, *Science and Health*, 164.

32. See, for example, Donald Meyer, *The Positive Thinkers* (New York: Pantheon Books, 1965), 101.

33. From letters written during the late nineteenth century published in the *Christian Science Journal*, quoted in McDonald, "Nineteenth-Century Public Woman," 106–107.

34. Meyer, *Positive Thinkers*, 39.

35. Rabbi Maurice Lefkovits, "The Attitude of Judaism Toward Christian Science," *CCAR Yearbook* (henceforth *CCARY*) 1912, vol. 22 (Cincinnati: CCAR, 1913), 300.

36. John J. Appel, "Christian Science and the Jews," *Jewish Social Studies* 31, 2 (April 1969): 120, erroneously cites Lefkovits as saying that " 'less than one-fifth of one per cent' " had joined, leading Appel to conclude that if Lefkovits was correct, six thousand Jews had joined Christian Science. See Lefkovits, "Attitude of Judaism toward Christian Science," 300.

37. Wise, "Why Jews Turn to Christian Science," 141–143.

38. This information, as well as some of the figures cited earlier can be found in John J. Appel, "Christian Science and the Jews," *Jewish Social Studies* 3, 2 (April 1969): 119–121.

39. Appel, "Christian Science," 101.

40. Eddy, preface to *Science and Health*, xi.

41. For a fuller discussion, see Carolyn Cobb, "Sue Harper Mims, C.S.B.," *Atlanta Historical Bulletin* 4, 16 (January 1939): 77–89.

42. *Atlanta Journal*, April 5, 1914.

43. Wesley Jackson, "Christian Scientists in State Once Subject to Persecution," *New Orleans Times-Picayune*, May 12, 1974.

44. As cited in Appel, "Christian Science and the Jews." According to Eichhorn, Wertheimer later left Christian Science for Baptist fundamentalism.

45. Julian Miller, "Rabbi Must Oppose Christian Science," *American Israelite* 58, 30 (January 25, 1912): 4.

46. Kaplan, "A Program for the Reconstruction of Judaism," 193.

47. Isaac Mayer Wise, excerpt from his writings, 1898, cited in Dena Wilansky, *Sinai to Cincinnati: Lay Views on the Writings of Isaac M. Wise, Founder of Reform Judaism in America* (New York: Renaissance Books, 1937), 154.

48. Isaac Mayer Wise, "Editorial," *American Israelite* 46, 38 (March 22, 1900): n.p.

49. Rabbi Max Heller, "Editorial," *American Israelite* 58, 15 (October 12, 1911): 4.

50. "Resolution on Judaism and Christian Science," *CCARY* 1912, vol. 22, 148.

51. Rabbi William Rosenau, *CCARY* 1917, vol. 27 (Cincinnati: CCAR, 1918), 199–200.

52. Samuel Schulman, "Jewish Self-Criticism," *Beth-El Pulpit* (New York: Congregation Beth-El, n.d.), 12.

53. Samuel Schulman, "The Searching of the Jewish Heart," *Menorah Journal* 4, 2 (April 1918): 95–97.

54. Samuel Schulman, discussion following Kohler, "The Mission of Israel and Its Application to Modern Times," *CCARY* 1919, vol. 29 (Cincinnati: CCAR, 1920), published separately in pamphlet form, 34–35.

55. Julian Morgenstern, "Were Isaac M. Wise Alive Today: A Program for Judaism in America," *CCARY* 1919, vol. 29, 230–242.

56. Leo M. Franklin, "Presidential Address," *CCARY* 1920, vol. 30 (Cincinnati: CCAR, 1921), 170.

57. Harry W. Ettelson, "Conference Sermon," *CCARY* 1920, vol. 30, 208.

58. Louis Witt, "The Spirit of the Synagogue—Conference Lecture," *CCARY* 1921, vol. 31 (Cincinnati: CCAR, 1922), 129.

59. Kaufmann Kohler, "The Mission of Israel and Its Application to Modern Times," 20.

60. Louis Grossman, "Presidential Message," *CCARY* 1919, vol. 29, 120.

61. Edward N. Calisch, "Presidential Message," *CCARY* 1922, vol. 32 (Cincinnati: CCAR, 1923) 112.

62. Stephen S. Wise, "Liberal Judaism," *Free Synagogue Pulpit* (1921): 3.

63. Wise, "Why Jews Turn to Christian Science, 160–161.

CHAPTER 2

1. Alfred Geiger Moses, *Jewish Science: Divine Healing in Judaism* (Mobile, Ala.: published by the author, 1916), 11.

2. Alfred G. Moses, *A History of the Jews of Mobile*, reprinted from the *Publications of the American Jewish Historical Society*, no. 12 (Baltimore: Lord Baltimore Press, 1904), 8.

3. Robert J. Zietz, *The Gates of Heaven: Congregation Sha'arai Shomayim, the First 150 Years* (Mobile, Ala.: Congregation Sha'arai Shomayim, 1994), 27.

4. Alfred G. Moses, "Synopsis of Congregational History," in *A Congregation in the Name of God* (Mobile, Ala.: Brisk, 1905), 1.

5. For a fuller discussion, see Zietz, *Gates of Heaven*, 27–29.

6. Alfred G. Moses, "Our Present Condition as a Jewish Community," sermon delivered in celebration of Sha'ari Shomayim's Sixtieth Anniversary, in *A Congregation in the Name of God*, 10.

7. Adolph Moses, "Yahvism," in *Yahvism and Other Discourses*, ed. H. G. Enelow (Louisville: Louisville Section of the National Council of Jewish Women, 1903), 10–29.

8. Adolph Moses, cited in W. Gunther Plaut, ed., *The Growth of Reform Judaism: American and European Sources to 1948* (New York: World Union for Progressive Judaism, 1965), 35.

9. Zietz, *Gates of Heaven*, 100.

10. This information was provided to me by Phyllis Feibelman, chair, Archives Committee, Spring Hill Avenue Temple (Sha'arai Shomayim), Mobile, Ala. She received this information from a Christian Science practitioner in Mobile who based his information on a brief article focusing on Christian Science in Mobile by Frances Beverly, published in 1938.

11. Moses, *Jewish Science* (1916), 48.

12. Leon Schwarz, "Reminiscences," Mobile, Alabama, 1872–1919 (unpublished manuscript, 1936), AJA, box 1938.

13. Moses, *A Congregation in the Name of God*, 8.

14. A[lfred] G[eiger] Moses, "Annual Report of the Superintendent of the Sabbath School," Board of Trustees file, 1914, Sha'arai Shomayim Archives, Mobile, Alabama (henceforth SSA).

15. Moses, *Jewish Science* (1916), 48.

16. Taped reminiscences of Samuel Brown, Mobile, Alabama, in response to my letter of April 13, 1984.

17. Moses, *Jewish Science* (1916), 50.

18. Moses, *Jewish Science* (1916), 20–21.

19. Moses, *Jewish Science* (1916), 18–19.

20. Moses, *Jewish Science* (1916), 10.

21. Alfred Geiger Moses, *CCARY* 1919, vol. 29 (Cincinnati: CCAR, 1920), 302.

22. Emil W. Leipzinger, "Alfred G. Moses," *CCARY*, vol. 66 (New York: CCAR, 1957), 178.

23. Board of Trustees Minutes, SSA, March 1904, n.p.

24. Leipziger, "Memorial Tribute," 179.

25. It should be noted that other early proponents of mind cure, including Mary Baker Eddy and many leaders of the loosely organized movement known as New Thought, also developed an interest in healing because of personal problems with mental health.

26. Moses, *Jewish Science* (1916), 40.

27. Moses, *Jewish Science* (1916), 57, 69.

28. Moses, *Jewish Science* (1916), 48.

29. Moses, *Jewish Science* (1916), 20.

30. Max Heller, letter to Alfred Geiger Moses, January 5, 1917. Moses Papers, AJA.

31. Alfred Geiger Moses, *Jewish Science: Psychology of Health, Joy and Success or The Applied Psychology of Judaism* (New Orleans: Searcy and Pfaff, 1920), 95.

32. Moses, *Jewish Science* (1920), 97–98.

33. Moses, *Jewish Science* (1920), 242. For a greater understanding of applied psychology, see the textbook by A. L. Hollinworth and A. T. Poffenberger, *Applied Psychology* (New York: Appleton, 1917). Revised editions of this work appeared in 1920 and 1923. See also Bernard C. Ewer, *Applied Psychology* (New York: Macmillan, 1923).

34. Moses, *Jewish Science* (1920), 65.

35. Correspondents included the New Orleans manufacturer Marcel Krauss, Della Bloomstein, a Nashville woman who wrote to Moses on several occasions, and Bertha Strauss and Lucia Nola Levy, who later approached Moses about leading a Jewish Science group in New York City.

36. Alfred Geiger Moses, letter to the editor, *New Orleans Times-Picayune*, March 10, 1920, Moses Papers, AJA.

37. Gail M. Harley, *Emma Curtis Hopkins: Forgotten Founder of New Thought* (Syracuse, N.Y.: Syracuse University Press, 2002), 90. Charles Braden, *Spirits in Rebellion: The Rise and Development of New Thought* (Dallas: Southern Methodist University Press, 1963), credits the spiritual healer and writer Phineas Quimby (1802–1866) as having been the founder of New Thought. While some New Thought writers, most notably Warren Felt Evans, were greatly influenced by Quimby (in 1862, Mary Baker Eddy, then known as Mrs. Patterson, became a patient and admirer of Quimby as well), New Thought as a movement did not develop until approximately twenty years after Quimby's death.

38. Warren Felt Evans, "Mental Medicine" (1872), cited in Braden, *Spirits in Rebellion*, 116.

39. Lilian Whiting, *The World Beautiful* (Boston: Roberts Brothers, 1895), 16.

40. Ralph Waldo Trine, *My Philosophy and My Religion* (New York: Dodd, Mead, 1921), 25–26, 30. Note that while Emerson's identification of the "still, small voice" with the "Christ within me" is explicitly Christian in nature, the concept of God as an inner "still, small voice" can be traced back to the Hebrew prophets, more specifically to the Book of Isaiah.

41. According to Braden, *Spirits in Rebellion*, during the 1920s and 1930s, the early years of the church's growth, members of the Church of Religious Thought,

later known as the Church of Religious Science, did not consider themselves to be part of New Thought (285). Yet Holmes studied with Emma Curtis Hopkins in New York in 1924, two years before publishing his most important work, *Science of Mind*, and Holmes himself was an active member of the International New Thought Alliance, speaking frequently at INTA congresses and serving as an officer or chairman of several important committees and as editor of one of their few publications.

42. Moses, *Jewish Science* (1920), 65.

43. Ernest Shurtleff Holmes, *The Science of Mind*, rev. and enl. ed. (New York: Dodd, Mead, 1938; originally published 1926), 137–156.

44. Moses, *Jewish Science* (1920), 135.

45. Moses, *Jewish Science* (1920), 143.

46. Moses, *Jewish Science* (1920), 144.

47. Moses, *Jewish Science* (1920), 145.

48. Moses, *Jewish Science* (1920), 149.

49. Moses, *Jewish Science* (1920), 150.

50. Moses, *Jewish Science* (1920), 10.

51. As discussed in the previous chapter, those who argued this most forcefully at annual meetings of the CCAR were Rabbis Julian Morgenstern, Leo Franklin, Harry Ettelson, Edward Calisch, and Abraham Simon.

52. Moses, *Jewish Science* (1920), 23.

53. Moses, *Jewish Science* (1920), 27.

54. While for the most part Moses focused on mental ailments, he did discuss such physical ailments as constipation and other stomach troubles (which doctors today would agree can be caused by anxiety and worry) as well as diabetes and Bright's disease, which Moses assumed, in opposition to the leading medical opinion of his day and ours, were often caused by a "dark and despairing attitude that . . . poison[ed] the secretions of certain organs and promote[d] the[se] diseases." *Jewish Science* (1920), 42.

55. Moses Gaster, letter to Alfred Geiger Moses, July 10, 1919. Moses Papers, AJA.

56. Rabbi Emil Leipziger, letter to Alfred Geiger Moses, October 14, 1919. Moses Papers, AJA.

57. Martin A. Meyer, letter to Alfred Geiger Moses, May 25, 1917, Temple Emanuel, San Francisco, Calif., and Louis Mann, announcement sent to Alfred Geiger Moses, n.d., Moses Papers, AJA.

58. Marcel Krauss, letter to Alfred G. Moses, November 12, 1920, Moses Papers, AJA.

59. Claire Fabricant, letter written to S. S. Rosen, NYC, n.d., Moses papers, AJA. Rosen, a supporter of efforts to form a Jewish Science group in New York, apparently sent this letter to Alfred Moses.

60. I am not certain when *Primary Lessons in Christian Living and Healing* was first published. The cover of the earliest edition I have discovered cites 1918 as the book's publication date, while an inside page lists 1914 as the date of copyright. Either Militz first published the book in 1914, publishing a new, presumably revised edition in 1918, or she first published the book in 1918 but gave 1914 as the copyright date, referring to its initial publication, presumably in 1914, as a series of essays in *Unity*,

the magazine published by New Thought's Unity School of Christianity, founded by Charles and Myrtle Fillmore.

61. Rolla W. Calloway, letter to Alfred Geiger Moses, August 28, 1919, Moses Papers, AJA.

62. Marcel Krauss, letter to Alfred G. Moses, March 11, 1920, Moses Papers, AJA.

63. Della H. Bloomstein, letter to Alfred Geiger Moses, July 2, 1922, Moses Papers, AJA.

64. Hattie Seidenbeum, letter to Alfred Geiger Moses, November 28, 1919, Moses Papers, AJA.

65. Lucia Nola Levy, letter to Alfred Geiger Moses, September 7, 1920, Moses Papers, AJA.

66. According to an announcement in the *New York Times*, reprinted among Alfred Moses' private papers, with an indication of the date (January 11) but not the year, though presumably it was 1921; Moses Papers, AJA.

67. Lucia Nola Levy, open letter to James A. Edgerton, February 21, 1921, Moses Papers, AJA.

68. J[ames] A. Edgerton, letter to Lucia Nola Levy, February 26, 1921, Moses Papers, AJA.

69. Bertha Strauss, letter to Alfred Geiger Moses, June 21, 1921, Moses Papers, AJA.

70. *New York Times*, December 10, 1921, 24.

CHAPTER 3

1. Scholarly references have listed 1889 as the year Lichtenstein was born. Indeed, the date of birth given on his gravestone is January 1, 1889. However, a copy of Morris Lichtenstein's school records from HUC, sent by request to his son, Immanuel, in March 2003, includes a copy of his application for admission. Handwritten by Morris Lichtenstein in August 1911, it gives his date of birth as October 4, 1888.

2. His master's thesis was entitled "A Study in Religious Changes among Jewish Immigrants."

3. *Athens Daily Banner*, September 28, 1920.

4. Morris Lichtenstein, editorial note, *JSI* 1, 1 (February, 1923): 1.

5. Interview with Immanuel Lichtenstein, June 4, 1985, Princeton, New Jersey.

6. *Athens Daily Banner*, December 9, 1921, 1.

7. *Banner Herald*, January 1, 1922, 6, and May 31, 1922, 4.

8. Interviews with Immanuel Lichtenstein, June 4, 1985, Princeton, New Jersey, and Michael Lichtenstein, June 17, 1985, New York City.

9. Rebecca T. Alpert, "From Jewish Science to Rabbinical Counseling: The Evaluation of the Relationship between the Religion and Health by the American Reform Rabbinate" (Ph.D. diss., Temple University, 1978), 77, notes: "whether or not Lichtenstein received rabbinical ordination in Bialystok is disputed by the available sources. The [1938 *Universal Jewish*] *Encyclopedia* article states that he did; the Memorial Address by Abraham Holtzberg (1939 *CCAR Yearbook*, 298) [simply] states that he studied at yeshivot in Bialystock and Lomza." Perhaps most tellingly, in his HUC applica-

tion, dated August 28, 1911, in answer to the questions "What schools have you attended?" and "Have you received any Hebrew education? If so, where and from whom?" Morris Lichtenstein described his yeshivah background but made no mention of having received rabbinic ordination.

10. Morris Lichtenstein, "Application for Admission to the HUC," August 28, 1911, AJA.

11. *New York Times*, January 7, 1922, 24.

12. *New York Times*, March 11, 1922, 20.

13. Bertha Strauss apparently became a member of the Centre of Jewish Science, created under the leadership of Rabbi Clifton Harby Levy at the end of 1924. Indeed, he may have established the center largely at her instigation. See chapter 5.

14. "Constitution and By-Laws of the Society of Jewish Science," 1925, Society of Jewish Science Archives (henceforth SJSA).

15. "Constitution and By-Laws," 1925, SJSA.

16. "Society of Jewish Science Financial Report, 1927–1929," SJSA.

17. *JSI* 15, 12 (January 1938): 7.

18. *JSI* 1, 1 (February 1923): 1.

19. *JSI* 1, 2 (March 1923): 6.

20. Membership lists, Harry Hartman files, SJSA.

21. "Constitution and By-Laws for The Women's League of Jewish Science, adopted April 7, 1926," SJSA.

22. "Constitution and By-Laws for Women's League, 1926," SJSA.

23. Rebecca Dreyfuss, "Jewish Science," unpublished poem, SJSA.

24. Minutes, Annual members' meeting of Society of Jewish Science, October 24, 1927, SJSA.

25. Minutes, Annual meeting of the Society, October 28, 1938, SJSA.

26. *Society of Jewish Science Year Book* (New York: Society of Jewish Science, 1927), SJSA.

27. *Society of Jewish Science Year Book* (New York: Society of Jewish Science, 1934), SJSA.

28. T. L. Ansbacher, letter to the editor, *JSI* 1, 7 (August 1923): 5.

29. Mrs. M. Livingston, letter to Etta Naftal, *JSI* 1, 6 (July 1923): 5.

30. Mrs. M. Brandman, letter to Morris Lichtenstein, *JSI* 1, 9 (October 1923): 7.

31. Mrs. Celia Kraus, "Personal Document," *JSI* 6, 11 (December 1928): 5.

32. Julius Schwartzwald, "Personal Document," *JSI* 6, 11 (December 1928): 5, 7.

33. S.V. Rosenblum, letter to Morris Lichtenstein, *JSI* 5, 10 (November 1927): 7.

34. (Mrs. I. E.) Esther Davis, letter to the editor, *JSI* 1, 10 (November 1923): 6–7.

35. Nathaniel Casden, letter to Morris Lichtenstein, *JSI* 1, 9 (October 1923): 7.

36. E. G. R., letter to editor, *JSI* 4, 9 (October 1926): 4.

37. Sam Moser, "A Personal Note," *JSI* 10, 4 (May 1932): 5.

38. Harry Hartman, "What Does Jewish Science Mean to Me?" May 19, 1939, handwritten draft, SJSA.

39. Jeannette F. Mayer, "What Jewish Science Means to Me," *JSI* 10, 7 (August 1932): 5.

40. Interview with Bertha Schwartz, January 18, 1984, Barbizon Plaza Hotel, New York City.

41. Interview with Abraham Goldstein, Barbizon Plaza Hotel, April 23, 1985.

42. Morris Lichtenstein, "Knowing God," *JSI* 12, 3 (April 1934): 2.

43. Morris Lichtenstein, "The Road to Spirituality," *JSI* 13, 8 (September 1935): 2.

44. Lichtenstein, "Road to Spirituality."

45. Morris Lichtenstein, *Judaism* (New York: Jewish Science, 1934), 148.

46. Lichtenstein, *Judaism*, 128, 145.

CHAPTER 4

1. Jack Botwin, letter to David Goldstein, July 8, 1988, forwarded by David Goldstein to me.

2. Morris Lichtenstein, "How to Choose Your Life Work," *JSI* 1, 3 (April 1923): 1.

3. Lichtenstein, "Life Work," 2.

4. Morris Lichtenstein, "Men, Women and Their Differences," *JSI* 8, 11 (December 1930): 1.

5. Morris Lichtenstein, "Conquering Fear," *JSI* 8, 1 (February 1930): 4.

6. Morris Lichtenstein, "Right Thinking," *JSI* 9, 10 (November 1931): 4.

7. Morris Lichtenstein, "A Life of Regrets," *JSI* 11, 3 (April 1933): 2.

8. Morris Lichtenstein, "Perpetual Youth," *JSI* 1, 5 (June 1923): 2.

9. Morris Lichtenstein, "On Being Critical," *JSI* 8, 9 (October 1930): 4.

10. Morris Lichtenstein, "When Silence Is Eloquent," *JSI* 11, 10 (November 1933): 1.

11. Morris Lichtenstein, "With Patience," *JSI* 11, 3 (April 1933): 3.

12. Morris Lichtenstein, "The Tonic of Laughter," *JSI* 11, 10 (November 1933): 3, 5.

13. Samuel R. Goodkind, letter dated August 21, 1936, *JSI* 14, 8 (September 1936): 5.

14. Mrs. Jennie Bloom, *JSI* 12, 5(June 1934): 5.

15. Mrs. Sarah Fellerman, "My Experiences in Jewish Science," *JSI* 12, 2 (March 1934): 3.

16. Mrs. C. Roosefelt, New York City, letter to Morris Lichtenstein, *JSI* 13, 1 (February 1935): 7.

17. Hannah Klotz, Baltimore, Md., letter to Morris Lichtenstein, *JSI* 12, 12 (January 1935): 5.

18. In lay terms, *neuritis* refers to the inflammation of a nerve, causing continuous pain and often paralysis and sensory problems.

19. (Mrs. J.) P.S.C., letter to Morris Lichtenstein, *JSI* 12, 9 (October 1934): 5.

20. Mrs. Isabelle Gordon, New York City, letter to Morris Lichtenstein, *JSI* 12, 7 (August 1934): 7.

21. Mrs. Sadie Feinberg, Kingston, N.Y., letter to Morris Lichtenstein, *JSI* 11, 2 (March 1933): 7.

22. S.F.H., St. Paul, Minn., letter to Morris Lichtenstein, *JSI* 14, 4 (May 1936): 5.

23. Morris Lichtenstein, "The Jewish Science-God Conception," *JSI* 1, 2 (March 1923): 4.

24. Morris Lichtenstein, "Practical Religion," *JSI* 7, 11 (December, 1929): 2.

25. Abba Hillel Silver, "My Quest for God" (1926), in *Therefore Choose Life: Selected Sermons, Addresses and Writings*, vol. 1, ed. Herbert Weiner (Cleveland: World, 1967), 40.

26. Maurice N. Eisendrath, *Can Faith Survive? The Thoughts and Afterthoughts of an American Rabbi* (New York: McGraw-Hill, 1964), 292.

27. Roland Gittelsohn, *Man's Best Hope* (New York: Random House, 1961), 120, 185.

28. Mordecai Kaplan, "What Judaism Is Not," *Menorah Journal* 1, 1 (January 1915): 215.

29. Mordecai M. Kaplan, *The Future of the American Jew* (New York: Macmillan, 1948), 41. Kaplan expressed these ideas in his earlier works as well. See, for example, *The Meaning of God in Modern Jewish Religion* (New York: Reconstructionist Press, 1962; originally published 1936), 14–20.

30. Kaplan, *Meaning of God*, 28, 29.

31. Mordecai M. Kaplan, *Judaism as a Civilization: Toward a Reconstruction of American-Jewish Life* (Philadelphia: Jewish Publication Society of America, 1981; originally published 1934), 179.

32. Morris Lichtenstein, "Our God Conception," *JSI* 2, 4 (May 1924): 1.

33. "Our God Conception," 2.

34. Morris Lichtenstein, *Judaism* (New York: Jewish Science, 1934), 177.

35. Lichtenstein, *Judaism*, 128.

36. Lichtenstein, *Judaism*, 148.

37. Lichtenstein, *Judaism*, 149.

38. Lichtenstein, *Judaism*, 40.

39. Lichtenstein, *Jewish Science and Health*, 137.

40. Morris Lichtenstein, "Faith and Superstition," in *Joy of Life: Jewish Science Essays* (New York: Jewish Science, 1938), 302–303.

41. Lichtenstein, *Jewish Science and Health*, 36.

42. Lichtenstein, *Jewish Science and Health*, 37.

43. Lichtenstein, "When Silence Is Eloquent," 2.

44. Morris Lichtenstein, "Some Aspects of Jewish Science," *JSI* 8, 12 (January 1931): 3.

45. Morris Lichtenstein, *Jewish Science in Judaism*, pamphlet (New York: Society of Jewish Science, n.d.), 9–10.

46. Morris Lichtenstein, "Healing in the Old Testament," *JSI* 1, 1 (February 1923): 3.

47. Morris Lichtenstein, "The Miracle of Healing," *JSI* 15, 9 (October 1937): 2.

48. "Explanation of Affirmations," *JSI* 1, 2 (March 1923): 6. While the ideas expressed are clearly those of Morris Lichtenstein, the explanations themselves may well have been written by Tehilla Lichtenstein, editor of the *Jewish Science Interpreter*.

49. Harry Hartman, "Notes from Practitioners' Course," lecture 6, December 5, 1927, typed notes, SJSA.

50. Hartman, "Practitioners' Notes," lecture 6.

51. Hartman, "Practitioners' Notes," lecture 7, December 8, 1927, SJSA.

52. Hartman, "Practitioners' Notes," lecture 9, December 19, 1927, SJSA.

53. Harry Hartman, "Practitioners' Notes," lecture 29, Thursday, March 8, 1928, SJSA.

54. Hartman, "Practitioners' Notes," lecture 17, January 23, 1928, SJSA.

55. Hartman, "Practitioners' Notes," lecture 14, January 12, 1928, SJSA.

56. Hartman, "Practitioners' Notes," lecture 29, March 8, 1928, SJSA.

57. Lichtenstein, *Judaism*, 174–175.

58. Lichtenstein, *Judaism*, 228.

59. Lichtenstein, *Judaism*, 195–196.

60. Lichtenstein, *Judaism*, 210–211.

61. Lichtenstein, *Judaism*, 212.

CHAPTER 5

1. Clifton Harby Levy, "The Program of Jewish Science," talk presented to the New York Board of Jewish Ministers, printed in pamphlet form, n.d., AJA.

2. Clifton Harby Levy, "Jewish Science: A System and a Method," reprint from *CCARY* 1927, vol. 37 (Cincinnati: CCAR, 1928), 5.

3. [Morris Lichtenstein, as edited by Tehilla Lichtenstein], "Jewish Science versus Christian Science," *JSI* 1, 1 (February 1923): 2.

4. Clifton Harby Levy, "Why the Jew Can Not Accept Christianity," *Jewish Life* 1, 1 (March 1925): 13.

5. Levy, "Why the Jew Can Not Accept Christianity," 14.

6. Mary Baker Eddy, *Science and Health with Key to the Scriptures* (Boston: First Church of Christ Scientist, 1875), 495–497.

7. Gary Zola, "Isaac Harby," in *Reform Judaism in America: A Biographical Dictionary and Sourcebook*, edited by Kerry M. Olitzky, Lance J. Sussman, and Malcolm H. Stern (Westport, Conn.: Greenwood Press, 1993), 83. For a more detailed study of Harby's life, see Gary Philip Zola, *Isaac Harby of Charleston, 1788–1828: Jewish Reformer and Intellectual* (Tuscaloosa, Ala.: University of Alabama Press, 1994).

8. Whether or not his immediate family settled in Mobile is unclear. While Levy never indicated as such, he did mention in his brief handwritten autobiography that his maiden aunt, Addie (Adeline C. Moses), lived in Mobile and was founder of its first circulating library in around 1875. He also wrote that he remembered well his maternal grandmother, who lived with Addie, presumably after her husband died. Given the fact that Levy studied after his confirmation in 1880 with James Gutheim of New Orleans, he either lived in Mobile for a short time (with his mother and possibly other members of the family), then returning to New Orleans, or continued to live in Mobile, preparing for HUC with Gutheim through correspondence or extended visits. The only extant source alluding to this period in Levy's life is his brief "handwritten autobiographical outline" in his papers at the American Jewish Archives.

9. Levy, "Autobiographical Outline," [1951], unpublished autobiographical information supplied by Levy to the American Jewish Archives, Levy Papers, AJA.

10. Clifton Harby Levy, "A Spiritual Conference," *Jewish Life* 2, 1 (September 1925): 2.

11. Levy, "Autobiographical Outline."

12. See, for example, "Clifton Harby Levy," *American Jews: Their Lives and Achievements*, vol. 1 (New York: Golden Book Foundation of America, 1947), 128; the memorial tribute to Levy by Rabbi Maurice J. Bloom, *CCARY* 1962, vol. 72 (New York: CCAR, 1963), 192–193; and the biographical entry on Levy in *The Encyclopedia Judaica* (Jerusalem: Keter, 1971), 11:157–158.

13. Tremont Temple Society minutes, April 13, 1906–May 16, 1907. Tremont Temple Papers (henceforth TTP), Scarsdale Synagogue–Tremont Temple, Scarsdale, New York.

14. Tremont Temple Society Minutes, November 19, 1908, and Congregational Minutes, February 18, 1909, TTP.

15. See Levy, "Autobiographical Outline," and Rebecca T. Alpert, "From Jewish Science to Rabbinical Counseling: The Evaluation of the Relationship between the Religion and Health by the American Reform Rabbinate" (Ph.D. diss., Temple University, 1978), 72.

16. Minutes of Meetings of Board of Trustees and Annual Congregational Meetings, February 18, 1909–February 19, 1919, TTP.

17. Minutes of Board of Trustees Meetings, November 14 and December 5, 1912, TTP.

18. Minutes of Board of Trustees Meeting, February 4, 1913, TTP.

19. Minutes of Board of Trustees Meetings, April 2, 1913–July 2, 1913, TTP. This of course does not mean that Shavuot services were not held, or that some arrangements for seating weren't made. But it does give some indication of the ways the board dismissed Levy's suggestions and disliked being reminded by him of what they needed to do.

20. Minutes of Board of Trustees Meetings, June 7, 1915, and July 12, 1915, TTP.

21. Minutes of Board of Trustees Meetings, February 6, 1917– May 7, 1918, TTP.

22. Minutes of Board of Trustees Meetings, February 11, 1919, TTP.

23. Clifton Harby Levy, "Letter to the Board of Trustees and Members of the Tremont Temple," February 14, 1919, attached to Minutes of Board of Trustees Special Meeting, TTP.

24. Minutes of Board of Trustees Meetings, March 4, 1919–August 12, 1919, TTP.

25. Minutes of Board of Trustees meetings, August 8, 1920, and September 7, 1920, TTP.

26. Levy, "Jewish Science: A System and a Method," CCARY 1927, vol. 37, 4.

27. In his "Autobiographical Outline," written in 1951, Levy maintained that his group approached him for the second time in 1923. It is more likely that the correct date was December 1924—the date given by Levy in his 1927 address to members of the CCAR.

28. Levy, "Jewish Science: A System and a Method," 4.

29. Lucia Nola Levy was also not one of the original members of the incorporated Society of Jewish Science. There was a Mrs. Mathilda Jacobs, who joined with her husband, Hyman. While issues of the Jewish Science Interpreter and yearbooks issued by the society do not mention their names, suggesting that their membership was short-lived, I have discovered no evidence that the Mathilda Jacobs and the Mrs. Jacobs who approached Clifton Harby Levy in 1924 were the same individual. Indeed, unless Hyman Jacobs died prior to December 1924, the fact that Levy did not mention a "Mr. Jacobs" suggests they were not. See "Certificate of Incorporation of Jewish Science, Society of Jewish Society," SJSA.

30. [C. H. Levy], "Founder's Day," Jewish Life 5, 2 (January 1928): 1.

31. [C. H. Levy], "What's in the Name?" Jewish Life 1, 4 (June 1925): 2.

32. [C. H. Levy], "A Positive Program," Jewish Life 2, 4 (December 1925): 1.

33. [C. H. Levy], "The Course in Spiritual Culture," *Jewish Life* 2, 2 (October 1925): 1.

34. These included the Hebrew Tabernacle and Temple of the Covenant in New York (presumably Manhattan); Union Temple and Beth Emeth in Brooklyn; Beth Israel in Atlantic City; and "The Temple" in East Orange, New Jersey.

35. Listed were newly established circles at the Free Synagogue in Flushing under the leadership of Rabbi Meyer and at Unity Temple in Manhattan, led by Rabbi Tintner. *Jewish Life* 5, 2 (January 1928): 2.

36. In 1928, the Jewish Science Centre of Union Temple published Louis Gross's own interpretation of Levy's views in *What Is Jewish Science?*

37. Alpert, "From Jewish Science to Rabbinical Counseling," 100.

38. [C. H. Levy], "Jewish Science Circles," *Jewish Life* 6, 2 (January 1929): 2.

39. [C. H. Levy], "The Rabbis Are with Us," *Jewish Life* 1, 3 (May 1925): 1.

40. [C. H. Levy], "The Soul Clinic," *Jewish Life* 2, 5 (January 1926): 1.

41. [C. H. Levy], "New Headquarters," *Jewish Life* 2, 5 (January 1926): 1.

42. [C. H. Levy], "Religion in Hospitals," editorial, *Jewish Life* 4, 2 (March 1927): 5.

43. [C. H. Levy], "Jewish Science Rally," *Jewish Life* 5, 4 (June 1928): 1.

44. [C. H. Levy], "Spiritual Help and Healing for To-day," *Jewish Life* 5, 5 (October 1928): 1.

45. [C.H. Levy], "Temple of Jewish Faith," *Jewish Life* 4, 1 (November 1926): 1.

46. Lichtenstein, *Jewish Science and Health*, 10.

47. Lichtenstein, *Jewish Science and Health*, 128–133.

48. Levy, *The Helpful Manual* (New York: Centre of Jewish Science, 1927), 9.

49. Levy, *Helpful Manual*, 2 (note: the manual has no page 1; it begins on page 2).

50. Levy, *Helpful Manual*, 11–13.

51. Levy, *Helpful Manual*, 39. The affirmation can also be found in *Jewish Life* 1, 1 (March 1925): 7–8.

52. This view was apparently shared by a contemporary critic of Jewish Science, the Reform rabbi Philip Waterman, who angrily maintained in 1926 that "the more one reads of the particular branch of Jewish Science that is called 'Jewish Science Incorporated,' the less one knows what it is all about. . . . The fault may lie in me, but [Levy's theological ideas and biblical] commentaries convey no meaning whatever to my outraged intelligence. . . . If a man talk at length, surely it is not too much to expect that he say something." Philip Waterman, "This Jewish Science," *Menorah Journal* 12 (August 1926): 364.

53. Clifton Harby Levy, "Discussion-Committee on Resolutions," *CCARY* 1925, vol. 35 (Cincinnati: CCAR, 1926), 165.

54. Clifton Harby Levy, "Significant Jewish Science," *Jewish Institute Quarterly* 3, 1 (November 1926): 3.

55. "Report of Committee on Relation of Synagog[ue] to Healing," *CCARY* 1927, vol. 37 (Cincinnati: CCAR, 1928), 166, 174–175.

56. In 1930, he became rabbi of Temple Rodeph Sholom in New York City.

57. Louis I. Newman, "Christian and Jewish Science," *Jewish Tribune*, September 23, 1927, 56.

58. Levy, "Jewish Science: A System and a Method," 1–2, 4–5, 7–9.

59. *CCARY* 1928, vol. 38 (Cincinnati: CCAR, 1929), 106–107.

60. For a fuller discussion of Reform rabbinic responses to Jewish Science, see Alpert, "From Jewish Science to Rabbinic Counseling," 87–117.

61. Press announcements, HUC-JIR, available online: July 25, 2000, http:/huc .edu/news/blaustein.html January 29, 2001, http:/huc.ed/news/kalsman.html.

62. Rebecca T. Alpert, "Clifton Harby Levy," in *Reform Judaism in America: A Biographical Dictionary and Sourcebook,* edited by Kerry M. Olitzky, Lance J. Sussman, and Malcolm H. Stern (Westport, Conn.: Greenwood Press, 1993), 125.

CHAPTER 6

1. "Certificate of Incorporation of Jewish Science, Society of Jewish Science," SJSA.

2. While Immanuel and Michael Lichtenstein remember their mother as keeping a kosher home, Michael remembers that while his mother only bought kosher meat, did not allow *treif* (nonkosher food, including shellfish) in the house, and did not mix meat and dairy, they only had one set of dishes. According to Michael, about five years after his father died, his mother became more lax in her observance. She began to eat treif in and outside of their home, though for the most part continued to buy kosher meat. Michael told me: "My mother enjoyed experiencing life. Anything that deprived her of the experience of doing something [including strictly following the dietary laws], made her unhappy. She had fears, but not a fear of life." Interviews with Michael Lichtenstein, June 17, 1985, and Immanuel Lichtenstein, March 27, 2003.

3. According to their son, Immanuel, the Lichtensteins also supported his paternal grandmother, Hannah, who lived in Lithuania. After Ozer Lichtenstein died (in the early 1930s if not before), Tehilla and Morris Lichtenstein sent Hannah money each month. As her 1939 tax return reveals, Tehilla continued to do so after Morris Lichtenstein died. Phone interview with Immanuel Lichtenstein, March 27, 2003; Tehilla Lichtenstein, 1939 Tax Return, SJSA.

4. The secular dates of death for Chava and Chaim Hirschensohn are on file in the office of Riverside Cemetery in Saddle Brook, New Jersey, where they, as well as Tehilla and Morris Lichtenstein, are buried. According to these records, Chava died on November 22, 1931, and Chaim on September 15, 1935. These dates correspond to the Hebrew dates of death on their gravestones. To determine their dates of birth, I took into consideration the following. (1) In her study of her grandmother, called "Sara Bayla and Her Times," reprinted in Adlerblum, *Memoirs of Childhood: An Approach to Jewish Philosophy* (Northvale, N.J.: Jason Aronson, 1999), Nima Adlerblum writes in a footnote that her parents, Chaim and Chava Hirschensohn, were married for fifty-eight years. If so, they got married in 1873. (2) The Hebrew inscription on Chava Hirschensohn's gravestone says she died "in her 70th year of life." If so, she was born in 1862. However, the note card filed in the office at Riverside Cemetery indicates that she was sixty-seven at the time of her death. If so, she was born in 1864. (4). The note card filed at Riverside Cemetery says that Chaim was seventy-nine when he died. If so, he was born in 1856. (5) If, as Nima writes, Chaim was eighteen and Chava twelve when they got married, and if they got married in 1873, he was born in 1856 (in agreement with my conclusion in [4]), and she was born in 1861 or

1862. My own guess is that she was born in 1862, though it is certainly possible that she was born slightly earlier or later.

5. Nima H. Adlerblum, "Sara Bayla and Her Times," in Adlerblum, *Memoirs of Childhood*, 190.

6. Press release, n.d., Tehilla Lichtenstein Papers, AJA.

7. Adlerblum, "Sara Bayla," 192.

8. Michael Lichtenstein, telephone conversation with author, April 3, 2003.

9. Adlerblum, "Sara Bayla," 194.

10. Adlerblum, "Sara Bayla," 193.

11. Nima H. Adlerblum, "Memoirs of Childhood—An Approach to Jewish Philosophy," in Adlerblum, *Memoirs of Childhood*, 4.

12. Cited in Adlerblum, *Memoirs of Childhood*, 172.

13. Nima Adlerblum, "Appendix: Rabbi Hayyim Hirschensohn—An Intimate Portrait," in Adlerblum, *Memoirs of Childhood*, 307–308.

14. Ivria Sackton [daughter of Nima Adlerblum], "Journey to the Present, 1847–1989," vol. 1 (unpublished), 7. My thanks to Ivria Sackton's daughter, Margaret Sackton Rosan, for giving me a copy of this two-volume work by her mother. This work includes numerous letters written by family members that make it clear that Tehilla was known as Rachel before and for many years after the family came to the United States. The Hebrew inscription on her gravestone identifies her as Rachel Tehilla; the English inscription simply as Tehilla.

15. Marjorie Lehman, "Tamar de Sola Pool," in *Jewish Women in America: An Historical Encyclopedia*, edited by Paula Hyman and Deborah Dash Moore, vol. 2 (New York: Routledge, 1997), 1095.

16. Sackton, "Journey to the Present," vol. 1, sec. 1, chap. 2, "Departure from Jerusalem," 5–6.

17. Sackton, "Journey to the Present," vol. 2, handwritten vita by Chaim Hirschensohn, chap. 16, 2.

18. See, for example, Rebecca Trachtenberg Alpert, *The Life and Thought of Tehilla Lichtenstein*, pamphlet (New York: Society of Jewish Science, n.d.), 2.

19. Ivria Sackton, telephone interview, September 3, 1985.

20. Adlerblum, *Memoirs of Childhood*, 165.

21. Sackton, "Journey to the Present," vol. 1, "Departure from Jerusalem," 8.

22. See Sackton, "Journey to the Present," vol. 1, sec. 1, "The Years in Constantinople," 9 n.

23. That she was reluctant to become leader of the society was told to Rebecca Alpert by Tehilla's sister, Tamar de Sola Pool. Alpert, "From Jewish Science to Rabbinical Counseling: The Evaluation of the Relationship between the Religion and Health by the American Reform Rabbinate" (Ph.D. diss., Temple University, 1978), n. 1, p. 167.

24. Tehilla Lichtenstein, "To My Friends," *Jewish Science JSI* 16, 11 (December 1938): 5.

25. R.T.L., ad of thanksgiving, in *The Society of Jewish Science Yearbook, 1939* (New York: Society of Jewish Science, 1939), 34.

26. *New York Times*, December 5, 1938, 25.

27. [Tehilla Lichtenstein], "Jewish Science Broadcasts," *JSI* 20, 12 (July 1944): 22.

28. Tehilla Lichtenstein, "Jewish Science," in *Universal Jewish Encyclopedia* (New York: Universal Jewish Encyclopedia, 1942), 6:142.

29. Cited in Alpert, *Life and Thought of Tehilla Lichtenstein*, 6.

30. Telephone interview with Mildred Goldstein, March 18, 2003.

31. "Seventy Years of Jewish Science: Sarah Fellerman," *JSI* (summer 1992): 6.

32. Tehilla Lichtenstein, *JSI* 2 (April 1958): 2; Tehilla Lichtenstein, "Tribute to Sarah Fellerman," cited in *JSI* (summer 1992): 8.

33. Interview with Helen Harwood and Sarah Rosenfeld, Barbizon Plaza Hotel, December 18, 1983.

34. *JSI* 17, 2 (March 1939): 7.

35. *JSI* 17, 9 (October 1939): 10.

36. Phone interview with Mildred Goldstein, March 18, 2003.

37. Correspondence with Jack Botwin, March 8, 2003.

38. Letters from J. J. Taubenhaus, *JSI* 2, 8 (September 1924): 7, and *JSI* 3, 5 (June 1925): 3, 5. See Professor J. J. Taubenhaus, "Jewish Science—An Appreciation," *JSI* 4, 2 (March 1926): 2–3.

39. Esther Taubenhaus, letter to Tehilla Lichtenstein, September 11, 1952. The letter begins: "Darling, sweetheart, Tehilla," and is signed "Lovingly, Esther." Tehilla Lichtenstein Papers, AJA.

40. Lehman, "Tamar De Sola Pool," 1095–1096.

41. Abraham Goldstein, letter to Rev. Dr. Louis C. Gerstein, Congregation Shearith Israel, June 9, 1981, SJSA.

42. In a newspaper article published in May 1979, Tamar was reported as having said that "if she had to choose where she would live permanently Jerusalem would top the list. Then she would pick Fire Island where she and her husband spent their summers." Sue Gardner, "Tamar de Sola Pool: Daughter, Wife, Mother, Grandma of Celebrities Is Very Much Herself!" *Jewish Week–American Examiner*, May 17, 1979, 28.

43. Coincidentally, David de Sola Pool and Tehilla Lichtenstein, though eight years apart in age, shared a birthday. Both were born on May 16.

44. [Tehilla Lichtenstein], "Tribute," *JSI* 16, 12 (January 1939): 5.

45. Tehilla Lichtenstein, "Recapitulation," unpublished essay, n.d., Tehilla Lichtenstein Papers, AJA.

46. Eleanor Roosevelt, letter to Tehilla Lichtenstein, May 8, 1962, SJSA.

47. Golda Meir, telegram to Rev. Dr. [David] de Sola Pool, May 10, 1962, SJSA.

48. Tehilla Lichtenstein, *What to Tell Your Friends about Jewish Science* (New York: Society of Jewish Science, 1951), 3.

49. In looking at these examples, one should note that they are not just gender-bound but class-bound (i.e., middle-class) as well.

50. Tehilla Lichtenstein, "The Changing Relationships between Men and Women" and "Have You Straightened Your Accounts?" Tehilla Lichtenstein Papers, AJA. Tehilla Lichtenstein, "About Ruling Others and Yielding to Others," in *Applied Judaism: Selected Jewish Science Essays by Tehilla Lichtenstein*, ed. Doris Friedman (New York: Society of Jewish Science, 1989), 585.

51. Tehilla Lichtenstein, "What Our Children Can Teach Us," *JSI* (December 1962): 3–4.

52. Tehilla Lichtenstein, "Two or Three Important Words," in *Applied Judaism*, 36–37.

53. Tehilla Lichtenstein, "Controlling the Tongue and the Temper," *JSI* 23, 5 (1951): 15.

54. Morris Lichtenstein, "Civilization and Stress," *JSI* 10, 9 (October 1932): 5–6.

55. Tehilla Lichtenstein, "Cures for Minds in Distress," sermon, n.d., Tehilla Lichtenstein Papers, AJA.

56. Tehilla Lichtenstein, "Believing Is Seeing," in *Applied Judaism*, 135.

57. Tehilla Lichtenstein, "Don't Be Afraid," sermon, n.d., Tehilla Lichtenstein Papers, AJA. Tehilla Lichtenstein, "A Corsage for Mother," *JSI* 18, 3 (May 1940): 9.

58. Tehilla Lichtenstein, "How Much Do You Count?" sermon, n.d., Tehilla Lichtenstein Papers, AJA.

59. Among the many sermons containing these lines is "When to Pray and How to Pray," *JSI* 18, 3 (April 1940): 3–4.

60. Tehilla Lichtenstein, "Does Denying Things Make Them Disappear: Christian Science versus Jewish Science," *JSI* 17, 10 (November 1939): 2.

61. Apparently, however, Hirschensohn dedicated one of his volumes of *responsa* to Morris and Tehilla Lichtenstein, in appreciation of their efforts to bring Jews back to Judaism (presumably, through Jewish Science). This dedication was brought to my attention by Rabbi Perry Berkowitz, personal communication, June 8, 2003.

62. Tehilla Lichtenstein, "Know Thyself," *JSI* 17, 6 (July 1939): 7.

63. Tehilla Lichtenstein, "What Does Jewish Science Offer to the Jew?" *JSI* 17, 11 (December 1939): 3.

64. Lichtenstein, *What to Tell Your Friends about Jewish Science*, 13.

65. [Tehilla Lichtenstein], "The Goodly Tents of Jacob," *JSI* 18, 6 (August 1940): 7.

66. Lichtenstein, *What to Tell Your Friends about Jewish Science*, 13.

67. Tehilla Lichtenstein, "Are We a Chosen People?" sermon, n.d., Tehilla Lichtenstein Papers, AJA.

68. Tehilla Lichtenstein, "Ablutions before the Feast," *JSI* 19, 7 (September 1941): 2.

69. [Tehilla Lichtenstein], "Your Harvest of Health and Happiness—How to Gather It In," *JSI* 18, 8 (October 1940): 7.

70. Tehilla Lichtenstein, "Passover Brings You Three Gifts," *JSI* 25, 7 (April 1954): 5–6, 9.

71. Tehilla Lichtenstein, "The Law Upholds Those That Uphold It: The Meaning of Shavuos," *JSI* 21, 4 (March-April 1945): 4–8.

72. "Guiding Principles of Reform Judaism" (1937), in *The Reform Judaism Reader: North American Documents*, edited by Michael A. Meyer and W. Gunther Plaut (New York: UAHC Press, 2001), 200–201.

73. Cited in Jennifer Breger, "Nima Adlerblum," in *Jewish Women in America: An Historical Encyclopedia*, edited by Paula Hyman and Deborah Dash Moore, vol. 1 (New York: Routledge, 1997), 22.

74. [Tehilla Lichtenstein], "What It Means to Be a Jew," *JSI* 20, 5 (September 1943): 19–20.

75. [Tehilla Lichtenstein], "A Pattern for Successful Living," *JSI* 17, 11 (December 1939): 7.

76. [Tehilla Lichtenstein], "Cyclorama of the Future," *JSI* 17, 5 (June 1939): 7.

77. [Tehilla Lichtenstein], "Which Shall Prevail?" *JSI* 16, 12 (January 1939): 4.

78. [Lichtenstein], "Which Shall Prevail?" 5.

79. [Tehilla Lichtenstein], "The Uses of Adversity," *JSI* 17, 3 (April 1939): 7–10.

80. [Tehilla Lichtenstein], "How Does God Answer Your Prayers?" *JSI* 18, 12 (February 1942): 3–4.

81. [Tehilla Lichtenstein], "How to Face Life These Days," *JSI* 19, 6 (August 1941): 7.

82. [Tehilla Lichtenstein], "What Is America? And Who Are Americans?" *JSI* 19, 4 (June 1941): 3.

83. [Tehilla Lichtenstein], "A Formula For Courage," *JSI* 17, 2 (March 1939): 2.

84. Tehilla Lichtenstein, quoted in Henry Beckett, "Rabbi's Widow Discounts Leader Title Claimed for Her," *New York Post*, January 26, 1951, SJSA.

85. Tehilla Lichtenstein, "Shall Women Have Religious Equality?" lecture, Park Avenue Synagogue, 1951, Tehilla Lichtenstein Papers, AJA.

86. Norman Vincent Peale, *The Power of Positive Thinking* (New York: Fawcett Columbine, 1952), 126.

87. Tehilla Lichtenstein, "Pattern for Successful Living," in *Applied Judaism*, 388–389.

88. Interview with Michael Lichtenstein, June 17, 1985.

89. Tehilla Lichtenstein, "Don't Say It's Too Late," in *Applied Judaism*, 508–509.

CHAPTER 7

1. [Tehilla Lichtenstein], "What Do You Wish For Most?" *JSI*, 18, 1–2 (February-March 1940): 1.

2. John J. Appel, "Christian Science and the Jews," *Jewish Social Studies* 31, 2 (April 1969): 115. According to Rebecca Alpert, this idea was corroborated by Tehilla's son, Michael. Rebecca T. Alpert, "From Jewish Science to Rabbinical Counseling: The Evaluation of the Relationship between the Religion and Health by the American Reform Rabbinate" (Ph.D. diss., Temple University, 1978), 167, n. 2.

3. Lichtenstein, "What Do You Wish For Most?" 3–4.

4. Bernard Mehlman, "Joshua Loth Liebman," in *Reform Judaism in America: A Biographical Dictionary and Sourcebook*, edited by Kerry M. Olitzky, Lance J. Sussman, and Malcolm H. Stern (Westport, Conn.: Greenwood Press, 1993), 127.

5. Joshua Loth Liebman, *Peace of Mind* (New York: Simon and Schuster, 1946), 178.

6. Liebman, *Peace of Mind*, 10.

7. Liebman, *Peace of Mind*, 83.

8. Liebman, *Peace of Mind*, 83–84.

9. Liebman, *Peace of Mind*, 143.

10. Liebman, *Peace of Mind*, 122, 124.

11. Liebman, *Peace of Mind*, 132.

12. Liebman, *Peace of Mind*.

13. Alpert, "From Jewish Science to Rabbinical Counseling," 155.

14. Liebman, *Peace of Mind*, 171.

15. Jacob Weinstein, cited in Rebecca Alpert, "From Jewish Science to Rabbinical Counseling," 154.

16. Alpert, "From Jewish Science to Rabbinical Counseling," 155.

17. Samuel Cohon, *Judaism: A Way of Life* (1948), cited in Alpert, "From Jewish Science to Rabbinical Counseling," 155.

18. Donald Meyer, *The Positive Thinkers* (New York: Pantheon Books, 1965), 327.

19. Louis Binstock, *The Power of Faith* (Englewood Cliffs, N.J.: Prentice-Hall, 1952); *The Road to Successful Living* (New York: Simon and Schuster, 1958); and *The Road to Maturity* (New York: Hawthorne Books, 1969).

20. Hyam J. Schachtel, *The Real Enjoyment of Living* (New York: Dutton, 1954); *The Life You Want to Live* (New York: Dutton, 1956); *The Shadowed Valley* (New York: Knopf, 1962). For a fuller discussion of the writings of Schachtel, Binstock, and Magnin, see Alpert, "From Jewish Science to Rabbinical Counseling," 157–162. For further discussion of Binstock and Liebman, see Meyer, *Positive Thinkers*, 327–330.

21. Meyer, *Positive Thinkers*, 327–329.

22. Meyer, *Positive Thinkers*, 331.

23. Meyer, *Positive Thinkers*, 329.

24. Tehilla Lichtenstein, "How to Release Your Power," *JSI* (October 1961): 19.

25. Tehilla Lichtenstein, "A Balance between Communal and Personal Religion," typed draft, written for October 1951 issue of *JSI,*. AJA.

26. Lichtenstein, "Balance between Communal and Personal Religion," 170.

27. I am indebted to the archivist Kevin Proffitt at the Jacob Rader Marcus Center of the American Jewish Archives in Cincinnati for finding for me the date in which the synagogue joined the Union of American Hebrew Congregations (UAHC) in the *Proceedings of the UAHC*, 1955. The year of their departure is confirmed in a letter from Esther Laibson, Secretary to Rabbi Erwin Herman, Director of Pacific Southwest Council of UAHC, to Rebecca Alpert, March 17, 1975, given to me by Alpert.

28. S. P. Mendes, letter to Rebecca Alpert, May 2, 1977. Alpert, "From Jewish Science to Rabbinical Counseling," 169, n. 3.

29. S. Pereira Mendes, *What Is the New Thought Synagogue and Why . . .* (Santa Monica, Calif.: published by the author, n.d.), cited in Alpert, "From Jewish Science to Rabbinical Counseling," 171.

30. S. Pereira Mendes, letters to John Appel, cited in Alpert, "From Jewish Science to Rabbinical Counseling," 170.

31. Appel, "Christian Science and the Jews," 118.

32. Alpert, "From Jewish Science to Rabbinical Counseling," 170.

33. Reva Mendes, *Words for Quiet Moments* (Santa Monica, Calif.: published by the author, 1956), cited in Alpert, "From Jewish Science to Rabbinical Counseling," 171–172, n. 1.

34. Alpert, "From Jewish Science to Rabbinical Counseling," 170.

35. Alpert, "From Jewish Science to Rabbinical Counseling," 171–189.

36. At the meeting, the society's honorary chairman and attorney, Harry Hartman, apparently also serving that evening as acting secretary, reported that the price of the property was $82,000, with a required cash down payment of $35,000. An additional $13,000 had to be paid annually, with the entire amount met by 1961. As of

November 1951, monies received for the temple fund totaled $20,400. Harry Hartman, draft of minutes of the annual membership meeting of the Society of Jewish Science, November 19, 1951. Society of Jewish Science Archives (SJSA).

37. Harry Hartman, Draft of Minutes of November 19, 1951, Membership Meeting, SJSA.

38. The day and location of Jewish Science services in the Forest Hills area were ascertained by looking through copies of the *Jewish Science Interpreter*. However, I was not able to find copies from the end of 1956 until September 1957. The October 1957 issue of the *Interpreter* suggested that those in Queens or the Farmingdale area wishing information about services call the society's administrative office in Manhattan.

39. Letters written in October 1953 from Mrs. Ginsberg of Brooklyn, Miriam and Joseph Jacobson, Elizabeth Frank, and Mr. and Mrs. Jacob Frank requesting that their pledges be partially or fully refunded on the grounds that they were not in favor of supporting a building outside of New York City, SJSA. Apparently up through October, when the majority of members voted to build the synagogue in Long Island, erecting a synagogue in Manhattan was still a possibility.

40. According to David Goldstein, his parents owned fifteen acres of land in Old Bethpage. Their home was on the property and was in walking distance of the synagogue, which was built on the property as well. Conversation with David Goldstein, May 27, 2003, offices of the Society of Jewish Science, New York City.

41. Letters to Board of Trustees, members of the society, and notes from congregational meeting, October 1953, SJSA.

42. Copy of deposition of Mildred Goldstein, February 1955. A letter to Abraham and Mildred Goldstein dated November 21, 1960, SJSA, acknowledges an additional gift of a parcel of land adjoining the synagogue valued at $14,000.

43. Abraham Goldstein, letter to members of the Society of Jewish Science, October 27, 1953, SJSA.

44. These and other references to the dedication service are from the audiotape of the society's synagogue dedication service, May 30, 1956, a copy of which was given to me by Jack Botwin.

45. The deed executed in February 1955 said that the property began "at a point on the northeasterly corner of Round Swamp Road and Smiths Road." Once constructed, the synagogue was said to be located on the northeast corner of Round Swamp Road and Claremont Street. SJSA.

46. "Society of Jewish Science Plan [sic] Consecration Services," *Farmingdale Post*, November 2, 1955, 7, SJSA.

47. Placard announcing Sabbath services at the Synagogue of Jewish Science, n.d., SJSA.

48. Gerald Jacobs, Esq., letter to Morris Gershbaum, Esq., in regard to the termination of Rabbi Michael Werthman's contract with the Society of Jewish Science, April 27, 1977, SJSA.

49. Conversations with David Goldstein, office of the Society of Jewish Science, Plainview, Long Island, July–August, 1985. If Werthman did instigate the lawsuit, albeit behind the scenes, and if the Board of Directors had proof of his actions, this was most likely the reason for his termination.

50. Tehilla Lichtenstein, letter to those enrolled in the Jewish Science healing class at the Old Bethpage synagogue, n.d., SJSA.

51. Notes from practitioners' meeting, March 10, 1960, SJSA.

52. Interview with Michael Lichtenstein, June 17, 1985.

53. Bernard Martin, "In Memoriam, Tehilla Lichtenstein," April 29, 1973, *JSI* (special issue, n.d.).

54. Conversation with Perry and Leah Berkowitz, June 7, 2003, Headquarters of the Society of Jewish Science, New York City. Leah also studied at the seminary and was ordained within the Jewish renewal movement.

55. As I witnessed when attending the class on Sunday, June 7, 2003. Nine men and women of various ages were in attendance, which, given the society's current membership of 120, can be considered fairly good.

56. Conversations with Immanuel and Michael Lichtenstein, Abraham Goldstein, David Goldstein, and Doris Friedman from 1985 to 2003.

57. Simkha Y. Weintraub, "Jewish Healing?" *Sh'ma* 24, 475 (May 27, 1994): 5.

58. Nancy Flam, "Reflections toward a Theology of Illness and Healing," *Sh'ma* 24, 475 (May 27, 1994): 3.

59. Her husband, the writer Paul Cowan, had recently died of leukemia.

60. "Conference," *Outstretched Arm* 1, 1 (fall 1991): 3.

61. Amy Eilberg, "Dying Alone," *Sh'ma* 24, 475 (May 27, 1994): 4.

62. "About the Jewish Healing Center," available online at: www.jewishhealingcenter.org and www.sfjcf.org. Accessed on June 11, 2003.

63. Marina Krakovsky, "Rabbi Amy Eilberg Teaches Women to Be Spiritual Guides," *Jewish Bulletin News* (San Francisco), January 17, 2003. Published by the Bay Area Jewish Healing Center.

64. Simkha Weintraub, cited in Susie Kessler, "Women Leaders of the Healing Movement," *Journey* (published by Mayan, a project of the Jewish Community Center in Manhattan) (spring 2002): 14.

65. Kessler, "Women Leaders," 15.

66. *Healing of Soul, Healing of Body*, a project of the National Jewish Healing Center, appeared in paperback in 2000, published by Jewish Lights, Woodstock, Vermont.

67. Gail Quets and Hannah Greenstein, *The Outreach Potential of Jewish Healing Centers* (New York: Jewish Outreach Institute, 2002), 1, n. 2.

68. Figure supplied by Simkha Weintraub, phone interview, June 11, 2003.

69. In the spring of 2003, for example, he taught a course entitled "Out of the Depths: Jewish Healing and the Spiritual Caregiver," and he plans to offer this course in 2004 as well. Interview with Simkha Weintraub.

70. This information is readily available through Elat Chayyim's yearly calendar, available in print and online.

71. Joshua Hammerman, cited in Mara Dresner, "A Time to Heal: Area Healing Services Provide Spiritual Support for Those in Need," *Connecticut Jewish Ledger*, May 15, 1998, 18.

72. Michael Lerner, *Jewish Renewal: A Path to Healing and Transformation.* New York: Putnam, 1994), 283–284.

73. The same is true of the Kabbalah Centre International, "which boasts 50 branches worldwide, including several in Israel and a five-story building on East 48th Street [in Manhattan], and study groups cropping up in places like Louisiana and Kenya" and continues to attract Jews and non-Jews, including celebrities like Mick

Jagger and Madonna. Founded in New York in 1965, it espouses the spiritual precepts of the Zohar, the major work of medieval Jewish mysticism, and "claims to have touched the lives of 3.5 million people," a number that its director, Rabbi Yehuda Berg, admits is arbitrary. Julia Gold, "Into the Mystic," *Jewish Week*, May 2, 2003, 15.

74. Telephone interview with Kerry Olitzky, June 11, 2003; telephone interview with Simkha Weintraub, June 11, 2003.

75. Quets and Greenstein, *Outreach Potential of Jewish Healing Centers*, 7.

76. Michael D. Lemonick, "Your Mind, Your Body," in a special issue that devoted sixty-four pages to exploring "How Your Mind Can Heal Your Body," *Time*, January 20, 2003, 63.

Bibliography

PRIMARY SOURCES

Interviews and Correspondence

Botwin, Jack. Personal correspondence, July 8, 1988; series of letters and phone conversations, March–June 2003.

Brown, Samuel. Personal correspondence, April 1984.

Feibelman, Phyllis. Ongoing interviews and correspondence, March 1983–June 1988; January–July 2003.

Flam, Nancy. Telephone interview, June 9, 2003.

Friedman, Doris. Ongoing interviews and correspondence, November 1983–February 1998.

Friedman, Kate. Telephone interview, April 28, 1987.

Goldstein, Abraham. Interview, April 23, 1985. Ongoing personal correspondence, 1985–1998.

Goldstein, David. Ongoing interviews and correspondence, June 1985–July 2003.

Goldstein, Mildred. Telephone interview, March 18, 2003.

Harwood, Helen. Personal interview, December 18, 1983.

Hauptman, Harry. Personal interview, November 1983.

Lichtenstein, Immanuel. Personal interviews, June 1985; correspondence and telephone interviews, May–June 1985, March–June 2003.

Lichtenstein, Michael. Personal interview, June 17, 1985; correspondence and telephone interviews, June 2003.

Olitzky, Kerry. Telephone interview, June 11, 2003.

Rosenfeld, Sarah. Personal interview, December 18, 1983.

Sackton, Ivriah. Telephone interview, September 3, 1985.

Saldick, Evelyn Diamond. Telephone interview, March 17, 2003.

Schwartz, Bertha. Personal interview, January 18, 1984.

Teller, Jeanne. Personal correspondence, April 20, 1984.
Weintraub, Simkha. Telephone interview, June 11, 2003.

Selected Journals, Newspapers, and Published Conference Proceedings

American Hebrew. New York, N.Y., 1879–1938. Microfilm, New York Public Library, New York, N.Y.

American Israelite. Cincinnati, Ohio, 1880–1907. Microfilm, Klau Library, Hebrew Union College–Jewish Institute of Religion, Cincinnati, Ohio.

Athens Banner. September 18, 1920–May 31, 1922. Microfilm, University of Georgia, Athens, Ga.

Atlanta Journal and Constitution. 1860–1922. Microfilm, Emory University Library, Atlanta, Ga.

CCAR Yearbook, 1912–1929, 1938, Cincinnati, Ohio; 1956, 1962, New York, N.Y. *(CCARY)*

Jewish Life. New York: Jewish Science Advance, 1925–1929.

Jewish Science Interpreter. New York: Society of Jewish Science, 1923–June 2003. *(JSI)*

Outstretched Arm. Jewish Healing Center/The National Center for Jewish Healing. Fall 1991–spring 2001.

Society of Jewish Science Year Book. New York: Society of Jewish Science, 1930–1984.

Times Picayune. New Orleans, La. 1974. Microfilm, Emory University Library, Atlanta, Ga.

Unpublished Documents and Archival Sources

Congregation Sha'arai Shomayim Archives, Spring Hill Avenue Temple, Congregation Sha'arai Shomayim, Mobile, Ala.

Clifton Harby Levy Papers. American Jewish Archives, Cincinnati, Ohio.

Morris Lichtenstein Papers. American Jewish Archives, Cincinnati, Ohio.

Tehilla Lichtenstein Papers. American Jewish Archives, Cincinnati, Ohio.

Alfred Geiger Moses Papers. American Jewish Archives, Cincinnati, Ohio.

Sackton, Ivria. "Journey to the Present, 1847–1989." 2 vols. Personal possession, Ellen Umansky. Unpublished family memoir and letters.

Schwartz, Leon. "Reminiscences." Unpublished memoir. Mobile, Ala., 1872–1919. American Jewish Archives, Cincinnati, Ohio.

Society of Jewish Science Archives, New York, N.Y.

Tremont Temple Papers. Scarsdale Synagogue–Tremont Temple Archives, Scarsdale, N.Y.

Published Sources

Cohon, Samuel. *Judaism: A Way of Life*. Cincinnati: Union of American Hebrew Congregations, 1948.

Cowan, Paul. *An Orphan in History*. Toronto: Bantam Books, 1982.

Deinard, Samuel N. *Jews and Christian Science*. Minneapolis: Deinard, 1919.

Eddy, Mary Baker. *Science and Health with Key to the Scriptures*. Boston: First Church of Christ, Scientist, 1875.

Eichhorn, David Max. "The Genesis of Two 'Sciences' (Christian and Jewish)." *Hebrew Union College Monthly* 19, 2 (December 1931): 12–14, 25.

———. "Science Plus and Minus." *Hebrew Union College Monthly* 19 (March 1932): 12–15.

Eisendrath, Maurice N. *Can Faith Survive? The Thoughts and Afterthoughts of an American Rabbi*. New York: McGraw-Hill, 1964.

Ellsworth, Paul [pseud. of Paul Ellsworth Triem]. *Health and Power through Creation*. Holyoke, Mass.: Elizabeth Towne, 1916.

Evans, Warren Felt. *Healing by Faith or Primitive Mind Cure*. London: Reeves, 1885.

Ewer, Bernard C. *Applied Psychology*. New York: Macmillan, 1923.

Fauer, Ruth G. *The Influence of Jewish Science in Healing*. New York: privately printed, 1935.

Fillmore, Charles. *Christian Healing*. Kansas City, Mo.: Unity, 1919.

Frank, Henry. *Why Is Christian Science Luring the Jew away from Judaism?* San Francisco: Princess Press, 1919.

Freeman, David L., and Judith Z. Abrams, eds. *Illness and Health in the Jewish Tradition: Writings from the Bible to Today*. Philadelphia: Jewish Publication Society, 1999.

Gittelsohn, Roland. *Man's Best Hope*. New York: Random House, 1961.

Gross, Louis. *What Is Jewish Science?* Brooklyn: Jewish Science Centre of Union Temple, 1928.

Hollinworth, A. L., and A. T. Poffenberger. *Applied Psychology*. New York: Appleton, 1917.

Holmes, Ernest Shurtleff. *The Science of Mind*. Rev. and enl. ed. New York: Dodd, Mead, 1938.

———. *This Thing Called Life*. New York: Dodd, Mead, 1948.

Hopkins, Emma Curtis. *Scientific Christian Mental Practice*. Marina Del Rey, Calif.: DeVorss, n.d.

Kallen, Horace M. "Can Judaism Survive in the United States?" *Menorah Journal* 11, 2 (April 1925): 101–113.

———. "Can Judaism Survive in the United States?" 2nd article. *Menorah Journal* 11, 6 (December 1925): 544–559.

Kaplan, Mordecai M. *The Future of the American Jew*. New York: Macmillan, 1948.

———. *Judaism as a Civilization: Toward a Reconstruction of American-Jewish Life*. New York: Schocken Books, 1967 (originally published 1934).

———. *The Meaning of God in Modern Jewish Religion*. New York: Reconstructionist Press, 1962 (originally published 1936).

Kohler, Kaufmann. *Guide for Instruction in Judaism*. New York: Philip Cowen, 1907.

Lerner, Michael. *Jewish Renewal: Path to Healing and Transformation*. New York: Putnam, 1994.

Levy, Clifton Harby. *The Helpful Manual*. New York: Centre of Jewish Science, n.d.

———. *Jewish Life: Discourses on Judaism Applied to Living*. New York: Jewish Science Advance, 1925.

Lichtenstein, Morris. *Cures for Minds in Distress*. New York: Jewish Science, 1936.

————. *The Healing of the Soul.* New York: Society of Jewish Science, 1974.

————. *How to Live.* New York: Jewish Science, 1929.

————. *Jewish Science and Health.* New York: Jewish Science, 1925.

————. *Jewish Science in Judaism.* New York: Jewish Science, n.d.

————. *Joy of Life.* New York: Jewish Science, 1938.

————. *Judaism.* New York: Jewish Science, 1934.

————. *Peace of Mind.* New York: Jewish Science, 1927.

Lichtenstein, Tehilla. *Applied Judaism: Selected Jewish Science Essays by Tehilla Lichtenstein.* Edited by Doris Friedman. New York: Society of Jewish Science, 1989.

———— *What to Tell Your Friends about Jewish Science.* New York: Society of Jewish Science, 1951.

Liebman, Joshua Loth. *Hope for Man: An Optimistic Philosophy and Guide to Self-Fulfillment.* New York: Simon and Schuster, 1966.

————. *Peace of Mind.* New York: Simon and Schuster, 1946.

Mendelsohn, S. Felix. *Mental Healing in Judaism: Its Relationship to Christian Science and Psychology.* Chicago: Jewish Gift Shop, 1936.

Mendes, Reva. *Words for the Quiet Moments.* Los Angeles: self-published, 1956.

Mischkind, Louis A. "Taking Stock of 'Reform': A Personal Impression of the [1920] Rabbinical Conference." *Menorah Journal* 66, 5 (October 1920): 295–300.

Moses, Adolph. *The Religion of Moses.* Louisville, Ky.: Flexner, 1894.

————. *Yahvism and Other Discourses.* Louisville, Ky.: Louisville Section of the Council of Jewish Women, 1903.

Moses, Alfred Geiger. *A Congregation in the Name of God.* Mobile, Ala.: Brisk, 1905.

————. *A History of the Jews of Mobile.* Baltimore: Lord Baltimore Press, 1904.

————. *Jewish Science: Divine Healing in Judaism.* Mobile, Ala.: self-published, 1916.

————. *Jewish Science: Psychology of Health, Joy, and Success, or the Applied Psychology of Judaism.* New Orleans: Searcy and Pfaff, 1920.

————. *A Peace Anthology.* Mobile, Ala.: self-published, 1916.

Moses, Clara Lowenburg. *Clara Lowenburg Moses: Memoir of a Southern Jewish Woman.* Edited by Wendy Machlovitz. Jackson, Miss.: Museum of the Southern Jewish Experience, 2000.

Newman, Louis I. *Rodeph Sholom Pulpit.* New York: Rodeph Sholom, 1932.

Ochs, Carol, and Kerry M. Olitzky. *Finding Our Way to God.* San Francisco: Jossey-Bass, 1997.

Olitzky, Kerry M. *One Hundred Blessings Every Day: Daily Twelve Step Recovery Affirmations, Exercises for Personal Growth, and Renewal Reflecting Seasons of the Jewish Year.* Woodstock, Vt.: Jewish Lights, 1994.

Peale, Norman Vincent. *A Guide to Confident Living.* New York: Prentice Hall, 1948.

————. *Positive Imaging: The Powerful Way to Change Your Life* (formerly titled *Dynamic Imaging*). New York: Ballantine Books, 1982.

————. *The Power of Positive Thinking.* New York: Prentice Hall, 1952.

Quimby, Phineas. *The Quimby Manuscripts.* Edited by Horatio W. Dresser. New York: Crowell, 1921.

Scher, Bertha. *Hebrew Science: The "I."* New York: Oneness of Life, n.d.

Schulman, Samuel. *Beth-El Pulpit, 1919–1927.* New York: Congregation Beth-El, 1927.

BIBLIOGRAPHY 233

Sheen, Fulton. *Peace of Soul.* New York: McGraw-Hill, 1949.

Shield, Jacob S. "Christian Science and the Jewish People." *Christian Science Journal* 19 (February 1902): 690.

Silver, Abba Hillel. *Therefore Choose Life: Selected Sermons, Addresses, and Writings.* Vol. 1. Cleveland, Ohio: World, 1967.

Stern, Elizabeth (pseud. Leah Morton). *I Am a Woman—And a Jew.* New York: Sears, 1926.

Trine, Ralph Waldo. *My Philosophy and My Religion.* New York: Dodd, Mead, 1921.

Walton, George Lincoln. *Those Nerves.* Philadelphia: Lippincott, 1909.

Waterman, Philip. "This Jewish Science." *Menorah Journal* 12 (August 1926): 359–370.

Whiting, Lilian. *The World Beautiful.* Boston: Roberts, 1895.

Wise, Stephen S., *Free Synagogue Pulpit: Sermons and Addresses by Stephen S. Wise.* 7 vols. New York: Bloch, 1910–1928.

Witt, Louis. *Judaism and Healing.* Cincinnati: Union of American Congregations Tract Commission, n.d.

SELECTED SECONDARY SOURCES

Adlerblum, Nima H. "The Philosophy of 'Judaism as a Civilization.'" New York: Society for the Advancement of Judaism, 1929.

———. *Memoirs of Childhood—An Approach to Jewish Philosophy,* edited by Els Benheim. Northvale, N.J.: Jason Aronson, 1999. [Includes "Memoirs of Childhood," "Sara Bayla and Her Times," and "A Biography of the Rabbinic Spirit"]

Alpert, Rebecca T. "From Jewish Science to Rabbinical Counseling: The Evaluation of the Relationship between Religion and Health by the American Reform Rabbinate." Ph.D. diss., Temple University, 1978.

———. *The Life and Thought of Tehilla Lichtenstein.* New York: Society of Jewish Science, n.d.

Appel, John J. "Christian Science and the Jews." *Jewish Social Studies* 31, 2 (April 1969): 100–121.

Braden, Charles. *Spirits in Rebellion: The Rise and Development of New Thought.* Dallas: Southern Methodist University Press, 1963.

Breger, Jennifer. "Nima Adlerblum." In *Jewish Women in America: An Historical Encyclopedia,* vol. 1, edited by Paula Hyman and Deborah Dash Moore. New York: Routledge, 1997.

Cobb, Carolyn. "Sue Harper Mims, C.S.B." *Atlanta Historical Bulletin* 16 (January 1939): 77–89.

Garrett, Franklin M. *Atlanta and Its Environs.* New York: Lewis Historical, 1954.

Golin, Paul. *The Coming Majority: Suggested Action on Intermarried Households for the Organized Jewish Community.* New York: Jewish Outreach Institute, 2003.

Harley, Gail M. *Emma Curtis Hopkins: Forgotten Founder of New Thought.* Syracuse, N.Y.: Syracuse University Press, 2002.

Korn, Bertram Wallace. *The Jews of Mobile, Alabama, 1763–1841.* Cincinnati: Hebrew Union College Press, 1970.

Kraut, Benny. *From Reform Judaism to Ethical Culture: The Religious Evolution of Felix Adler*. Cincinnati: Hebrew Union College Press, 1979.

——. "Judaism Triumphant: Isaac Mayer Wise on Unitarianism and Liberal Christianity." *AJS Review* 78 (1983): 179–230.

——. "Reform Judaism and the Unitarian Challenge." In *The American Jewish Experience*, edited by Jonathan D. Sarna. New York: Holmes and Meier, 1986.

Lehman, Marjorie. "Tamar de Sola Pool," in *Jewish Women in American: An Historical Encyclopedia*, edited by Paula Hyman and Deborah Dash Moore, vol. 2. New York: Routledge, 1997.

Malone, Bobbie. *Rabbi Max Heller: Reformer, Zionist, Southerner, 1860–1929*. Tuscaloosa, Ala.: University of Alabama Press, 1997.

McDonald, Jean A. "Mary Baker Eddy and the Nineteenth-Century 'Public' Woman." *Journal of Feminist Studies in Religion* 2, 1 (spring 1986): 89–111.

Meyer, Donald. *The Positive Thinkers*. New York: Pantheon Books, 1965.

Meyer, Michael. *Response to Modernity: A History of the Reform Movement in Judaism*. New York: Oxford University Press, 1988.

Olitzky, Kerry M., Lance J. Sussman, and Malcolm H. Stern, eds. *Reform Judaism in America: A Biographical Dictionary and Sourcebook*. Westport, Conn.: Greenwood Press, 1993.

Peel, Robert. *Mary Baker Eddy: The Years of Authority, 1892–1910*. New York: Holt, Rinehart, and Winston, 1977.

——. *Mary Baker Eddy: The Years of Discovery, 1821–1875*. New York: Holt, Rinehart, and Winston, 1966.

Plaut, W. Gunther, ed. *The Growth of Reform Judaism: American and European Sources to 1948*. New York: World Union for Progressive Judaism, 1965.

Quets, Gail, and Hannah Greenstein. *The Outreach Potential of Jewish Healing Centers*. New York: Jewish Outreach Institute, 2002.

Sachar, Howard M. *A History of the Jews in America*. New York: Vintage Books, 1992.

Satter, Beryl. *Each Mind a Kingdom: American Women, Sexual Purity, and the New Thought Movement, 1875–1920*. Berkeley: University of California Press, 1999.

Smith-Rosenberg, Carroll. *Disorderly Conduct*. New York: Knopf, 1985.

Umansky, Ellen M. *Lily Montagu and the Advancement of Liberal Judaism in England: From Vision to Vocation*. Lewiston, N.Y.: Edwin Mellen Press, 1983.

Wilansky, Dena. *Sinai to Cincinnati: Lay Views on the Writings of Isaac M. Wise, Founder of Reform Judaism in America*. New York: Renaissance Book, 1937.

Zietz, Robert. *The Gates of Heaven: Congregation Sha'arai Shomayim, the First 150 Years*. Mobile, Ala.: Congregation Sha'arai Shomayim, 1994.

Zola, Gary Phillip. *Isaac Harby of Charleston, 1788–1828*. Tuscaloosa, Ala.: University of Alabama Press, 1994.

Index

Page numbers in italics refer to figures.